RIGHT THIS WAY

RIGHT THIS WAY

A HISTORY

of the

AUDIENCE

———

ROBERT VIAGAS

APPLAUSE
THEATRE & CINEMA BOOKS

Essex, Connecticut

APPLAUSE
THEATRE & CINEMA BOOKS

An imprint of Globe Pequot, the trade division of
The Rowman & Littlefield Publishing Group, Inc.
4501 Forbes Blvd., Ste. 200
Lanham, MD 20706
www.rowman.com

Distributed by NATIONAL BOOK NETWORK

British Library Cataloguing in Publication Information Available

Library of Congress Cataloging-in-Publication Data
Names: Viagas, Robert, author.
Title: Right this way : a history of the audience / Robert Viagas.
Description: Essex, Connecticut : Applause, [2023] | Includes
   bibliographical references and index.
Identifiers: LCCN 2023005835 (print) | LCCN 2023005836 (ebook) | ISBN
   9781493064557 (cloth) | ISBN 9781493064564 (epub)
Subjects: LCSH: Performing arts--Audiences. | Arts audiences.
Classification: LCC PN1590.A9 V53 2023 (print) | LCC PN1590.A9 (ebook) |
   DDC 302.2308--dc23/eng/20230320
LC record available at https://lccn.loc.gov/2023005835
LC ebook record available at https://lccn.loc.gov/2023005836

Printed in India

For Donna Viagas, whose edits, comments, laughter, and occasional frowns made this book so much better. She is a great audience.

ACKNOWLEDGMENTS

I extend special thanks to Susan Schulman, Chris Chappell, Barbara Claire, Nicholas Viagas, Benjamin Viagas, Howard Sherman, Garen Daly, Jay Michaels, Mira Felner, Jonathan Kalb, Robert Davis, Dongshin Chang, Claudia Orenstein, Rosalia Gioia, Stephen Russo, Patricia Hoag Simon, Howard Siegman, John Cerullo, Trisha Doucette, the Library of Congress's The Civil War in America collection, and John L. Calhoun of the New York Public Library's Billy Rose Collection.

Plus, all the producers and press agents who granted me press tickets to the thousands of shows at hundreds of theatres I got to see during my half century as a critic and entertainment journalist. All those experiences informed this book.

Author's Note: This book covers a wide variety of audience experiences from many countries and many time periods. The vast reach of the subject made it impossible to include every title, artist, and team from every culture in every era, though effort was made to be as inclusive as possible. The author has a wide background in live theatre, science fiction and adventure movies, and certain other niche entertainment forms from the time period in which he has lived. That is reflected in many of the citations within the text and in the bibliography.

The audience in a theater is changed ev'ry night,
As a show runs along on its way,
But to people on the stage, the audience looks the same,
Ev'ry night, ev'ry matinee.
A big black giant who looks and listens
With thousands of eyes and ears,
A big black mass of love and pity
And troubles and hopes and fears,
And ev'ry night the mixture's diff'rent,
Altho' it may look the same.
To feel his way with ev'ry mixture
Is part of the actor's game.
One night it's a laughing giant;
Another night a weeping giant.
One night it's a coughing giant;
Another night a sleeping giant.
Ev'ry night you fight the giant
And maybe if you win,
You send him out a nicer giant,
Than he was when he came in . . .

"The Big Black Giant" (excerpted) from *Me and Juliet*
Lyrics by Oscar Hammerstein II
Music by Richard Rodgers

CONTENTS

Introduction

Rolling in the Aisles

The COVID-19 pandemic of 2020–2022 took many things away from us, including jobs, freedoms and, of course, loved ones. But one of the least-noticed treasures pilfered from our lives, and one for which we all hungered, was the experience of being in a group, participating in life as part of an audience.

The word *audience* is derived from Latin and means simply "those who hear." It has the same root as *audio* and *auditorium*. And to that extent, it's an OK word, but it doesn't go far enough. An audience doesn't just hear. What happens on the stage or the screen isn't really where entertainment happens, though we pretend it does. Every movie, or Netflix show, or play, or concert isn't really where the story happens. It happens inside the hearts and minds of the audience.

Virtually everyone has been part of an audience at one time or another. But have you ever wondered what really was going on, what deep human need was being fulfilled?

It's one thing to watch TV or play YouTube videos alone. But there is a strongly definable fulfillment when you have that experience as part of a group. There is you and there is the entertainer, giving to you and you giving back to them with cheers or applause or with respectful, intense concentration. You also pick up energy from those around you, and they pick up energy from you. There is a mystical consensus that arises from a shared experience. Sometimes it is ecstatic, like when the crowd rises to its feet, or you see the number of Facebook and Twitter likes mounting into the thousands and hundreds of thousands. Sometimes it's ugly, such as when a mob decides to attack someone of a different ethnicity, or tries to invade government buildings and harm political leaders.

But in both those cases, there is a shared, atavistic, and powerful human activity that can be experienced only as a group. How powerful? During COVID-19, people's impatience to rejoin in mass groups often led to super-spreader events where the disease was transmitted en masse. People were literally dying to be part of a group.

Why? What do they get from it?

At a concert venue, a musician completes a virtuoso guitar solo and the audience, which has paused for a moment from their dancing in the aisles, erupts in screaming cheers.

In a lull during a sports game, fans in the stadium keep the action going by creating a wave, seemingly spontaneously, but with perfect timing and control as it rolls from one end of the deck to the other.

In a grand opera house, fans hustle down to the ends of the aisles closest to the orchestra. When the idolized diva comes forward to take her bow, she's showered with flowers.

A congregation at a gospel church feels the energy from the choir and begins to stamp, clap, and chant along with the music, punctuating it with shouts and praise breaks, drawing strength and devotion, not just from the music, but from one another.

At a mass political rally, the crowd shouts answers to the charismatic leader's rhetorical questions. "Are you going to stand for that??" Back comes the response, "Noooo!!"

A class of schoolchildren gathered around their teacher and sings "If You're Happy and You Know It," clapping their hands, patting their heads, and otherwise illustrating the song with movements that bring life to the lyrics.

A tired office worker kicks back at the end of a long day, eating Häagen-Dazs out of the container with a spoon, and chuckling over an internet meme. He clicks the up arrow to become the 1,345th person to like it.

The chorus of *Hamilton* sings its final line—"Who lives, who dies, who tells your story"—and the voices hold the close a cappella harmony longer, longer, a bit longer. They then fall silent for a fraught moment . . . before the audience bursts forth with cheers and applause.

A couple, stretching out in their sweatpants, cocooned under a comforter, immerses themselves in the quick wit and ever-changing costumes of the new season of *The Marvelous Mrs. Maisel.*

A line of moviegoers shifts impatiently as they wait to spend more than the price of the tickets for what looks like a bathtub full of popcorn at a multiplex so they can rejoin their dates inside as the trailers roll.

A troop of Scouts huddles around a crackling campfire, listening—some wide-eyed, some guffawing in an attempt to show they're not afraid—as one of the older scouts tells a classic ghost story while shadows from the fire flicker on the surrounding woods.

On July 4, stretched out together on the warm grass, a family hears a soft *pfoomf* and watches a tiny spark of a rocket arc into the sky and then blossom into an explosion of color that whistles and pops as it tumbles earthward accompanied by a chorus of "oohs" from those on the ground. The parents hold hands.

In prison, the greatest punishment short of death is solitary confinement. Enforced solitude robs you of your humanity. Group activities experienced in common, such as the ones above, are not just something that humans do. They are a defining aspect of a social species. They are *required* for humanity. With that in mind, let's take a closer look.

1

GATHERING AROUND THE FIRE

Our lives as part of an audience begin even before we are born. The first sounds a human hears, from the depths of the womb, are those of its own family speaking. After the child is born, she or he hears the sound of a parent cooing, of that artificially high voice grown-ups direct at babies, of someone singing a lullaby.

Our mouths, lips, tongue, teeth, and larynx all evolved to create noises organized into a mutually intelligible code called speech, abetted by facial expressions, hand motions, and body language. Our ears, auditory nerves, and the auditory cortex of the brain's temporal lobe developed to turn this bedlam of sounds and images into coherent and orderly thoughts. We are information-processing creatures.

Speech itself, in the form of a good loud voice, also came to serve as the first mass medium. The urge to gather to hear a story is as old as humankind. People drew around a knowledgeable and articulate speaker to get all kinds of hard information about food sources and hunting techniques. At some point it was discovered that allegory and metaphor could convey even more complicated information that penetrated on many levels instead of just one.

The Birth of the Audience

Where was the audience born?

It was born all over the world in different ways in different cultures. But for the first recognizable community audience that supported a body of magnificent playwrights, fragments of whose work are still performed today, you need to go to the city of Athens on the Aegean Sea, a little over five hundred years before the birth of Christ.

The population of Athens numbered about three hundred thousand (about one-third of them slaves) at its classical peak, slightly less than Greensboro, North Carolina, today. Yet the minds that were bred there developed advanced mathematics, charted and named the stars in the heavens, wrote philosophical works that are still quoted today, devised the idea of democracy to rule themselves, and gave birth to generations of playwrights whose insights into human life still move the hearts of audience members twenty-five hundred years later.

The Athenians built their seat of government on a hill called the Acropolis, and into the side of that hill they carved a seventeen-thousand-seat amphitheatre, the Theatre of Dionysos. There, every spring, they would host a celebration in honor of the eponymous god, which was called the Great Dionysia or the City Dionysia: there were many theatres sprinkled around classical Greece, but the Theatre of Dionysos in Athens was the biggest one. It was the Broadway of its day.

The annual festival grew out of individual poetry readings and expanded into mass performances in which epic, story-length poems were recited in unison by a group called the chorus. Sometimes the chorus was divided into two groups who would alternate in reciting sections, creating a kind of primitive dialogue.

According to legend, the first actor was named Thespis. Before his time, the chorus would recite a poem about the activities of, say, a particular god from the pantheon and narrate what was happening. Thespis, who traveled around Greece and performed as part of these poetry/storytelling events, decided to take it one step further. Instead of saying "God X did this. God

X did that," Thespis took the revolutionary step of presenting himself *as* the god, and would say, "*I* did this. *I* did that." Instead of telling the story in the third person, he turned it into a story about himself as the character, and he became that third person. He is, therefore, credited with being the first actor, and his name is what gives us the term *thespian* for actors.

For years afterward, the chorus would speak with the main character, known as the protagonist, who would answer them in character as whatever role he was playing. The playwright Aeschylus came up with the next revolutionary step, which was to introduce a second character so that the protagonist and the secondary character could speak to each other without the chorus intervening. The chorus would often come in and comment on what these two characters said and did, but this was the first time you had characters speaking to each other in character. Often, the secondary character would be placed at odds with the main character and became known as the antagonist. In the years to come, Sophocles added a third character, and gradually more characters were added until plays began to take the shape we know today.

It was many years before a play was written that did not include the chorus speaking in unison as a separate character. In today's plays and movies, audiences rarely see a group of characters speaking in unison. The one common exception is in musicals, when a chorus will sing together, commenting on the action, and essentially fulfilling the function of an ancient Athenian chorus.

The six-day Dionysia showcased plays by five or so poets who presented a trilogy of tragedies each day, punctuated by comedies, musical performances, the consumption of great quantities of wine, and celebratory orgies—the festival's namesake, Dionysos, being the god of theatre, wine, and fertility. (The word *Bacchanalia* comes from "Bacchus," the Latin name for Dionysos.)

Many of these plays were adapted from the rich Greek mythological tradition, and from the works of the epic storyteller Homer. Playwrights included Euripides and the aforementioned Sophocles and Aeschylus, names we know because a few of

THEATRE OF DIONYSOS AT ATHENS.

Theatre of Dionysos, fifth century BCE; Athens, Greece (UNESCO World Heritage List, 1987).
North Wind Picture Archives / Alamy Stock Photo

their works managed to survive to the present day—there were many others whose plays have been lost. Dramas like *Oedipus Rex, Medea, The Bacchae, Antigone,* and the *Oresteia* trilogy were thrilling explorations of what audience members owed to their family, their country, their gods, and themselves.

At the conclusion of the Great Dionysia, the judges would put their heads together and announce a prize for Best Play. Athenian theatre fans and the many visitors who converged on the city each March to see all the latest plays discussed the contenders and looked forward to the announcement of the winners with the same fervor as fans of today's Tony or Olivier Awards. (In 2022, Broadway held its seventy-fifth annual Tony Awards. By comparison, the Great Dionysia awards were given for nearly two hundred years.)

In Athens alone, sixteen thousand to seventeen thousand people would pack the great theatre for premieres of the latest plays by their favorites. The trilogies—three linked tragedies interrupted by a satirical and often dirty Satyr play—would last all day and into the early hours of the evening. When the plays were done, audiences would feast and drink themselves into a stupor (don't forget, the whole event was ostensibly a celebration of the god of theatre and wine).

The popularity of these plays was such that wherever the Greeks built a city, they made sure to build a theatre. The Greek empire spread throughout the Mediterranean basin and into the Black Sea, with Greek-speaking colonies extending from the Rock of Gibraltar to the Middle East. And along the way the Greeks spread theatres, like Johnny Appleseed sowing apple trees across North America, or Native Americans farming the woods, planting hickory, chestnut, and other food trees so they would have something to eat wherever they went.

For the Greeks, their nourishment was theatre. And they didn't always need to send armies to conquer new territory. Word of the wonderful Greek living stories spread to the cities in their path, which would submit to Greek rule if their new overlords would bring theatre. These proto-audiences were hungry to be the real thing.

The 530s to the late 300s BCE was a period of explosive innovation in theatre in Athens, accompanied by an equally explosive growth in the sophistication of the audience, which responded to the innovations and proved themselves open to more. The transformations in storytelling helped bring about a variety of technological changes as well, although the innovations were fairly primitive by the standards of today. The playing space changed from a simple bare oval to one occupied by a prop box, to one with multiple entrances, to spaces of various sizes accessed through huts that allowed the surprise introduction of props and characters. The huts evolved into structures that allowed a multilevel playing space and introduced cranes to fly gods in and out of the action.

The introduction of the eccyclema, a small platform on wheels, allowed actors to make dramatic entrances with entourages, and allowed "dead" bodies to be wheeled on to show that a terrible battle had taken place offstage. As eccyclemas became larger and more complex, they were used to move more sophisticated sets and props on and off the stage. The increasingly complicated sets were prompted by the addition of first, second, and third characters into the tragedies. This helped encourage greater and more complicated dramatis personae and the gradual decline of the chorus as the principal performer.

The introduction of the gods as separate characters was later termed by the Romans as *deus ex machina*, the "god in a machine" that enabled playwrights to wrap up the seemingly unsolvable conflicts in their plays by bringing in gods to set things right. This opened the door to ever greater sophistication and complexity of character and action.

The introduction of additional actors also led to the development of a primitive "star" system in which certain individuals came to be in demand for performances. Higher pay for these individuals, and the increasing cost of more advanced scenery, costumes, and props, led to increased expense for the polis, and greater financial demands on the wealthy citizens who funded the plays and used them to enhance their social status. As these increased, so did the pressure to create greater pageantry in the performances, which in turn placed pressure on playwrights to incorporate more spectacular stage effects.

Of the hundreds of Greek plays written and produced during the centuries from the 500s to the 200s BCE, only about three dozen survive. We have fragments of many more, along with descriptions of the lost plays, but the complete originals are indeed lost, an irreparable calamity for audiences. The few scripts we have were preserved by accident, translated into Latin by the Romans, or used by medieval monastery copyists for practice before they were permitted to copy the sacred verses of the Bible.

It's likely that copies of these plays were stored at the great Library at Alexandria in Egypt. At the time, the city on the north coast of Africa was a center of culture and scholarship. The city had been settled by the Greeks, evidenced by its namesake, Alexander the Great. Scholars there spoke Greek and were heavily influenced by Greek education and way of life. The library, or a great part of its collection, was accidentally burned by Julius

Caesar in 48 BCE during the Roman civil war. The surviving library declined over the ensuing centuries, was vandalized and burned again. What was left was finally demolished in 391 CE. This resulted in the destruction of a priceless legacy of classical scholarship and literature that is likely gone forever.

But evidence of the continued influence of Greek theatre can be found in the most obvious place: the word *theatre*. The ancient Greeks called it *theatron* ("a place to behold"), and it persisted as *theatrum* (Latin), *teatro* (modern Italian), *théâtre* (French), *teatro* (Spanish), *theatre* (German, pronounced tay-ata), *teatru* (Romanian), *theatro* (modern Greek), *tiyatro* (Turkish), *teatrone* (Hebrew), *queat* (Arabic), *teatr* (Polish), *teatr* (Russian), *shiatā* (Japanese), *teater* (Indonesian), *thiyetar* (Hindi), and many more.

As the Greek empire declined and the growing Roman empire to the west gradually supplanted it in importance, much of Greek culture was adopted and adapted to Roman tastes. For their part, Roman audiences by and large clamored for very different forms of entertainment. Yes, the Romans had access to many of the Greek tragedies, thanks to translations by Livius Adronicus and others. And, thanks to a considerable Hellenophile audience in Rome and its provinces, the empire supported its homegrown drama writers such as Terence and Seneca the Younger. But Roman audiences generally preferred gladiatorial contests, clowns, acrobats, and jugglers.

Among the most popular attractions were *venationes* ("animal hunts"), featuring exotic animals from the distant districts of the empire. The venationes would start with a parade of the animals around the arena. Sometimes the animals would have been costumed as familiar Roman personalities, which would prompt laughs of recognition from the crowd. But this was no *Animal Planet*.

In the *venatio direptionis*, members of the audience were allowed to hunt the animals and take home the pelts or meat of whatever they killed.

In the *munus gladiatorum*, the animals were released into arenas that had been decorated to look like jungles. Humans, generally prisoners of war, convicted criminals, or later, Christians, would be marched into the arena with the animals to kill them or, more often, to be killed by them for the crowd's entertainment. The animals were also goaded to do battle to the death with one another.

Venationes did not simply use a few animals here and there. In one notable 120-day marathon, eleven thousand animals were slaughtered for the crowd's amusement. The venationes were instrumental in bringing about the extinction of African lions and elephants in lands north of the Sahara. But these were not the only animals killed. The crowds watched ostriches, ibexes, stags, boars, leopards, sheep, giraffes, onagers, hyenas, rhinoceroses, tigers, and so on, meet bloody ends. And if the poor creatures weren't ferocious (predators) or terrified (prey) enough to satisfy the audience, the animals would be dispatched with arrows or spears—five thousand in a single day in one notorious case.

But not all Roman entertainment involved death, dismemberment, and cruelty to animals. Among the most popular entertainments were the raucous comedies of Titus Maccius Plautus, often familiar to modern audiences thanks to the musical *A Funny Thing Happened on the Way to the Forum*, which had characters and situations adapted from Plautus.

Greek theatre had a profound effect on all that came afterward, but this is not to say that theatre did not exist in other parts of the world, developing independently of the Greek and Roman models and styles. There were rich traditions in places like Aztec Mexico, Shang China, sub-Saharan and Nilotic Africa, and the Middle East, many of them growing out of religious ceremonies with various degrees of separation between the performers and the audience. These traditions came to be disrupted and banned in many places by European imperialism. But elements have survived and are being rescued from extinction by modern historians and theatre folk.

One of the most interesting traditions that has survived more or less intact was developed in ancient India, starting in the second millennium BCE. The complex theology of Hinduism is encoded in four Vedas: the Rigveda, the Yajurveda, the Samaveda, and the Atharvaveda, which outline how to live and how to worship. According to tradition, the people of India implored the god Brahma for a fifth Veda, one specifically for rituals and theatre. Brahma responded with the *Natya Shastra*, an encyclopedic treatise on every aspect of the performing arts, including drama, music, dance, and poetry. Although it is full of minute, nuts-and-bolts technical details on how to do everything from construct a musical scale to how to hold your hands and direct your eyes on stage, the point of the *Natya Shastra* is to make performing arts central to the expression of Hindu religious devotion. The gods want to be entertained, and entertained properly. Significantly, the caste system of social strata, which is important to much of the history of Hinduism, does not apply to the performing arts: the processes outlined in the *Natya Shastra* are open to all castes, from Brahmans to Untouchables. All are equal when it comes to performing for the supernatural audience of the gods.

The Audience in the Middle Ages

The Western Roman Empire, centered on Rome, endured its final collapse in the late 400s CE. However, the Catholic Church persisted like a ghost of the empire, with its emperor-like pope in Rome, the bishops like governors of the provinces, which the Romans also had called dioceses. The churches, built with increasing magnificence in the centuries that followed, preserved the performative qualities of theatre: music, lavish costumes and props, storytelling, a central character (the priest) and subsidiary characters (deacons, altar boys, etc.), and above all, ceremony, which built to the miraculous climax of transubstantiation: the supposed changing of bread and wine into the body and blood of the man believed to be the Son of God, Jesus Christ.

"Offstage," in the rectories, monasteries, and convents, ancient texts were preserved, copied, and sometimes studied. tenth-century German nun Hroswitha of Gandersheim (who was also one of the first acknowledged female playwrights) was so inspired by what she found that she wrote plays on Christian religious themes modeled on the ancient Greek dramas that chronicled the doings of their gods. Her work was part of a small flowering of morality plays that taught Biblical lessons. Who were the audiences for Hroswitha's plays? It's doubtful that they were performed in any kind of formal theatre because none existed in her time. Perhaps they were performed at the convent, but more likely they were what is known as closet dramas—plays created only to be read. Whatever their original audience, her fellow nuns liked her plays enough to preserve them, and that's the only reason we have them today.

European audiences of the Middle Ages had little education—or, more often, none at all. There were no public libraries. The only book any of them ever saw or heard of was the Bible. Masses were conducted in classical Latin, a language they understood less and less as it evolved into what we now know as Italian, French, Spanish, Romanian, and other descendant languages. Congregations heard Bible stories only from droning priests, barely more literate than they, in their homilies.

These stories came alive for medieval audiences through miracle plays performed as an adjunct to church services, usually to celebrate holy days like Easter and Christmas. More sophisticated versions of these parish plays, known today as Civic Cycles, were performed on a parade of carts or wheeled platforms called pageant wagons in medieval villages. The wagons would gather in the village square or snake through the streets of the town, each presenting a different scene in the play, with audiences walking from one to the next. Among the most popular pageants that survive today: "The Fall of Man" and "The Crucifixion."

Some wagons were fairly simple; some were complex: two or three stories tall, with moving parts and primitive machinery to create special effects. Workers of the time were often organized into guilds to train newcomers, set standards, and determine prices. Each wagon was assigned to a different guild, and the guilds competed with one another to dazzle unsophisticated audiences with the most impressive setting and costumes for their wagons. There being no professional actors, the roles in the pageants were taken by guild members or other people from the community. A popular attraction of these miracle plays was the Hell Mouth, usually depicted as a terrifying dragon head, sometimes complete with smoke and flame special effects, featuring a fanged mouth opened wide to gobble up unwary souls and swallow them down to Perdition.

The pageant wagon performances were entertaining. But more important, they were instructive to the viewers who had never seen anything like them. By dramatizing scenes from the Bible, they taught medieval audiences to fear God, fear damnation, love the Savior, and obey the church.

For simple people living simple lives, the Bible, with all its miraculous tales, adventures, miracles, frightening villains, and supernatural characters, seemed immediate and real. And because the roles were performed by people they knew, these pageants drove home the New Testament story of God made man, having decided to be born and live as a human being and share their pains, desires, illnesses, and appetites. And who, it was said, died for them. It was potent theatre for a receptive audience and helped keep Christianity alive.

But the presence of pageant wagons was the exception, not the rule, in most towns across Europe. What little news and entertainment they got from beyond the fields surrounding their villages came from traveling entertainers known as troubadours or minstrels. They served many roles: musicians, singers, dancers, jugglers, acrobats, jesters, and storytellers. They often carried fiddles, lutes, or other easily portable musical instruments. They told stories of distant places and wonders, some of which began as truthful accounts, but gradually grew in the telling to become myths and legends.

In a time long before newspapers, troubadours also often brought news about what was happening in the next town and the wider world. With no mass communication, news moved slowly—even directives from the king, duke, bishop, or whatever noble ruled their lives. It was a sad fact of medieval life that people were all too often horribly surprised when enemy armies or ships full of Vikings descended on their towns to rape and pillage. Troubadours sometimes brought urgent warnings that saved lives. (Most troubadours were men, though there were some bold and talented women, known as trobairitzes, who fulfilled the same role.)

The role and popularity of these minstrels is reflected in the story of Blondel de Nesle, who was a real historical figure but who lives on today in what is widely considered a pleasant legend. Blondel was a twelfth-century performer who served in the court of the English King Richard I, the Lion-Hearted. Richard and Blondel even composed a love song together.

Returning from the Crusades through the section of the Holy Roman Empire now known as Austria in 1192 CE, King Richard was taken prisoner by a rival, Duke Leopold of Austria. Blondel set out to find his lost master by traveling as a troubadour from castle to castle throughout Europe, singing their song, and hoping Richard would hear it. While performing the song in the city of Dürnstein, Blondel completed the first verse, only to hear a voice from below singing the second verse. With Blondel's help, this royal audience of one was able to win his freedom.

Shakespeare's Audience

Many people have some sort of mental image of William Shakespeare—balding guy with quill pen, perhaps—and at least some vague idea of what his plays looked like when staged, with doublets and swords and such. They know he was considered "great."

But who came to see his plays? The Globe Theatre wasn't easy to get to, on the other side of the Thames, away from the heart of London. But they came back again and again, high born and low, and supported him whether he was writing raucous comedies, moony romances, deeply philosophical dramas, or sword-clanging action-adventures.

Naturally, these audiences had their preferences. Mistaken identity, cross-dressing, witty wordplay, lots of glimpses into the private lives of the high and mighty. And the ever-popular sword fights. How do we know this? Shakespeare titled one of his plays *As You Like It*, which contained all these elements.

Each morning the theatre owner would advertise what kind of play would be presented by hoisting a color-coded flag: a white flag meant that a comedy would be performed that day; a black flag announced a tragedy, a red flag advertised a history.

Tickets might seem cheap by modern standards. Bottom price was a penny, but in those days that was enough to buy a loaf of bread. That detail reveals a great deal about those audiences. They were doing just well enough to not need that extra loaf of bread to survive. They could spend it on fun.

Prices went up from there: twopence to sit on benches at the back of the Yard. Threepence paid for a seat in the ground-level section of the gallery. Four to sixpence paid for increasingly nice seats on increasingly high levels of the gallery. Cushions could also be rented for a further penny.

Today, we think of the seats right in front of the stage as the most desirable. But in Shakespeare's day that was not the case. The open area directly in front of the stage, an area called the yard, had no seats. People holding the cheapest tickets, called "groundlings" or more descriptively, "stinkards," got to watch the play from below, while the wealthier people sat in the shade of a three-level gallery and got to see the action head-on,

The curtain call for a performance of The Tempest *by Shakespeare at Shakespeare's Globe, London, 2000; Master of Design: Bjanka Ursulov, Master of Music: Nigel Osborne, Master of Play / Director: Lenka Udovicki.*
Donald Cooper / Alamy Stock Photo

or from above. The groundlings would stand for hours on the straw-covered yard, cracking and eating (and sometimes throwing) hazelnuts and cockles while watching some of the greatest dramas ever written.

According to historians from Winthrop University, Shakespeare's audiences would become "restless if there's no action; they talk, and get up and walk around, and sometimes even throw things. They hoot if the hero kisses the heroine. This is a mild version of what the people in the pit were like. They might have been able to appreciate the subtleties of Hamlet's soliloquy; but they wanted a sword fight or a good, bloody murder. And if too much time went by without one, they'd amuse themselves by booing or jeering the people on stage, or throwing rotten fruit or eggs at the actors. Thus, keeping the pit happy was one of Shakespeare's (or any playwright's) major concerns. One of the things he liked most about the Blackfriars Theatre was that it catered to a wealthier and more educated audience, and had no pit."

In his essay "Walking Shadows," historian Ed Simon painted a vivid picture of the collaboration between Shakespeare and his first audiences. "Shakespeare didn't have in mind an arid graduate seminar, but rather wrote for the Globe Theatre in the warm dwindling sunlight—the length of acts had to be timed to end before it became too dark. The background noise of theatregoers loudly munching on concessions would require consideration as well. Scenes would need to be scheduled so that Blackfriars' stagehands could cut candlewicks, lest smoke sting the eyes of performers. So prevalent is the contention that Shakespeare was 'not of an age, but for all time,' as Jonson wrote, that we can forget how he was very much of his own age, one that he shared with the actors who performed his words."

Advancing Technology

Theatre enjoyed explosive growth in the first half of the seventeenth century, especially the 1630s and 1640s. The Renaissance was in full bloom in northern Italy, with the principalities achieving enough wealth to pursue their curiosity about the magnificent ruins of the Roman Empire they lived amid. With surviving ancient texts rescued from the collapse of the Eastern Roman Empire in 1453 and the discovery of long-lost scripts by Plautus and other Roman writers, the theatre artists of Renaissance Italy sought to recreate the great works of the past. Reading the writings of Vitruvius inspired them to recreate the technological innovations of the late empire, especially in terms of theatre design.

But the intellectual reawakening of the period also inspired new innovations. Among them, were Filippo Brunelleschi's development of point perspective, which led to a revolution in set design that lent the stage the illusion of depth.

Recreations of classical stage design revealed its weaknesses. Where could crews hide those increasingly lavish sets, and how could they move them on and off stage without slowing the action unduly? The development of machinery above the stage led to the building of the Teatro Farnese in Parma, the first pro-scenium stage. Theatre technicians of the period experimented with different ways of hiding and revealing action, which led to the various means of raising, lowering, or parting the curtains.

Moving the action of plays indoors out of the elements also demanded lighting. Experiments with methods of lighting the stage, mainly through candles, led to the invention of devices that could be dimmed to varying degrees.

Another major innovation was the development of the chariot-and-pole device that allowed the stage crew to change scenery fluidly, seemingly by magic, though actually using a system of pulleys that slid scenery off and on simultane-ously. These innovations influenced theatre throughout western Europe, notably in France, where the shows that used them came to be known as machine plays.

The ability to change location more fluidly and to gain con-trol over lighting also helped undermine the neoclassical preoc-cupation with the Aristotelean unities of place, time, and action. It freed playwrights to explore a wider range of subjects, char-acters, and locations. These changes enabled audiences to stay engrossed in the action rather than being jolted back to reality by the mechanics of changing scenery, lighting, et cetera.

As in ancient Greece, novelty came to be associated with the demonstration of wealth by the princes who sponsored the theatre of the period. Competition to outdo one another in theatrical spectacle inspired innovations in playwriting and design, along with an arms race in theatrical technology that continues today.

2

WHAT DOES THE
AUDIENCE WANT?

The 1998 Broadway musical *Ragtime* contains a lyric by Lynn
Ahrens (set to music by Stephen Flaherty) that explains simply
and clearly—yet profoundly—what all audiences want. In the
song "Buffalo Nickel Photoplay, Inc.," the character of Tateh, a
pioneer in the movie business, tries to describe why his simple
nickelodeon (the primitive film format, not the cable TV service
of today) featurettes are so wildly popular in early twentieth-
century America. He sings:

> *Life shines from the shadow screen,*
> *Comical, yet infinitely true.*
> *People love to see what people do*

> ("Buffalo Nickel Photoplay, Inc.,"
> excerpted from *Ragtime*.
> Lyrics by Lynn Ahrens,
> music by Stephen Flaherty)

That's it. People are curious animals. They like to watch other
people and see how they behave.

In role-playing games, it's possible to simply watch other
people play the game. It may seem odd, but how is that different from people watching baseball or tennis? Most of them
could easily play it themselves, but they like to see how others

work their way through the game. For that matter, that's also why people watch plays and movies and TV shows. They want to see how other people solve their problems. A lot of theorizing can stem from such a simple thought. But that's what it all boils down to. We like to watch. And listen.

One of the earliest theorists of this phenomenon was the Greek philosopher and polymath Aristotle, who assembled his *Poetics* nearly twenty-four hundred years ago. He gave voice to feelings and principles that playwrights, actors and, most importantly, audiences had always sensed and intuited, but to which they had never given names.

One of the most important of these principles was the concept of *katharsis*—the purging of negative emotion. Aristotle believed that theatre was not just "entertainment" but was actually necessary for the mental and emotional health of human beings, and therefore necessary for the proper functioning of the *polis*, the city-state of Athens itself.

Watching the great tragedies like *Medea* or *Oedipus Rex* or the *Oresteia* trilogy provoked sensations of "terror and pity" as Aristotle put it, leading to the cleansing release of tears. One way audiences accomplish this is by identifying with one or more of the characters—characters we admire, or those whose predicament we can sympathize with.

The horrors that the central characters encountered firsthand could be experienced secondhand by the audience watching and enduring them vicariously at minimal personal cost or danger. This enabled the audience to think "What would I do in a similar situation?" "How would I react?" Or better yet, "What could I do to avoid getting in a situation like that?" Such plays usually dealt with powerful people, and sometimes even the gods, which allowed audience members to measure themselves against great personages. These experiences also helped prepare the audience in case similar disasters should ever befall them, and therefore inoculated them emotionally.

Life comprises conflicts, great and small. And so does drama. Politics, sports, stories, and just about every narrative presented to an audience does too. Conflict is the central engine of drama, and it gives birth to both comedy and tragedy. The audience's surrogate is the protagonist—the hero/heroine. The protagonist wants to do or be or get something, but is opposed by an adversary, the antagonist or villain. In some stories the protagonist overcomes the adversary. That's usually comedy. Sometimes the protagonist is defeated and the antagonist is the winner. That's usually tragedy.

Ultimately, both of those things happen. They are part of life. And the audience gets to experience their happening vicariously. They watch to see how the conflict will be resolved. And they come away a little bit better equipped to face the vicissitudes of real life.

Psychology of the Audience

The audiencing experience begins with the lights going down. In live theatres and cinemas there is usually a moment of literal darkness. Even on television there's often a momentary pause between one show and the next, or between a commercial and a show, or between the "bumper"—the station identification or promo or other transitionary clip—and the main program.

This moment approximates falling asleep or blinking your eyes. It is designed to approximate the beginning of a dream, a period when we willingly enter into that suspension of disbelief—that moment discussed earlier when we agree to immerse ourselves in a story, to submit to a kind of light hypnosis when we enter the world of the video game or film or TV show or sports, and agree to pretend that we're not just a person sitting in a dark room looking at shadows on a wall, but flying into space, or walking dangerous streets or following whatever journey the storyteller wants to take us on.

Sometimes the piece we're watching serves the same purpose as a dream. It runs us through a variety of emotional paces, allowing us to exercise our minds and straighten out mental clutter in an environment that doesn't necessarily threaten us physically—no matter how terrifying the nightmare might be, or how forbidden the sexual scenario may be.

It's a remarkable feat of mutual trust. Jump cuts in storytelling fill in what is not absolutely necessary to the narrative. We know what a long car ride is like. We don't need to see every minute of it in order to follow the story. Our minds just fill in the missing scene. In real life, we have to take the car ride. In a movie, we only need to see the character entering or leaving the car to know what happened in between. We trust the storyteller that nothing important happened during the ride, or it would have been shown.

Once the audience is under this spell, the variety of sensory input from what we're watching begins to engage the emotions, of course. That brings up memories, both pleasant and unpleasant. We may recall a game or favorite toy we played with as children. When watching sports we may recall good (or bad) times we had on the field with our friends and parents. Love scenes may bring up lost or current loves. Scenes with children may remind us of something our own children said or did. What we're watching engages the intellect. "Oh, yes, I read something about this." "My teacher once said something like that." It engages skepticism. "Wait, I know that's nonsense." "This is set in 1955 and I know that model car didn't come out until '59 or '60." "There's no sound in space!"

The thing we're watching stirs our hopes, our libidos, our subconscious yearnings. The best things we watch reach psychological depths, of which we may scarcely be aware. We may laugh or cry at what we're watching, and not even be sure why.

We constantly measure the story against our previous experience, adding bits of information where we find a gap, reinforcing a notion or a prejudice or a belief ("Great movie—I know just how they felt!"), and sometimes rejecting what we see if it fails to match what we know—or think we know ("Lousy movie—it just wasn't believable").

We find ourselves caught up in the story, or not, as the individual case may be.

Everyone has their unique reaction to what they see on the screen, the stage, or the sports field. Things that *he* finds dull might fascinate *her*, and vice versa. It depends not just on what's in the story or the song or the game, but on what we bring to the experience. Our lives, our prejudices, our interests, our personal tastes, our upbringing, our little obsessions, our socioeconomic group, the era in which we were raised, the environment in which our interests were formed, the ups and downs of our life, our education, our ethnic background, our level of maturity—these all play into our audience experience. One person may hate roller coasters or horror movies or a particular band. The person next to them may love all those things, or be bored by them.

Sometimes the protagonist says things we cannot say, which allows us to test out new ideas and words in a safe way. We can see what may happen when those words are said. The characters may have adventures we wish we could have, or are afraid of having. They take chances. They succeed and we share in their success, as with a sports star. Or they come crashing down in flames as failures, and we see how they deal with it, as with a singer who forgets the words or suffers from a sour note. We measure our knowledge and learn things when we watch a game show like *Jeopardy!* We measure our own voice or other talent against contestants on a competition show, like *America's Got Talent*. These TV shows I mention are mostly recent, but the principle has been in force since we gathered around storytellers in caves millennia ago.

Indeed, scriptwriters and actors both owe a debt to the first storytellers described in chapter 1. The skills honed while telling stories around a fire are the same skills used today. Their primary tool is conflict. Two people enter a room. One wants something. The other wants to stop her or him from getting it. Who will get their way, and how? We're already interested.

But the storyteller doesn't resolve the conflict right away. That's when the second tool comes into play: suspense. They talk, they argue—will there be a fight? Will one of them deliver a devastating comment that will smash the other one's confidence? *How will it end?*

Then the storyteller adds a countdown of some kind. One person in the room has to meet a train and must be out within a half hour! A decision has to be made before a third person arrives in five minutes!! One is carrying a bomb that will explode in ninety seconds!!! A skilled storyteller or musician or athlete knows how to hold the audience's attention, and when, finally, to let it go.

As Frank N. Furter says in *The Rocky Horror Picture Show*, "I see you shiver with antici—
(He pauses for what seems like an eternity, then . . .)
—pation!"

Another important factor in storytelling is the rate at which each of us can absorb and process information about plot and character, even the rate at which we are able to absorb and process the very words being spoken. There was a time when actors were trained to enunciate: to speak clearly and understandably. This was important when theatres were 100 percent acoustic. But with the introduction of electronic amplification and the miked recordings of film and digital entertainment, actors found they could speak more colloquially, could mumble or rush their words to sound less artificial and more "realistic."

Many audiences prefer to absorb the words and the story at a leisurely pace, comparable to the musical tempo of *largo*. They like to savor each word and think over each turn of phrase. Other audiences find that pace frustratingly slow. I get it already! Get a move on! I haven't got all day! They like things *andante*.

And then there are those audiences who like speed and complexity just as they might enjoy spicy food. They crave *presto*. It's not a new concept. Shakespeare's ideas, images, and gems of poetry sometimes tumble out at a dizzying rate. Jump to the patter songs of Gilbert and Sullivan, Mozart's "too many notes" as described in *Amadeus*, the interlocking puzzles of Stephen Sondheim's counterpoint songs, the machine-gun story-weaving of rap choppers like Twista and Busta Rhymes.

Audiences who prefer their information input *presto*, or even just *allegro con moto*, love drinking from the fire hose when they sit down to be entertained. The others protest, "I can't understand a thing they're saying!" That's legitimate too.

Many audiences like a bold story told with a lot exciting incidents. Others like to enjoy vicarious romance with beautiful costumes and lush settings. Some like their stories to be presented like complex mysteries or even as a kind of dramatic crossword puzzle. Think of the "nonsense" that suddenly reveals itself as brilliance in James Joyce's *Finnegans Wake*, the unapologetic dada of Gertrude Stein's *Four Saints in Three Acts*, the realization that characters are traveling both forward and backward in time simultaneously in *Tenet*. Fans of works like these like to *solve* what they're watching.

For many, this is great fun. For many others, it's a headache.

Movement

There are other, more fundamental ways audiences absorb story information. Mime and dance seem to be restricted in what they can communicate because they eschew anything verbal. And yet, watching them, we realize how much we use our hands, eyes, and the stance of our entire bodies to communicate with others. For instance, no mere words can convey as eloquently what a sultry, side-eyed look over the shoulder can.

Think of Mr. Noodle (Bill Irwin) on *Sesame Street*. He never says a word, but his struggles to put on a hat or catch a ball

The Busking Project on the streets of New York, with Bill Irwin and a young audience member.
Photo by Howard Sherman

or get his feet into his shoes are instantly recognizable to any child. He offers kids who don't know how to do these things a sense that they're not alone. And it allows those who *do* know how to do them to feel a flush of pride that they have mastered something that's not easy, even for a seeming grown-up like Mr. Noodle.

This processing of information from various sources in different ways at the same time reaches its acme in the *bharata natyam,* considered the national dance theatre of India. It developed in what is now the southern Indian state of Tamil Nadu and is spreading gradually throughout the world.

Originating as a form of religious devotion in the region's Hindu temples, it has a strong narrative element, employing densely choreographed hand movements (*mudras*) and eye movements (*dhrishti bheda*) as distinguishing features. These are designed to tell stories and recreate adventures drawn from the great Indian epic the *Mahabharata* in a way that would be understandable to all viewers. The choreographed movements contain strong elements of what would be termed mime in the West.

The central action of traditional bharata natyam consists of a single body (usually a woman—bharata natyam is traditionally a female-practiced art form) moving through space to a set of highly stylized and choreographed steps and movements. Sets and props are generally dispensed with, though makeup and costuming are bold and vivid.

Formal bharata natyam performances are divided into segments. The first part (*nritta*) consists of pure dance. Subsequent segments (*varnam*) are used to tell a story or stories. The *varnam* sections are designed literally to speak without words. Originally quite simple and easily understandable to a general audience (as many performances still are), the intensely choreographed movements have evolved and become more complex over the centuries to the point that they now require some study for a sophisticated audience. In its more advanced forms, these movements become a kind of sign language.

All parts of the body are choreographed, including the hands, the head, the neck, the feet, and notably the eyes. The torso is generally erect, with knees usually bent. The *mudras* can be very simple. A thumbs-up movement (*shikara*) denotes courage. Three fingers held up together (*trishula*) indicates a trident (three-pronged weapon). Others have metaphorical meanings, like a palm held flat with the thumb crossing in front of it (*chatura*), which denotes cleverness. Some mudras mean different things in different contexts.

Similarly, the eyes themselves have choreographed movements that include the *pralokita* (moving the eyes from side to side), the *anuvritta* (flicking the eyes up and down), and the *nimilita* (focusing the gaze at the heart through half-shut eyes). The whole head, the arms, and even the neck have similar specifically significant movements.

Like mimes, these dancers speak a physical language that can be understood by onlookers with even the most limited experience. We know that people don't communicate only with spoken words. Facial expressions, hand gestures, and body motions can convey attitude and subtext, and greatly enhance verbal communication. But these gestures, polished and developed to a high degree, not only take the place of words, but they can render words unnecessary. The audience possesses the ability to extract meaning and significance from even the simplest of movements. Like the waggle dance of the honeybee that tells her hive mates where nectar-bearing flowers can be found, mime and dance movement can tell stories and move the heart as powerfully as the choicest *bon mot*.

The Mind Wanders

The narrative arts are designed to stimulate all parts of the audience's brain. It's not surprising, then, that sometimes the mind wanders during a performance. This is especially the case when the music or story at hand stimulate powerful emotions and memories. And, of course, the mind also tends to wander when it is bored or annoyed with what is being watched.

Naturally the performers and technical artists hope they are fully engaging everyone in the audience all the time. But the truth is, sometimes they just need to wake 'em up. The flash of a light, a finger-snap, a whistle. A cut from a slow, dark scene to a loud, bright scene. A dramatic modulation. A quiet scene that turns into shouts. A sudden confrontation with someone in the audience. You've probably seen a comedian actually make hay of his lack of reactions. He may pick on one person in the audience, or even poke the whole crowd for "sitting on their hands." An angry audience is an awake audience.

The Appeal of Comedy

Who doesn't like to laugh? Since before the days of royal court jesters, audiences have loved clowns and comedians, whether they're laughing with the performers or at them. *The Dick Van Dyke Show*, on TV in the early 1960s, found humor in the workplace, in marriage, and in parenthood, but it usually opened with Van Dyke coming home and immediately tripping over an ottoman and performing an elegant pratfall. Trying to help her granddaughter whose marriage is breaking up, Madea (Tyler Perry in *Diary of a Mad Black Woman*) offers her typically Solomonic solution: taking a chain saw to the couch they're fighting over.

Comedians look at life from an unusual angle, telling us unexpected truths, saying "forbidden" things we wish we could say, and doing things we dream of doing but are prevented by social strictures. They break normal rules, and sometimes turn normal situations upside down. They afflict the comfortable and comfort the afflicted. The more something or someone frightens us and has power over us, the more comedians work to puncture their self-importance and show us how weak and ridiculous they really are.

These clowns and comedians often pay the price for their transgressions, either on the stage or in their offstage lives. Ask Charlie Chaplin, Lenny Bruce, Sam Kinison, or the fictional Pagliacci. And still, we laugh. We feel superior to the people and situations they're making fun of, and sometimes we feel superior to the comedian. And sometimes, really skillful comedians will make us laugh at ourselves.

For a time, while we watch them make fools of themselves, or make fools of others, including us, we have the brief luxury of forgetting our own troubles, however considerable they may be. That, too, is a universal need of audiences everywhere.

The Appeal of Sex

Throughout history, audiences have also wanted to see sex, whether explicit or in the form of romance. In recent years the mass popularity of, and easy access to, pornography of all kinds via the internet has enabled audiences of one to indulge pretty much any kink you can imagine.

The desire to watch pretty girls and handsome boys transcends time, place, and cultural differences. They look nice and have offered audiences titillation and even arousal down through the ages via pinups, girlie magazines, stud calendars, erotic pottery, burlesque, peep shows, dirty movies, and all media ever used, used now, or may be developed in the future.

Despite endless efforts to suppress it, criminalize it, and portray it as a threat to our immortal souls, sex has never gone out of style.

The Appeal of Adrenaline

Sexual arousal is far from the only kind audiences enjoy. Look at the popularity of action movies that get the heart pounding. Audiences line up to see the likes of Chuck Norris, Jackie Chan, Sigourney Weaver, Robert Downey Jr., Sylvester Stallone, Arnold Schwarzenegger, Jennifer Lawrence, Chadwick Boseman, and Harrison Ford test their mettle against impossible odds in movies about Superman, Batman, Iron Man, Wonder Woman, Black Panther, Indiana Jones, and in earlier generations, Robin Hood, Buck Rogers, and Flash Gordon.

We enjoy their dangerous adventures vicariously, see how they managed to use brains, muscle (and money) to get themselves out of unsurvivable circumstances, solve impenetrable puzzles, and overcome massively overwhelming odds to win through to victory once again. Sometimes audiences learn lessons from their resourcefulness; sometimes they just go along for the crazy ride and surf the adrenalin rush.

The Appeal of Tears

The phenomenon is not that different from "weepers": stories, especially movies, that are designed to move the audience to tears. Among the classics are *The Notebook, Brief Encounter*, the opening sequence of Disney's *Up, Cyrano de Bergerac,* and the ultimate three-handkerchief heartbreaker, the 1945 movie *Mildred Pierce*. The latter tells the story of a woman, abandoned by her husband during the Great Depression, who gives up her own happiness to support her snobby and ungrateful daughter, who resents Mildred for the family's loss of social status. But Mildred will do anything for her daughter, including taking the rap for a murder she committed. Along the way Mildred also deals with the deaths of her other child and her second husband, and yet continues to soldier on bravely as the audience sobs.

Why would anyone want to see such a sad story and dab tears for 111 minutes? The same reason the ancient Greeks mobbed the great tragedies: catharsis—the healthy release of built-up emotion and the exercise of our emotional muscles.

Rehearsing Death

Exercising these emotional muscles is not just an end in itself. It prepares us, in a way, for how we will handle such sadness when it enters our own lives.

But the other side of Aristotle's "terror and pity" is, of course, terror.

Blood sports have always been perversely popular. Lynchings and sanctioned capital punishment have always drawn a crowd, as have plays where people are stabbed, slashed, have their eyes gouged out, or in the case of Oedipus, gouge their own eyes out. Bullfights, bearbaiting, dogfighting, cockfighting, and the gladiatorial contests in ancient Rome we saw in chapter 1 all ended in blood being spilled.

We may think we are so much more civilized because modern horror films, TV cop shows, and video games all use simulated or special-effects blood. Nevertheless, audiences love the shock of seeing the blood. The A. C. Nielsen Company estimated in 2013 that by the time an average American child finishes elementary school, they will have witnessed *eight thousand* murders on television. And that's only television. Movies and violent video games add far more.

And who was worse, ultimately? The people who made "snuff" (staged or not)? Or the people who avidly watched them?

So does that mean people who watch these gory acts are sick or perverted or evil? Or is the act of watching horrible death for entertainment just another way of exercising our emotional muscles, more akin to fans of weepy movies than mass murderers? Many will say no, that watching violent death again and again either desensitizes audiences or gives them an appetite for more. The same A. C. Nielsen survey that listed how many deaths people see on TV also found that 79 percent of Americans believe TV violence helps precipitate real-life mayhem: they point to the sickening rash of school and mall shootings over the past several decades as a symptom.

But most people don't react that way. For most audiences, seeing death dramatized is a way of preparing themselves for it—for the death of people we may hate or love, or even for the prospect of our own death. Rehearsing for it helps to put our emotional house in order.

Death may be "an awfully big adventure," as Peter Pan says. It may be the beginning of a second and eternal life in the hereafter, as many religions teach. It may be the irreversible end of everything. Death is the ultimate fate and the ultimate mystery. And when we're in an audience, we learn not only about ourselves, but about how others react to death. It puts death—with its horror, and perhaps, in the case of ghost stories and religion, a glimpse at what may follow—in a larger context.

Escapism

The other side of that coin is taking part in an audience to hide from pain, to relax and have a mindless good time. It's a way of dealing with what is known as the "tired businessman" syndrome—though the phenomenon is certainly not limited to men or to those in business. Anyone who's living through a dark time in their life or who has just had a hard day may want to be part of an audience that enjoys a laugh, hears some pretty music, or follows an undemanding storyline with a happy ending. They may want to watch an exciting sports contest in a stadium, with friendly strangers over beers in a sports bar, or just with good friends and family in a living room or movie theatre. These things just take their minds off what's bothering them, and for an hour or two allows them just to watch someone else dealing with their own problems with a positive outcome. The satisfaction may be personal, but there is also relief in watching other people peacefully having a good time without demanding anything of the viewer. There is something extra comforting about having a good time as part of an audience.

Suspension of Disbelief

One of the most remarkable—yet underrated—feats of human imagination is what's known as willing suspension of disbelief. We spend our lives trying to separate what's real from what is imaginary or illusory. It's a survival technique. Yet when we enter a theatre or a cinema, or even when we turn on a television or a radio, or log on to a website, we perform a feat of mental acrobatics. We *will* ourselves to ignore the curtains, ignore the fact that we're in a dark and crowded room with a sticky floor, ignore the fact that we're looking at shadows coming from a little box, ignore the fact that the people we see are actors pretending to be people they aren't—saying words written by someone else, and having adventures with special effects that were manufactured in a computer. Instead, we allow ourselves to enter the world of the show, to believe for a little while that we're flying through space, or riding the Hogwarts Express, or witnessing a furious battle, or watching real people falling in love. The distractions of reality become invisible and for the duration of the show, we believe.

In Japanese theatre, the stagehands are called *kuroko* (黒衣), which literally means "black-clad." They dress all in black as their name suggests and move about the stage doing their work in full view of the audience. The audience, however, knows to mentally subtract them from the action of the play. They are effectively invisible.

The concept of suspension of disbelief was first described by Aristotle, explored by Roman philosopher Marcus Tullius Cicero, and centuries later given the name by poet Samuel Taylor Coleridge as part of a "philosophical experiment" with his colleague William Wordsworth.

Coleridge described this "poetic faith" in his *Biographia Literaria*, writing,

> It was agreed, that my endeavors should be directed to persons and characters supernatural, or at least romantic, yet so as to transfer from our inward nature a human interest and a semblance of truth sufficient to procure for these shadows of imagination that willing suspension of disbelief for the moment, which constitutes poetic faith. Mr. Wordsworth on the other hand was to propose to himself as his object, to give the charm of novelty to things of every day, and to excite a feeling analogous to the supernatural, by awakening the mind's attention from the lethargy of custom, and directing it to the loveliness and the wonders of the world before us.

In other words, the goal is to create an effect so lifelike that the audience allows itself to believe for a time that what they are experiencing is real. This is theatre of the mind—not the self-hypnosis technique of the same name described by Maxwell Maltz, but the ability to listen to a storyteller and conjure in our minds pictures and characters and clashes, monumental or intimate, simply through the power of their words mated with our life experiences. We stop for a moment and allow ourselves to forget that we are hearing nothing more than the vibrations of their vocal cords or words scratched on paper, and instead convince ourselves that we are experiencing the most outlandish or outrageous events. We do this so often and so casually that we forget what a miracle human imagination can be.

The Appeal of Magic . . .

Even greater feats of suspension of disbelief are required, and happily achieved, by people who go to see magicians, take part in seances, submit to hypnotists, and sit for mind readers and psychics. Apart from true believers, most audiences know there is no way the magician can intuit which card you chose. They are aware that the dead can't communicate from beyond the grave. They're certain that there is no way they will succumb to the mesmerizing powers of a hypnotist. They are sure their thoughts can't be scanned like an email. And yet they *want* to believe in magic. They *wish* they could converse with their dear departed loved ones. They marvel when a psychic somehow knows so many personal details about their lives.

These audiences are willing collaborators in their own deception. They are the best assistants these talented charlatans could wish for. These audiences *love* being fooled, are grateful for the illusion of the supernatural, and cheerfully applaud the skill of their foolers.

. . . Or Not

That's all very well, but German playwright and director Bertolt Brecht (1898–1956) hated the notion of suspension of disbelief. He felt it was a con job perpetrated on audience members to put them in a sort of pleasant trance that distracted them from the political, social, and economic content of his plays. In his plays he constantly reminds the audience that what they are watching is fake, and they should not be deceived or pulled into the action because it's all make-believe. Brecht strove to break any spell that might be woven, and to remind the audience that they were there to be confronted by reality, not to escape from it. He called this *Verfremdungseffekt*—the "alienation effect."

To accomplish this, Brecht would often have his characters break the fourth wall (more on this in a moment) to address the audience directly, sometimes to point out unlikely plot developments in his own plays. Take, for example, his 1928 musical, *The Threepenny Opera*, one of Brecht's savage indictments of capitalism. In the "third finale," the show's antihero, master criminal Mackie Messer, aka Mack the Knife, is about to be hanged for his many crimes. He delivers one of Brecht's most famous lines: "What is robbing a bank compared with founding a bank?"

At the key moment, an emissary from the Queen arrives, pardoning Mack for all his crimes—and granting him a castle and a pension of ten thousand pounds a year as long as he shall live! The chorus then addresses the audience, admonishing them that, in reality, this is scarcely the fate of "the poorest of the poor, whose most arduous life you have seen portrayed here today. For, in fact, the poor come to very sticky ends. The saviors on horseback are far from frequent in practice."

I'm not sure if any audiences ever marched from his plays and started tearing down any capitalist enterprises, but it certainly helped them see things from a different perspective.

The Fourth Wall

In most plays, movies, and TV shows, the actors speak to each other, and the audience gets to listen in. We piece together the story from hearing what they say and seeing what they do, almost like we are watching them through a keyhole, or are invisible witnesses to even their most private, intimate conversations.

But every once in a while, an actor turns and speaks directly to the audience. This is called breaking the fourth wall, a reference to live theatre where the set is a room with three solid walls and an invisible fourth one through which the audience watches the action.

Sometimes the fourth wall is broken by a narrator, whose job is to help the audience by describing the background of the story and characters. Sometimes an actor will address an entire song or speech to the audience, to allow us to hear what they are thinking privately. Think of the opening speech of Shakespeare's *Richard III*, in which the bitter and plotting Richard tells the audience, "Now is the winter of our discontent" to describe how he hides his bitterness from his brothers, whom he intends to murder to make himself king.

Characters also are known to throw a line or a few to the audience, a practice known as an aside. But there are times where a character will treat the audience more like a friend and address entire speeches or even whole scenes to the audience.

For example, in the movie *Ferris Bueller's Day Off*, the lovable scamp Bueller (played by Matthew Broderick) is constantly confiding in the audience like they're his best buddies. At the end of the film, after the final credits finish rolling, he appears again, frowning a bit at those in the theatre who watched until the end, and tells them, "It's over. Go home!"

In both the original Broadway production and the film adaptation of *A Funny Thing Happened on the Way to the Forum*, the character of Pseudolus (played by Zero Mostel in both versions) spends the entire opening number, "Comedy Tonight," addressing the audience directly to describe the ancient Roman setting of the story. He describes the house of Erronius, "a befuddled old man, abroad now in search of his children, stolen in infancy by pirates." He next introduces the House of Marcus Lycus, "a buyer and seller of the flesh of beautiful women." He then leans in and adds, with a verbal wink, "That's for those of you who have absolutely no interest in pirates."

Filmmaker and comedian Woody Allen does a classic fourth wall break in his Oscar-winning comedy *Annie Hall*. Allen and costar Diane Keaton are waiting in line to buy tickets at a cinema, standing in front of a man who is gassing on and on to his date about the media theories of Marshall McLuhan. When Allen comments on him being a bloviating know-it-all, the man identifies himself as a Columbia professor and claims to be an authority on the subject.

Allen replies, "That's funny because I happen to have Mr. McLuhan *right here*." And, lo and behold, Allen pulls the actual McLuhan into the frame, and the theorist upbraids the loud-mouth: "I heard what you were saying. You know nothing of my work. . . . How you ever got to teach a course in anything is totally amazing."

Allen then breaks the fourth wall and tells the audience, rue-fully, "If life were only like this!"

In Thornton Wilder's Pulitzer Prize–winning play *The Skin of Our Teeth*, the fourth wall is violated repeatedly by several of the characters, who remind the audience they are watching actors in a play. At one point, the character of Sabina, the perpetually unhappy maid, confides, "I hate this play and I hate everyone in it."

Sometimes the audience, too, breaks the fourth wall. The 2022 Broadway revival of *The Music Man* drew a considerable crowd of theatre lovers to see this new take on the classic musi-cal. But it also attracted a considerable number of star Hugh Jackman's fans, some of whom had never seen a live stage musical before. An audience member, perhaps one of the latter group, broke the fourth wall in the scene where Jackman, as con man Professor Harold Hill, is trying to lure shy librarian Mar-ian Paroo (Sutton Foster) to meet him at the park footbridge—a traditional rendezvous for lovers. Marian coyly resists. Harold moves closer to her and turns up the high beams on his consider-able personal charm.

And in this moment, crackling with sexual energy, a woman at the back of the Winter Garden shouted, "Kiss her!" The audi-ence laughed. Jackman and Foster very nearly broke character to laugh as well. Foster blushed visibly. But they are pros, and they kept it together. They knew it wasn't time yet in the story structure for a kiss, but their live-theatre instincts told them they needed to do *something*. But what? After an uncertain moment Jackman did the only thing he could have done without break-ing character. He winked at the audience. The house erupted in applause and laughter. It was a Jackman wink, but it was also a con-man Harold Hill wink.

That's the beauty of live theatre. You can shout directions to a movie or TV screen until you're blue in the face, but it will never change. At *The Music Man*, the fans had the real thing right in front of them. And their charismatic idol changed his performance just that tiny bit for them. The audience changed the show.

In the following footbridge scene, where Harold finally lays a hot lip-lock on Marian as the script specifies, the audience exploded. It was finally the right moment, and it was received by the audience as if he had kissed *them*.

The Extensions of Man

Speaking of Marshall McLuhan, the Canadian communication theorist used so effectively as a prop in *Annie Hall*, enjoyed a vogue in the late 1960s and 1970s for his book *Understanding Media: The Extensions of Man*, which set forth several theories about how media affects the audience, and the society from which that audience is drawn.

Chapter 1 of that book was famously titled "The Medium Is the Message." It introduced the idea that the kinds of media we are absorbing are just as important, if not more important, than their actual content. As an example, he described how the neon lights in a marquee generate as much excitement about a given show as the name of the performer they spell out—that a story or star is in a big-budget movie on a huge screen is as important to the audience as the story being told.

McLuhan also examined the different ways and degrees to which various media involve the audience. He described certain media as "cool" or "hot," not owing to their sexual content or how famous the creators or performers might be, but to the amount of mental and emotional participation that particular medium demands of its audience. A hot medium is one that gives the audience everything it needs to understand and experience the content; movies (most of them, anyway) are an example because they involve the audience completely and tell them everything about the story, the characters, the costumes, the sights, and the sounds. All that is left to the audience is to absorb it, like a sponge. A cool medium is one that gives the audience only some information and calls for participants to supply the rest through their imaginations. Examples include radio, which gives only sounds and requires audiences to imagine everything else, and the spoken word, which stimulates the reader to fill in everything not directly supplied by the speaker.

Though a great deal of research and theorizing has been applied to this area of media studies, McLuhan's writings continue to be "cool media" themselves, especially since the internet revolution has changed the ways our society produces and consumes media.

Journalist Peter Hirshberg wrote about McLuhan,

> It is jarring to realize that the implication of this total media environment was also anticipated more than 40 years ago by McLuhan. When he spoke of the "global village," his point was not just that we'd be connected to one another. He was concerned that we'd all know each other's business, that we'd lose a measure of privacy as a result of living in a world of such intimate awareness. McLuhan called this "retribalizing," in the sense that modern media would lead us to mimic the behavior of tribal villages. Today, the effects of this phenomenon help define the media environment: we consciously manage ourselves as brands online; we are more concerned than ever with each other's business; and we are more easily called out or shamed than in the bygone (and more anonymous) mass communication era.

We understand what he's talking about when we watch a celebrity, politician, or industry leader get in trouble because of an old photo of something revealing or embarrassing they posted on the internet years ago. Or when we see innocent people stalked or subjected to revenge porn by rejected lovers or targeted by scams or phishing attacks. The very act of watching a video or looking at an online ad produces cookies that allow companies to track your interests and target you with customized ads—or worse things.

Fly on the Wall

It's interesting to note that audiences are expected to immerse themselves in a story or performance and feel they are in some sense a part of it—but very rarely do you see what's called POV (point of view) where the audience is watching as if through the eyes of one of the characters or participants and interacting with others.

Audiences for movies, TV shows, or concerts scan what's happening on the stage or screen as a separate party behind an imaginary fourth wall. This fly-on-the-wall experience means the audience goes wherever the creators want them to go and sees whatever the camera—or the position of their seat—allows. Audiences become voyeurs to moments of romance and spies during secret meetings. They can fly, pass through keyholes, and even breach solid walls. They see can see everything in a room, on a battlefield, or beneath the sea in a way that characters or performers cannot. But they are witnesses only. Audiences can shout at a screen or talk back to stage actors, but they are like ghosts: unseen, unheard, and unheeded by the actual participants.

The POV experience is much more common in role-playing video games like the seminal *Ultima Underworld* and *Wolfenstein 3D* or their descendants like *Prey*, *Bioshock*, *Skyrim*, and *Doom*. In these games, members of the audience are often among the participants. They experience the action not from beyond the safety of a fourth wall but through the eyes of one of the participants. They *are* participants, merging the roles of performer and audience. When they speak or act, they are heard and felt. No one watching *Saving Private Ryan* has to worry about being shot; in *World of Warcraft*, they worry about that all the time.

And talk about rehearsing for death: game participants are often wounded or even killed (virtually) and then return from the dead to game again. Are these games designed to train young and impressionable prospective conscripts to feel that dying in battle is no big deal? I'm being paranoid, perhaps. But perhaps not.

According to one survey, by age eighteen, the average TV watcher will have witnessed more than two hundred thousand "violent acts." Perhaps that needs to be updated to include valiant gamers, who may die dozens of times on a single weekend.

3

THE MIND AND BODY OF THE AUDIENCE

Understanding how humans function as members of an audience has attracted researchers from around the world. These include scientists with specializations in brain functioning who strive to explain exactly which lobes or neurons are stimulated during the audiencing experience, psychologists who explore the influence of childhood experiences, and social scientists and other scholars who try to understand how audiences relate to specific cultural or historical contexts. In all cases, they're trying to figure out just what it is that's going through the minds of audience members.

Beyond What Is Expected

In the book *Scales to Scalpels: Doctors Who Practice the Healing Arts of Music and Medicine,* about a group of Boston physicians who participate in the all-doctor Longwood Symphony Orchestra, coauthor Dr. Lisa Wong writes that what makes music interesting to audiences is

> the tension that you get from the variation beyond what is expected. That's why you can't listen to the same note over and over without getting bored and blanking out on it. The

human mind wants to hear the note do something a little different. Now, if the note tries to do something too far beyond the logic of expectation, the mind will reject it, and the person will say "I don't like that." But if the note changes just enough and for just the right interval, it will engage the brain and the person will continue to listen. Finding the right note and playing it the right way requires a fine sense of detail.

In music, as in storytelling overall, we expect things to go a certain way, but we get to enjoy the pleasure of surprise when it takes an unexpected turn that becomes exactly right and even better than what we anticipated.

Wong continues:

In music we get to exercise that propensity dozens of times over the course of a concert, playing notes that lead from one interesting place to another, keeping the audience engaged like a skilled storyteller telling an emotional story. That's what makes music exciting. That's what makes climaxes to pieces. That's what draws tears from your eyes: when you hear a tension between two notes that shouldn't be there and you're waiting for it to resolve. That's what's going to bring out the deeper emotion.

The Mirror Stage

The philosopher and psychoanalyst Jacques Lacan (1901–1981) wrote that humans go through a crucial phase in their psychological development called the mirror stage. Between the ages of six and eighteen months they learn to recognize that the image they see in a mirror is of themselves. It may appear to be separate, but it is indeed them.

According to Lacan, these children also see an idealized version of themselves that they spend their whole lives trying to live up to, sometimes fruitlessly. Some people hate what they see, or, more destructively, they love what they see in the mirror and come to hate their real selves for falling so far short of what they see—or think they see. In this they are like the wicked stepmother in *Snow White* who asks her magic mirror, "Who is the fairest of them all?" and is satisfied only when she is told that she is the most beautiful. But when the mirror tells her that someone else is, she becomes enraged.

Responding to criticism from his colleagues, Lacan modified his theory in later years to describe how the voyage of self-discovery, which starts with the mirror, continues through contact with metaphorical mirrors such as movies, plays, TV shows, and other representations. Most audiences need to identify with someone in a story in order to become emotionally involved. Usually it's the protagonist. We learn what they "want" early in the story and then watch them overcome obstacles, often including a villainous antagonist, on their way to getting it. The more urgent the want, the more interesting the obstacles, and the more hissable the villain—the more we enjoy the story. We see ourselves in that "mirror" and we root for them/us to succeed.

There has been a trend in commercial storytelling in recent years toward antiheroes. In these cases, the protagonist is deeply flawed or even evil, but there is something about the urgency of their want that makes us identify with and root for them. More often, however, the main character is idealized and heroic, making it easy to see our optimal selves in them. This accounts for the popularity of the Marvel Cinematic Universe, and all superheroes going back to the pulp comic book era and beyond. A lot of remakes and reboots claim to be "darker, grittier" takes on the story. But that may only be because our society as a whole has become more self-critical, and therefore more accepting that even our idealized versions of ourselves are far from perfect.

Stories We Love

There are certain archetypal stories that have enjoyed special resonance across the ages and across continents.

> Adventure—The main character or characters go on a quest to find something or achieve something, only to find the unexpected.

Romance—Lovers (of any gender identity) find each other, overcome adversity, part for a time over some disagreement, but then return with a deeper love.

Redemption—A disgraced character earns back their place in society through mighty or heartfelt deeds.

Rescue—Someone is saved from death, dismemberment, or other physical or spiritual disaster.

Revenge—You harmed me, and I will not rest until I harm you back.

Morality Tales—Parables that teach the difference between right and wrong.

Suspense—Someone achieves an objective, at the last minute and against all odds.

Triumph of the Underdog—The small and weak but worthy win out against stronger but unworthy opponents.

Life after Death—Everything from ghost stories and tales of the supernatural to religious texts.

Hypothesis, Antithesis, Synthesis—The foundation of all stories, whether we are conscious of it or not. Someone has a theory or idea, tests it out against all opposition, and then comes to a greater understanding.

There are more beyond these, and many stories combine aspects of more than one archetype. But what is it about these stories that resonate so deeply with humankind, to the extent that we like to hear them over and over? And what do they say about us? We want to understand the world. We want love. We want to live in a society with other human beings. We want others to recognize our worth. We want to explore the ultimate mystery of death, and what could possibly lie beyond it.

In any time and any place, stories of these wants have always drawn a crowd.

No Friendly Drop

But what happens, moment by moment, inside a typical audience member's mind as she or he is undergoing an audience experience? What is the jumble of thoughts, impressions, associations, digressions, distractions, and epiphanies that occur as the words and images come flying through their eyes and ears and collide with all the junk stored up in the warehouse of our minds?

As an example, let's look at what is happening in the final scene from *Romeo and Juliet*—remember, the important part here is not what's happening to the doomed young lovers playing out their tragedy on the stage, but what's happening inside the head of a person watching the scene.

For those not familiar with the story, Romeo Montague and Juliet Capulet have fallen in love even though their respective families are in the midst of a blood feud. Romeo gets in a fight with Juliet's cousin Tybalt, who wants him to leave Juliet alone. Romeo kills Tybalt in the fight and finds himself banished from their town, Verona.

The two lovers decide to marry in secret and flee together to a place where they can pursue their love in peace, far from the destructive feud. To escape from her overprotective family, Juliet takes a drug that knocks her out and makes her appear to be dead. She sends a message to Romeo to meet her at the tomb so they can steal away together when she awakens. But Romeo never gets the message that Juliet is faking death. When he comes to meet her, he thinks she has been killed by her family for wanting to be with him.

Romeo enters the Capulet tomb and sees Juliet lying on a catafalque.

Oh no. The poor guy doesn't know what he's in for. How pretty she is! Romeo sees her beauty too, which he notes is unusual in one who is dead.

> *O my love! my wife!*
> *Death, that hath suck'd the honey of thy breath,*
> *Hath had no power yet upon thy beauty:*
> *Thou art not conquer'd; beauty's ensign yet*
> *Is crimson in thy lips and in thy cheeks,*
> *And death's pale flag is not advanced there.*

That's right, Romeo! Glad you noticed! She looks alive because she *still is*! Oh, please act on your observation.

> *Ah, dear Juliet,*
> *Why art thou yet so fair? shall I believe*
> *That unsubstantial death is amorous,*
> *And that the lean abhorred monster keeps*
> *Thee here in dark to be his paramour?*

Romeo is actually jealous of Death. He imagines that Death wants to keep Juliet for himself!

> *Take your last embrace.*

Oh my God, that is so sad! This poor guy loved her so much it must be killing him to see her dead. His heart must be getting torn out. How can you take a last look into the eyes you loved so deeply?

> *Here, here will I remain*
> *With worms that are thy chamber-maids*

He's going to kiss her—except it's not going to be like the *Sleeping Beauty* kiss because she's never going to wake up. That poor sweet girl. Death can't be undone. I remember my friend who died. I wish I could have spoken to him one more time. I also remember losing somebody that I loved. She didn't die, but it was over for us *forever*. I don't remember a last kiss. We'd gone beyond kisses at that point.

Romeo is leaving! Good! But what kind of empty life could Romeo have without Juliet?

Oh, wait a minute. He's not leaving. He's turning back and reaching into his tunic. Does he have a knife? Can he be that devastated, that he would take his own life too? No, wait! He's got a small flask. Is it a medication of some kind for Juliet? Is it poison? Real poison? Oh my God, it's poison. He's pulling a plug to uncork it. Don't do it, you romantic idiot!

Eyes, look your last!
Arms, take your last embrace! and, lips, O you
The doors of breath, seal with a righteous kiss. . . .

He'd going to do it. He wants to be with her, and in order to join her, he must have such faith in the afterlife that he would drink poison like that to be with her. They say that love is eternal. If they're right, who would I meet in the afterlife? Do you get to see your lost friends and family?

He drank it! He's writhing in agony. My God, that must really hurt. Would I ever be in such despair that I'd kill myself for love? Would I be brave enough? Maybe it isn't about bravery. I wonder what it's like to take poison. Is there a way to commit suicide that is painless? Wasn't that a lyric to the theme of *M*A*S*H*? That lyric is certainly wrong. Look at that poor kid suffering. I wonder if he's having second thoughts. His beautiful young life is draining away.

Thus with a kiss, I die!

Oh, this is terrible. Terrible. Worse still, I don't know if I can watch what's going to happen when Juliet wakes up.

And here comes Friar Lawrence. A little late, now, aren't you, buddy? And, of course, here's Juliet awakening from her artificial death. I bet she's going to ask for Romeo.

Where is my Romeo?

Called it. Friar Lawrence has seen what happened to Romeo and now wants to get Juliet out of there before she sees too.

Lady, come from that nest
Of death, contagion, and unnatural sleep.

She doesn't want to go. She wants to wait for her Romeo. Don't look down, Juliet! Well, Friar, you can't hide this any longer. Let's see how you're going to break it to her.

> *A greater power than we can contradict*
> *Hath thwarted our intents. Come, come away.*
> *Thy husband in thy bosom there lies dead.*

She sees him lying beside her and suddenly the dawn breaks. She understands it all in a flash: Romeo thought she was dead, not asleep, because he never got the word about her plan! The full horror engulfs her like a tsunami. It was a horrible misunderstanding. A mistake. What a way to go! Oh Lord, that poor girl. But she won't leave with Friar Tuck!

> *Go, get thee hence, for I will not away.*

She's so faithful, so strong, so determined for such a young woman. She would have made a wonderful wife. But that can never happen now, can it? Unless she decides to go on living without him and finds someone new. That must be what's going to happen. She's too good to die too.

Uh-oh, she found the bottle of poison.

> *What's here? a cup, closed in my true love's hand?*
> *Poison, I see, hath been his timeless end.*

Without hesitating, she snatches the bottle from his hand. Stop! Don't do that! Not you too! She tilts back her head, only to find the bottle is empty! Thank God.

> *Drank all and left no friendly drop to help me after?*

Oh look, she's kissing him to try to get some of the poison from his mouth. I remember when they kissed early in the play to seal their love and join forever in life. Now she's kissing him to join him in death. A deep sexy kiss, but it's too late!

> *Thy lips are warm.*

She realizes she missed him by just moments. She sees that they were together so briefly, but now are separated forever in this life. Her plan has fallen apart. She's lost the man who loves her the most. Any time someone loses a love forever, it is heart-breaking. But in one so young, it's killer. Juliet bursts into tears, and so do we.

We hear the sounds of her family coming to get her. Maybe they will console her. But they hate Romeo and will probably be glad—and fiercely angry at Juliet. What can she do?

Then I'll be brief!

She grabs the knife that Romeo carried! Probably all men in that period carried some kind of weapon, as many do today.

Oh happy dagger, this is thy sheath.

No no no! Don't stab yourself! You have your whole life ahead of you! You don't realize how much it hurts!

There rust, and let me die.

OMG, she did it. She stabbed herself right in the freaking heart. Young people can be so damned stupid. And yet they love so much. So much! Am I crying? But this isn't real. It's just a play. And they're being so stupid. So why are tears rolling down my cheeks? I was once in love like that. I've suffered loss like that. Silly girl! Or am I the silly one? What's it like to love so desperately like that? I wish I had experienced that kind of love. But, wait, I have! I remember loving like that. It was wonderful at the beginning but terrible at the end. Was it worth it? In *West Side Story*, the character based on Juliet lives. Why couldn't Shakespeare have found a way to let his Juliet live?

The Prince of Verona is going to get the last word. He blames the Montagues and the Capulets for the deaths of the two finest flowers from both their families.

Some shall be pardon'd, and some punished:
For never was a story of more woe
Than this of Juliet and her Romeo.

You said it, brother.

I'm Going After That Truck

Here's another sample of what runs through the audience's mind during a typical scene. For purposes of wider familiarity, we'll examine the classic truck chase scene in *Raiders of the Lost Ark*, a masterpiece of storytelling, dramatic timing, homage, suspense, and wild camera effects. The scene was written by Lawrence Kasdan, based on a story by George Lucas and Philip Kaufman, and directed by Stephen Spielberg. The main character, Indiana Jones (Harrison Ford), is an American archaeologist with swashbuckling tendencies. The scene covers eight minutes and twenty-one seconds of screen time.

Here's the setup. Back in the 1930s, Indiana is sent by the US government to find one of the great lost treasures of all time: the Ark of the Covenant, a mythical gold chest that held the original tablets bearing the Ten Commandments, as described in the Bible. The Ark is believed to confer supernatural power on its owner. The US government has reason to believe that German führer Adolf Hitler has sent his goons to find it and take it back to Berlin. After a long and action-packed search by Jones, he finds the Ark deep in the Egyptian desert—only to see it stolen by the Nazi minions—including Indy's rival, René Emile Belloq (Paul Freeman). The Nazis load the Ark onto a heavily guarded truck and prepare to transport it over a long, twisting road to a place where it can be shipped by sea to Germany.

Here we go!

Look at this crowd! This isn't CGI; these are actual people. And now here are the bad guys, the Nazis with tilted hats, loading up some serious machine guns. They're shooting at the unarmed crowd! There is no way anybody or anything Indy has could possibly slow them down.

Indy is told about the Ark and the truck. Spying on the departing Germans, Indy sees that they have assembled a convoy: a convertible touring car carrying Belloq and some of the head bad guys, followed by the truck carrying the Ark, manned by nearly a dozen armed and swastika'd soldiers, and escorted

Harrison Ford goes after a truck carrying the Ark of the Covenant in Raiders of the Lost Ark *(1981). Directed by Steven Spielberg.*
Paramount Pictures / Photofest ©Paramount Pictures, Photographer: Albert Clark

by more soldiers in a jeep and a heavy motorcycle with a sidecar, and the aforementioned machine guns.

Indy delivers the greatest spoken line in the whole Indiana Jones franchise: "I'm going after that truck." It's one of the great lines in movie history, but Indy has no time for more. He's on the run! Ridiculous, of course. The Nazi convoy has a big lead and is pulling away.

No way is Indiana going to catch up with them. No way. No. way.

Smash cut to Indy riding a white horse.

Boom! A white horse! Hilarious! Then I suddenly stop laughing. Wait a minute . . . where the hell did he get a horse?

Ah, never mind, the scene is moving too fast to dwell on that or anything else. Because the soundtrack has begun to play that pulse-pounding Indiana Jones theme music, with all those John Williams trumpets. That reminds me of lyrics my boys and I wrote when we first watched the Indiana Jones films when they were kids. It has references to all the Indiana Jones pictures:

I am Indi-ana Jones
I make torches out of bo-o-ones
Yes, I'm Indiana Jones
And I do not like Nazis or snakes.

There's something really majestic about Indy's theme. What is there about brass that conveys so much power and adventure? An ancient military connection, probably. How did we inherit that?

Anyway, back at the Nazi convoy, the camera quickly reminds us that these vehicles are crawling with well-armed Aryan badasses. And we flash on the front car with that creepy guy in the black hat. Look at that degenerate face! Just like Goebbels and Himmler. How could they possibly have considered themselves the master race?

Now we're back to Indy on his white horse. Indy on white horse versus bad guys wearing black hats. Well, we certainly know where we stand. But how is a guy on a horse of any color gonna stop these bad guys in their vehicles? Well, somehow Indy went over a dusty hill and caught up with them. Now he's riding down that hill. Hope the horse doesn't stumble.

He has caught up with the truck! But now the Nazis on the motorcycles see him and are opening fire on him. It's a clear shot, how can they miss? But they miss. These guys are just as bad shots as the Storm Troopers in *Star Wars*!

We see Belloq twist around to see what's happening. Boo! Hiss!

Indy jumps from the horse and onto the truck carrying the Ark. The horse whinnies a goodbye: "Good luck, Indy!," it seems to say.

Indy's got the drop on the guys in the front seat of the truck. He yanks open the passenger side door and stone-cold flips the first Nazi out of his seat and onto the road. Not bad for a college professor. One down!

Next, Indy pounces on the driver. They're tussling, they're wrestling, they're punching. The truck swerves all over the road! Indy stamps on the brake and the truck slows down, causing the Ark to slide and the jeep behind them to slam into the back of the truck. This causes a Nazi guard to fall out of the back of the truck and onto the hood of the following jeep.

He gives the Wilhelm Scream! Classic. I was waiting for that. Two down!

Indy and the driver Nazi are fighting for control of the truck's steering wheel. Uh-oh, Indy sees something scary. What is it? Scaffolding! Something for them to crash into that won't stop the truck. Perfect!

Smashed scaffolding flies everywhere. One of the local workers lands on the hood of the truck and for a moment his startled face fills the windshield. It's this extra's big moment in cinema history. I wonder if he still gathers his grandchildren and shows them the scene and says, "Here I come! That's me!"

Indy and the Nazi driver have a little smiley moment over that. But it's a ruse. Indy was just lulling him. Socko! Out the door the driver goes, and over a conveniently placed cliff.

Three down!

Indy slams the truck door shut. He's in control of the truck with the Ark now, but he's baring his teeth. Ooh, he mad! He stomps the gas. He's going after that lead convertible with all the head bad guys in it. They all twist around to see him bearing down on them, looks of terror on their faces. Good. Suffer, Nazi scum.

Remember when Nazis were automatically the bad guys? My father fought in World War II and risked his life (and mine, apparently) to wipe them off the face of the earth. Hard to believe there are some people in our country today who think they were some kind of heroes. Assholes.

Indy crashes into the back of their car and runs them off the road. More scaffolding! More crashing!

But wait, Indy has a whole mob of Nazis still on his tail. We know he's in trouble because the orchestra suddenly plays the Indiana Jones theme in a minor key, where it definitely does not belong! The jeep with the machine gun tries to pull up next to him on the right and open fire. Indy swerves and runs it off the road. The driver says a bad word in German as his car plows into deep sand.

More down! Losing count now.

Indy gives one of his lopsided smiles through the windshield, but it doesn't last long. In his side-view mirror he sees the motorcycle now trying to pull up next to him on his left. Indy bares his teeth again. Don't mess with Indy when his teeth are bared! He pauses a moment to let the bad guys pull up juuuust enough, then he flicks the steering wheel and drives them off the road into a big puddle. They go flying. Bad guys fall in mud. Classic element of physical comedy. Now comes the part where I throw my head back and laugh. Ready? Ready! Ah-ha-ha!

Wait, no time to laugh yet. A second jeep has joined the conversation and is now creeping up on the left, having learned nothing from the fate of the motorcycle. Indy grins again. He flicks the steering wheel again. The goggles-wearing Nazi driving the jeep screams as he and his passenger go flying off . . . another cliff! This one looks to be hundreds of feet high. They wave their arms (and legs) goodbye as they fall. What happened to the mud puddle? I'd love to see a relief map of the countryside they're driving through.

But no time! There's still a whole buttload of bad guys in the bed of the truck Indy is driving, still guarding the Ark. Their leader, a gray-haired Nazi who has clearly had *enough*, barks out orders in German. They swing out the back and start clambering up both sides of the canvas-covered truck, guns drawn and ready to ruin Indy's afternoon. It's five to one against Indy! He spots them in those handy side-view mirrors. He scrapes off the two on the left side with some handy palm trees that have replaced the mud puddle and the cliff, then scrapes off the two on the right. Through the windshield we see Indy's bright, toothy smile of triumph.

Oh, but he hasn't won yet. Another bad guy sneaks up on Indy, draws his pistol, and shoots through the passenger-side door. It's point-blank, and he only manages to graze Indy's arm, but at last we have a bad guy who has some gumption and can shoot. To confirm that Indy's been hit, his blood spatters the windshield. Yuck! After some door-kicking, Indy finally manages to shake off the sharpshooter, who goes tumbling onto the road.

There's only one Nazi left on the truck, but this is the gray-haired commander who is clearly smarter than the others. Instead of trying to attack from the side yet again, Fritz (as I have very originally named this Nazi) climbs over the *roof* of the truck. He can be taught! As he's sneaking up on Indy, the slip-stream whips off his hat. Oh no, not his hat! I once lost a beloved hat that way (in the wind; not crawling up the roof of a truck).

As Indy winces in pain from his wounded arm, Fritz positions himself on the roof of the truck's cab. Then, with one graceful motion, thrusts himself feet-first through the driver's side window, kicking Indy away from the steering wheel. Nice! A worthy adversary at last.

Fritz tries to shove Indy out the passenger door. When Indy resists, Fritz helpfully rains hard punches on Indy's bullet-wounded arm. Wow, that hurts! I think I felt that myself. Teeth bared, they fight. Could Indy be losing? Fritz isn't kidding around. He seizes Indy and shoves him right through the windshield! Indy slides down the hood of the truck and falls off the front. That's it, he's doomed and will momentarily be run over. Fritz chuckles in delight.

But wait! Indy isn't down yet. He tries to hold on to the grille on the nose of the truck, but pieces keep coming off in his hand. He grabs the front fender. The barreling tire is mere inches from his crotch. I cringe. But he hangs on.

Meanwhile, Belloq and the other head Nazis are somehow back on the road and somehow back in front of them. They gesture for Fritz to speed up and smash Indy like a bug between their vehicles. Fritz gives a dastardly nod, shifts gears, and hits the gas. Indy sees their plan and realizes that he is totally dead . . . unless he can do something supremely and ridiculously insane to save his life. He can't climb up the truck, he can't slide around the sides of the truck. There is only one remaining route of escape.

Yes, he goes *under* the truck.

Belloq and the Nazis in the convertible watch with what looks like genuine interest as Indy slides under the speeding truck by holding on tight to the drive shaft. His pants and buttocks, apparently made of carbon steel, are unaffected by the friction from the stony, gravelly dirt road as he goes hand over hand from the front to the back of the truck, aided by his trusty whip, which keeps him from falling off. Is this the greatest moment in any action film?

In a grand reversal, it is now Indy's turn to climb onto the back of the truck and sneak up on Fritz. With a single graceful Fritz-like motion, Indy thrusts himself feet-first through the passenger-side door and serves Fritz his size-elevens right in the kisser. Flashing his scariest angry-face, Indy now seizes the steering wheel, slams Fritz's head against the dashboard a few times to soften him up, then returns the favor by hurling Fritz through what's left of the windshield.

How the tables have turned! Fritz is now the one clinging to the grille on the front of the truck. But for all his moxie, Fritz is no Indiana Jones. He loses his grip and we see the truck bounce merrily as it runs him over. Farewell, mighty (but misguided) warrior!

For those keeping score, Indy has now taken control of the truck with the Ark, cleansed it of Nazis, and shaken all their vehicles.

Except one. That convertible with Belloq and his unholy masters is still out front. Indy bares his teeth again, shifts gears, and guns the truck in pursuit. Indy's back, and there's gonna be trouble! The convertible serpentines on the dusty road but Indy wedges his truck next to them and runs them into a ditch. Belloq whaps the driver of the convertible with his hat, shouting "Idiot! Idiot!" as Indy barrels triumphantly past them, still grimacing with pain from his arm wound.

A moment later Indy zooms the truck into a crowded village marketplace and pulls the truck into a shelter, which the compliant villagers have conveniently prepared for him. In a moment, it is camouflaged and the villagers go back to selling their baskets and fruit, practically whistling with feigned innocence. Belloq and his bosses skid their big black convertible into the square, seeing that they have reached a dead end with no truck in sight. A villager tries to sell one of the uniformed Nazis a melon. The frustrated bad guy hurls the melon to the ground, depriving the poor local of probably half a day's wages. Jerk! It's all so sad until the black convertible and its careless crew huffily peels out and speeds away. Then the villagers rejoice! The white stranger in the truck has triumphed!

Encoding/Decoding

One of the masters of audience research is sociologist and cultural theorist Stuart Hall, who has created a model of how the mind functions in an audience setting in a model he describes as "encoding/decoding." And according to *Media Studies 101*,

> In terms of information received, we can generally say that information is decoded in three ways. There is the dominant reading, where the message intended is the message received. There is a negotiated reading, where the receiver accepts some of the intended message, and rejects other parts of it. Finally, there are oppositional readings, where the reader completely rejects the message intended.

Audiences sitting out there in the dark are constantly absorbing and sorting information like this, keeping what is fun or interesting or profound, and junking the rest. Whether we're watching Shakespeare or an Indiana Jones movie or the nightly news or a ballgame or listening to music . . . or doing audiencing of any kind, our hearts and minds are forever processing what we see and adding a little bit more to who we are.

4

RELIGION AND MORALITY

As touched on earlier, modern theatre—and all the storytelling forms and technologies that evolved out of it—can trace its roots back to religious ritual. Religious faith is a deeply personal phenomenon; a bond of worship between an individual and what is perceived as a higher power. But there are few religions that see such piety as a purely private practice. The unit of religion is the soul, but the next step upward is the congregation.

Religious rituals have many functions. High on the list is instruction in morality and belief in the form of readings from a Bible, Koran, or other holy book, and interpretations by a clergyperson of the lessons contained therein. As described in chapter 1, early modern Western theatre was largely a function of the church.

Many people derive religious lessons from reading their holy books, whichever they may be. But there is a special spirituality derived from listening to these stories and lessons read aloud in a church, temple, or other religious gathering place. Praying communally and listening to a clergyperson's interpretation of the holy books and how they relate to everyday life gains special significance when experienced in a group setting. Many faiths require attendance at religious services. Cynics can say this is to make sure the attendees put something in the collection baskets. But many of the faithful make their contributions privately, and some religions bar such collections during ceremonies to keep focus on matters of the spirit. Those who attend these ceremonies regularly speak of their feeling of community, the comfort of knowing that others believe what they do, and the transcendent emotion experienced when speaking the same words in concert with others.

The power of collective worship is rarely illustrated as lushly as when devotions are sung, either by a single cantor or by a choir, especially a big one like the Mississippi Mass Choir or the Mormon Tabernacle Choir. And that power is multiplied when the congregation sings along. Psalm 72 in the Christian Bible says, "He that sings praise, not only sings, but also loves him of whom he sings. In praise, there is the speaking forth of one confessing; in singing, the affection of one loving." As St. Augustine is supposed to have said, "When you sing, you pray twice."

Some denominations like Methodism regard singing hymns as a solemn and dignified practice. For many in those congregations, it is the only time in their lives they get to sing out loud in the company of others. Other denominations, especially modern Baptist churches, turn hymns into enraptured effusions, accompanied by rhythmic hand-clapping, foot-stamping, exclamations of "Hallelujah!," and various call-and-response singing that draws the entire congregation into the devotion and blurs the boundary between performer and audience.

Judaism demands a minimum gathering of ten—a *minyan*—in order for a religious ceremony to be legitimate. In Orthodox Judaism, ten males who have gone through the bar mitzvah ceremony (at age thirteen) are required for a "community of Israel" to be achieved. Reform Judaism recognizes a minyan as being ten worshippers of any gender.

Some sects of Islam adjudge music and singing to be *haram*, or forbidden, but the daily calls to prayer and the chanting of verses from the Koran provide a similar group participation experience. Muslims must answer to Allah five times a day when the *muezzin* calls them. These prayers are about themselves: a communication with a higher power, with the eternal. They are also a summons to share something in common with the faithful everywhere. To momentarily function as part of a worldwide audience, a shared mass experience that draws them closer to the deity, but also closer to one another. It's an implied audience, one that exists in fact, but also in the imagination of each Muslim who "sees" the others in a mental image.

But once in their lifetime, each Muslim is required to make a pilgrimage to the holy city of Mecca—an obligation known as a *hajj*—and take part in an in-person mass prayer experience as they circle the Kaaba shrine. As they pray, they hear the prayers of others and obtain a physical sense that they are not alone in their devotion.

The Power of Ecstasy

Some people, perhaps those who live humdrum or workaday lives, long for the transcendent. Deep in their hearts they yearn for magic, for miracles, for that momentary contact with the divine. This explains the allure of fundamentalist religions, like Pentecostal Christianity, where the faithful cross the line between audience and celebrant. They are sometimes elevated by their religious fervor into a kind of trance where speaking in tongues, frenzied dancing, and seizure-like bodily shaking unites them spiritually with their deity. In extreme situations, religion offers these audiences something that can only be called "ecstasy."

The spiritual teacher Eknath Easwaran wrote, "Lovers of God possess intense concentration. In prayer their attention rivets itself so completely onto God that nothing can tear it away. Even a suggestion of the divine may draw them into a higher state of consciousness." Easwaran gives a vivid example about teacher Sri Ramakrishna who found himself being swept away during a religious drama produced by his disciple. "The curtain went up and a character started singing the praises of the Lord. Sri Ramakrishna immediately began to enter the supreme state of consciousness. The stage faded; the actors and actresses faded. As only a great mystic can, he uttered a protest: 'I come here, Lord, to see a play staged by my disciple, and you send me into ecstasy. I won't let it happen!' And he started saying over and over, 'Money . . . money . . . money,' so as to keep some awareness of the temporal world."

H. L. Mencken, known as the "Sage of Baltimore," commented on many movements in early twentieth-century America, from politics to literature, but he is perhaps best known for his reporting on the 1925 so-called Scopes Monkey Trial. That trial focused on John T. Scopes, a teacher in Tennessee who had the temerity to teach evolution in a public school at a time when that theory was banned by state law. Sensing the potential for a grand show, Mencken hustled down to the town of Dayton to cover the trial (which, by the way, Scopes technically *lost*). Trying to understand the local religion, he decamped to the deep woods to serve as audience for a fundamentalist service. There, he witnessed a member of the congregation in the grip of the Holy Spirit, or something close to it:

> From the squirming and jabbering mass a young woman gradually detached herself. . . . Her head jerked back, the veins of her neck swelled, and her fists went to her throat as if she were fighting for breath. She bent backward until she was like half a hoop. Then she suddenly snapped forward. We caught a flash of the whites of her eyes. Presently her whole body began to be convulsed—great throes that began at the shoulders and ended at the hips. She would leap to her feet, thrust her arms in air, and then hurl herself upon the heap. Her praying flattened out into a mere delirious caterwauling.

Mencken observed that other members of the audience were not in the slightest alarmed by these transformations. On the contrary, they proved to be the point and goal of the proceeding:

> They were obviously not painful, for they were accompanied by vast heavings and gurglings of a joyful and even ecstatic nature. And they seemed to be contagious, too, and then came a third, and a fourth, and a fifth. The last one had an extraordinary violent attack. She began with mild enough jerks of the head, but in a moment she was bounding all over the place, like a chicken with its head cut off. Every time her head came up a stream of hosannas would issue out of it. Once she collided with a dark, undersized brother, hitherto silent and

stolid. Contact with her set him off as if he had been kicked by a mule. He leaped into the air, threw back his head, and began to gargle as if with a mouthful of BB shot. Then he loosed one tremendous, stentorian sentence in the tongues, and collapsed.

Public Affirmation

Naturally, not all religious practice entails such extreme devotion. Most just strive for communion in the lowercase sense: experiencing faith communally. That's especially the case with ceremonies that celebrate and affirm key passages in life. Events like the Christian baptism, the Jewish bris, the Muslim Shahada, and the ceremony of marriage in virtually all faiths are done in public, usually in the presence of family and friends who act as witnesses. The promise of two people to love one another for life might seem an intensely private thing. But it's done in public, before an audience, to publicize that they are a couple and not in isolation any longer, and to enlist the audience to help them as they move through life together.

During the COVID-19 pandemic, houses of worship of all faiths usually turned to the internet to enable their congregations to stay in touch with their churches, and with their faith. The Catholic Church, for example, when faced with the danger to health represented by its most sacred rite, the taking of the communion wafer, devised a virtual "Act of Spiritual Communion" for the faithful to recite while watching services on their electronic devices:

> My Jesus,
> I believe that You are present in the Most Holy Sacrament.
> I love You above all things,
> and I desire to receive You into my soul.
> Since I cannot at this moment receive You sacramentally,
> come at least spiritually into my heart.
> I embrace You as if You were already there
> and unite myself wholly to You.
> Never permit me to be separated from You.
> Amen.

Even when the churches were allowed to reopen, most followed health experts' restrictions regarding social distancing and mask wearing. But not all churches were content with virtual worship. For example, Tri Town Baptist Church in East Millinocket, Maine, insisted on holding a large wedding without requiring attendees to wear masks, which became a superspreader event that sickened many participants, who then went on to spread the disease to their families and friends. It became a common story at houses of worship across the United States and around the world. Churches in California, Louisiana, Colorado, Maryland, and many other locations defied local bans, often leading to illness and loss of life. And resistance came not just from church leadership, but from thousands of congregants who insisted that the restrictions violated their constitutional rights to freedom of religion. More extreme resisters believed that the restrictions were the work of Satan, a strategy to separate the faithful from their God.

They were willing to risk their health and their very lives to practice faith collectively. Being part of a group and experiencing the divine in a group setting was somehow essential to their religious experience. People were literally dying to become part of an audience.

The Lure of Pageantry

For most of human existence, the great mass of people lived in squalor and poverty. Even today, many members of the "99 percent" can only dream about the opulence and glamor they see on TV and in the movies. But for generations before the invention of those technologies, religion was the only means of experiencing dazzling visions of transcendent wonder. A lot of that was promised in the afterlife. But the sumptuous cathedrals and temples amazed and humbled the faithful with soaring columns, glistening stained glass windows, monumental statues, stately vestments, golden chalices, tabernacles, ciboria, patens, pyxes, menorahs, monstrances, and richly carved aron kodeshes.

Golden vessels are forbidden to Muslims, but their geometri-
cally decorated mosques compensate with their magnificence.

Theatres, cinemas, and concert halls all have their origins in
the mighty cathedrals, churches, temples, and mosques where
the faithful gather for their communal worship as audiences to
the divine. Many are crowned with steeples and minarets that
point and reach heavenward. To approach and enter one of these
awe-inspiring shrines is to feel that your every thought, word,
and deed are being conveyed heavenward. When the Jews' great
temple in Jerusalem was destroyed by the Romans in 70 CE, and
its people flung to the diaspora, they sought a spiritual place to
gather to take its place. Returning to the land of Israel with the
Wailing Wall, the only remaining part of the lost temple, is at
its heart a testament to the power of the audience experience in
religion. It's not enough to speak to God privately, though that is
important too. What's really important is the notion that adherents' prayers gain power when they are presented to Yahweh
in a theatre-like place of worship, surrounded by coreligionists
who gather there to place their petitions before God in common.

The grandeur to be experienced in these houses of worship
was not only architectural. Instead of the stink of the street, both
from overheated animals and unwashed humans, religions also
offered the heady perfume of incense. (Don't forget that two of
the gifts said to have been offered to the Christ child were frank-
incense and myrrh, both used as medicines and to perfume the
air.) These rich accoutrements sometimes came from wealthy
members of the congregation. But more often they were purchased through thousands of tiny contributions and bequests
from the faithful themselves. Their pious collective generosity
purchased sumptuous pageantry that they could only otherwise
dream about in their humble lives.

Oberammergau

Religious audience participation is taken to a kind of extreme
every ten years or so in the village of Oberammergau, Germany.
In 1633, its residents watched as whole families were wiped

out by the bubonic plague that was sweeping through Europe. Half the town's population succumbed. With no understanding of germ theory, nor of the role that fleas played in carrying the disease, the desperate citizens tried one last desperate measure. They gathered around a crucifix and made a solemn promise to God. They pledged to perform a play every year reenacting Jesus's life, suffering, death, and resurrection in return for Him sparing them from further horrors of the plague.

And true to their word, the residents of the tiny Bavarian village gathered every year from 1634 to 1680, handed out parts for Jesus, Mary, Joseph, Pilate, the Apostles, Herod, and so on to the local residents, and performed what came to be known as the *Oberammergauer Passionsspiele* (Oberammergau Passion Play), as the rest of the village watched and prayed. And, lo and behold, there were no further deaths. *None*, according to carefully preserved local records.

The tradition was modified in 1680, and the play has been performed in Oberammergau every ten years since then, drawing as many as half a million of the faithful (and theatre lovers) to be a part of the audience and to view the pretty village whose public buildings have been painted with scenes from history and from the play.

There were a few scheduling hiccups along the way, such as the two world wars, and ironically, a two-year delay in the 2020 performance due to a modern plague, COVID-19. But the play went ahead as rescheduled from May 14 to October 2, 2022, featuring a cast of nearly two thousand, all of them Oberammergau residents. Despite advances in medical knowledge, these people persist in paying homage to their ancestors' belief that theatre saved their lives, and only by gathering as an audience every ten years will they continue to protect themselves.

The Restoration

During the COVID-19 pandemic, theatres around the world closed for various lengths of time, as did all places where large groups gathered, to slow transmission of the airborne virus.

Most American theatres were closed for eighteen months, from March 2020 to September 2021.

But it was scarcely the first instance of such closures for health reasons. Theatres across medieval Europe were shuttered, sometimes for years at a time, to slow the spread of bubonic plague and other illnesses, though authorities didn't really understand how such illnesses were propagated. Throughout the career of William Shakespeare, for instance, the London theatres were frequently closed due to plague, which gave the Bard extra time to write his many plays.

Political considerations also sometimes led to closures—most notably in 1642, when the Puritan Long Parliament drove out King Charles I and installed a government that regarded theatre as sinful. The Puritans closed and, in many cases, demolished London theatres. This all occurred just over a quarter century after Shakespeare's death. For the next eighteen years, during what is known as the Commonwealth period, England was in the grip of a religious dictatorship under the thumb of Oliver Cromwell. Theatres were considered anathema.

Actors and playwrights pleaded with Parliament to reopen the playhouses. In January 1643, a group of them submitted that "Actors remonstrance or complaint for the silencing of their profession, and banishment from their severall play-houses" in which they plaintively promised, "wee have purged our stages of all obscene and scurrilous jests."

Their entreaties fell on deaf ears. Over the next few years, theatre continued to survive—barely—via secret performances and play readings. But these came to the ears of Cromwell and Parliament, which, in 1648, passed "An Ordinance for the utter suppression and abolishing of all Stage-Plays and Interludes, within the Penalties to be inflicted on the Actors and Spectators therein expressed." Around this time Charles I tried to retake his throne, but he was captured and, in 1649, beheaded.

But the English love their royalty—and their theatre. By the late 1650s audiences decided they had endured enough of the Puritans. After Cromwell died in 1658, the country was thrown into chaos until 1660, when the previous king's son, who had survived in exile, took the throne as Charles II.

Charles II was no Puritan. In fact, he was a hearty party boy who loved wine, women, song . . . and theatre. The Merry Monarch, as he was known, ushered in a renaissance of English theatre, reopening the playhouses, and issuing patents for two theatre companies: the King's Company and the Duke's Company.

He also fathered a reported twelve illegitimate children by various mistresses, including the actress Nell Gwyn. The king had a secret entrance built into the new Theatre Royal Drury Lane so he and Nell could enjoy each other's attentions without being observed by the hoi polloi.

London audiences had fallen out of the theatergoing habit during the eighteen years of suppression, and playwrights had to come up with something to stimulate their interest. That's partly why Charles II's ascension to power led to a whole genre of racy plays, now known as Restoration comedy, which lasted for the better part of half a century and influenced playwriting throughout Europe. Major playwrights of the time included William Wycherley (*The Country Wife*), William Congreve (*Love for Love, The Way of the World*), John Etherege (*The Man of Mode*), John Vanbrugh (*The Provoked Wife*), John Dryden (*All for Love*), and the first widely produced female playwright, the prolific Aphra Behn (*The Rover*).

A whole new audience flooded into the London theatres and developed a taste for naughty comedy—a taste, it must be said, that has not abated.

Liars

Actors spend their careers pretending to be someone they're not. Most of the words they speak describe things that never happened, and therefore are a kind of lie. (Actors who are really good at that kind of lying win awards.) For this reason and many others down through the years, religious organizations at various times have denounced performing arts, especially theatre and dancing, as immoral, sinful, politically subversive, an offense to general propriety, and a threat to the eternal souls of audience members.

Apart from the ancient Greeks and Hindus, for whom dramatic performance was an integral part of their religion, theatre folk traditionally have been held in low repute. Actresses (and some actors) were regarded as little or no better than prostitutes, displaying their bodies for the audience's lascivious attention. Of course, in some times and places, performers did sometimes work as prostitutes to feed themselves, or consorted with them. In Shakespeare's day, the problem was ameliorated by requiring that female roles be played by young men or boys in ladies' clothing trying their best to look and sound like women. It drove the clergy crazy anyway and became central to their efforts to "protect" the souls of the very congregants who formed the audiences for these same plays.

The English Parliament passed the infamous Act of 1545, which classed any adult person who did not belong to a guild as a "vagabond" and therefore eligible for arrest on that count alone. This targeted actors who earned their livelihoods touring from town to town. When the theatre-loving Queen Elizabeth I came to the English throne in 1558, she got around the Act of 1545 by allowing public performances—but only those approved by her Master of the Revels. Things loosened up in England in succeeding centuries, as the job of censor passed to the Lord Chamberlain. The Theatres Act 1843 restricted his power to ban a play only if "it is fitting for the preservation of good manners, decorum or of the public peace so to do." But that still left him with wide leeway. Censorship of the stage was not fully abolished in Great Britain until 1968, allowing audiences to see dramatizations of situations they encountered in their normal lives in other mediums, but not on the stage.

And then there was the dubious political and religious subject matter of many plays. Seventeenth-century French playwright Molière was in and out of trouble with the church and the aristocracy for virtually his entire career. He struck back in 1664 with *Tartuffe*, a scandalous portrait of a fanatically religious figure named in the title. Tartuffe is revealed to be a hypocrite who secretly wallows in all the sins he claims to despise in others. Historian W. D. Howarth writes, "The history of this great play sheds much light on the conditions in which Molière had to work and bears a quite remarkable testimony to his persistence and capacity to show fight. He had to wait five years and risk the livelihood of his actors before his reward, which proved to be the greatest success of his career."

Howarth continues,

> Molière was constantly harassed by the authorities, especially the ecclesiastical ones for the challenge to orthodoxy they saw in his plays. The church nearly won its battle against Molière: it prevented public performance, both of *Tartuffe* for five years and of *Dom Juan* for the whole of Molière's life. A five-act version of *Tartuffe* was played in 1667, but once only: it was banned by the President of Police and by the Archbishop on pain of excommunication.

"The Poisonous and Pregnant Depth of Depravity"

American theatre historians look back to the 1866 production *The Black Crook* as the first recognizable example of what we now know as the Broadway musical. There were other plays with music long before it, but this particular production offered a special combination of factors that could not have existed in quite that way previously. The owner of Niblo's Garden, a Manhattan theatre, found himself double-booked with both a lurid religious melodrama and a lively troupe of ballet dancers from France. With classic New York chutzpah, Niblo solved his problem in a simple (pre-labor-union) way. He combined the two shows, plugging the ballet dancers into the action of the melodrama on the slightest of pretexts.

It's hard to imagine how, without benefit of TV, radio, or internet, *The Black Crook* created such a sensation in its day. There were newspapers, of course, but *The Black Crook* got publicity from a medium that penetrated to nearly every Christian home in the metropolitan area, if not the nation: outraged ministers. In the weeks leading up to the opening in late summer 1866, word got out that something special and unusual was happening at Niblo's. Special—and sinful.

According to Joseph Whitton, even before it opened, the show was being denounced in editorials and sermons. It was called "infamous, scandalous and outrageous," and from one pulpit came the cry that "the poisonous and pregnant depth of depravity into which misguided New York would sink and the utter demoralization of society if such contemplated extravagance in color, song, and human form were [exposed] before the public."

One daily newspaper wrote in its editorial column:

> Nothing in any other Christian country or in modern times has approached [this] indecent and demoralizing exhibition. We can imagine there might have been in Sodom and Gomorrah such another place and scene, such another theatre and spectacle on the Broadway of those doomed cities just before fire and brimstone rained down upon them and buried them in the ruins.

What could possibly have upset them so much about a play that shows the triumph of good over evil, and the dragging of the satanic villain down to hell? Something far worse—sexy girls dancing in something New York had never seen before: tights.

Literary god Mark Twain himself weighed in on the show, observing, "Beautiful bare-legged girls hanging in flower baskets, others stretched in groups on great sea shells, others clustered around fluted columns, others in all possible attitudes; girls—nothing but a wilderness of girls—stacked up, pile on pile, away aloft to the dome of the theatre, diminishing in size and clothing."

One member of the clergy risked eternal damnation by visiting Niblo's and reported that all his worst fears had been realized:

> The first thing that strikes the eye is the immodest dress of the girls, the short skirts and undergarments of thin material, allowing the form of the figure to be discernible, the flesh-colored tights, imitating Nature so well that the illusion is

complete, with the exceedingly short drawers, almost tight-fitting, extending very little below the hip, arms and neck apparently bare, and bodice so cut as to show off every inch and outline of the body above the waist. The attitudes were exceedingly indelicate—ladies dancing so as to make their undergarments spring up, exposing the figure beneath, from the waist to the toe, except for such covering as we have described.

The journalist who quoted this account dryly observes, "The reverend gentleman was certainly a close observer, with a wonderful memory."

These and the supposed abominations that followed found an implacable enemy in Anthony Comstock (1844–1915), secretary of the New York Society for the Suppression of Vice who engaged in a lifelong battle against not just "obscene literature" but gambling, prostitution, contraception, abortion, and anything else he perceived as contrary to Christian principles. Comstock found plenty of supporters. In March 1873 Congress passed a law nicknamed the Comstock Act, which outlawed the distribution of contraceptives through the mail or across state lines. The act, and others that followed, emboldened both Comstock and his disciples to suppress any sort of literature, including the performance of plays, that violated his enumerated standards.

But despite this finger-wagging, *The Black Crook* proved to be an audience sensation. It ran sixteen months at a time when even the most successful shows stayed for just a few weeks. It had two major Broadway revivals in 1870 and 1871, and was widely imitated, to the point where many of its features—not least the pretty and talented chorus girls—became staples of what evolved into the American musical comedy form.

Mae West (1893–1980), America's favorite movie sexpot of the 1930s, famous for spouting double-entendre (and single-entendre), cut a swath through vaudeville and Broadway in the 1920s. She wrote and starred in several plays with "daring" subject matter including *The Drag*, about homosexuality; *Diamond Lil* about an outspokenly risqué woman in the 1890s; and *Pleasure Man*, in which the main character is castrated.

In April 1927, the New York Police Department's Municipal Vice Squad raided her play about a prostitute, unapologetically titled *Sex*. The cops arrested both West and the cast. West was charged with obscenity and "behavior designed to corrupt the morals of youth." She was offered a chance to go free after paying a $500 fine but opted to serve the judge's sentence of ten days in a municipal workhouse, hoping the publicity would boost her career. She was right.

The history of suppressing racy or politically charged entertainment is long and lurid. Lawyer Will H. Hays (1879–1954) was called in to "clean up" the moviemaking business on screen and off. He was responsible for inserting "morals" clauses into workers' contracts, and famously, for drafting the Hollywood Production Code in 1930, banning certain words, characters, and situations in films that he considered inappropriate. The code bedeviled and tied the hands of moviemakers until the mid-1960s.

New York Mayor Fiorello LaGuardia saw burlesque theatres and houses of prostitution as more or less equal in the 1930s and made a special mission of shutting them down. Thirty years later, police were still arresting comedians like Lenny Bruce for obscenity.

The New York City government soon got out of the business of censoring movies, plays, and comedy shows, but in 1971, the premiere of the Andrew Lloyd Webber–Tim Rice musical *Jesus Christ Superstar* was picketed by Christians who felt the show was irreverent, even blasphemous.

Christians have not been alone in their attacks on the arts. Chapter 8 will describe an attack by Islamists on a French concert hall.

Hot Buttons

In recent years there has been an epidemic of American schools canceling plays just before they are scheduled to be presented— often after the administration has already approved the production. Generally, the school administration either doesn't monitor the script choices closely, or is reacting to a complaint from a parent or community member who has gotten wind of the production and has decided to be offended by some aspect of the production—usually supposedly offensive language or "adult" situations in the plays. Some parents and community leaders feel that these situations should be discussed at home, if at all, between parents and their children. They feel that the audience experience is not the place for them. Others feel that the situations are a part of life like any other, and the audience experience is perfectly appropriate for them.

Hot-button plays targeted for cancellation, according to the Educational Theatre Association, include *The Vagina Monologues* by Eve Ensler; *Spamalot* by Eric Idle and John du Prez ("gay content"); *The Laramie Project* by Moises Kaufman and the Tectonic Theatre Project ("the play is too adult for a high school production but it does preach a great message"); *Rent*, book, music, and lyrics by Jonathan Larson ("language and what they consider to be inappropriately mature content."); *Blithe Spirit* by Noël Coward (might "encourage exploration of witchcraft and the occult" and "undermine students' commitments to monogamous relationships"); and even *Godspell* by Stephen Schwartz and John-Michael Tebelak ("breach of church-state separation").

This censorship (and self-censorship) also produced one of the most emotional endings to any movie. The Italian film *Cinema Paradiso* is the story of a boy who is befriended by an elderly cinema projectionist in the years after World War II. The old projectionist is very puritanical and takes it upon himself to protect the audience's perceived sensitivities by cutting the kissing scenes out of every movie he screens. But the boy falls in love with the movies anyway. At the end of the film, after the boy has become a famous movie director himself, he returns to the town where he grew up to attend the old man's funeral. The people who now run the cinema tell him the old projectionist left him something and hand him a film can. The boy (now man) asks to have the spool in the can screened. As the beautiful Ennio Morricone score swells, we see that it's all the kisses that were cut from all the old films, left to the boy as a gift of love. Alone in the cinema as an audience of one, the man can be seen with eyes glistening with tears. And so are ours.

Author's Message

And then there are shows that try to adjust audience behavior directly. Like classic parables and fables, many films and TV shows convey an author's message.

Charles Dickens's *A Christmas Carol* inspires us to look closely at our own selfishness and greed, and to see not only how it harms others, but how it harms ourselves. It wants to inspire audience members to live a better life, though many wind up feeling that they are already better just for having seen the show, whether it causes them to give any more money or care to the needy or not.

Morality tales like *The Apartment* and even *Little Shop of Horrors* have similar goals. In *Little Shop*, a nebbishy flower shop worker named Seymour discovers a plant that requires human blood to grow. Seymour is secretly in love with his coworker Audrey and tries to impress her by helping the plant become a media star, which requires him to murder people. Eventually, both Audrey and Seymour wind up in the plant's maw. The moral of the story: no matter how much you want something, there are limits to what you can do to get it.

Similarly, in *The Apartment*, another nebbishy office worker, Chuck Baxter, tries to climb the corporate ladder and impress Fran, a girl he likes, by loaning out his apartment to executives for their sexual liaisons. Chuck eventually discovers that one of those liaisons is with the object of his affections. This one has a happy ending. Once Chuck renounces his immoral shortcut and resolves to make his climb based on merit, not cheating, Fran finally notices him. Moral: do things the right way and you will be rewarded.

The original 1951 version of *The Day the Earth Stood Still* asked audiences to see how alien intelligence might view our headlong rush to acquire nuclear weapons. The 2008 remake shifted the warning to show how the same aliens might view and try to act on humanity's despoiling of the environment.

Do these stories immediately cause the audience to change their selfish ways? Perhaps not. But it makes them think about it, and maybe make the right choice when the chips are down.

Pornography

No tears are shed for pornography, though it's certain that other bodily fluids are.

Now, you might think that the audience for hard-core sex movies is not a fit subject for a book like this. But look at the statistics: online pornography alone powers a $2.84 billion industry that serves the needs of an estimated forty million Americans who regularly visit porn websites. Global use is many times that. Porn is thought of as a male-centric business, but it turns out that one-third of porn watchers are women. A little over one-third of all internet downloads are believed to be related to pornography. The most popular pornographic film actress, the Lebanese American Mia Khalifa, has had her film clips watched more than 3.7 billion times internationally.

That's a lot of audiencing.

The porn business started small, but it's been around for a long time. The most ancient surviving piece of sculpture is a crude representation of a naked (female) body known as the Venus of Hohle Fels, found in a cave in Schelklingen, Germany. Carved from the ivory tusk of a wooly mammoth (now extinct), it is estimated to be thirty-five thousand to forty thousand years old.

Our old friends the classical Greeks produced a bounty of erotic pottery, plates, and bowls, many involving homosexual activity. The sex manual *Kama Sutra* was written in India in the early centuries CE, as much for instruction as for titillation of the readers on its own. The caves of Ellora and Ajanta in India contain statues carved in the sixth to seventh centuries CE, depicting Hindu and Buddhist deities, some of whom are nude and some engaging in sexual congress. Pornographic images, poetry, and songs were popular in China, Persia, South America, and basically anywhere humankind created images. Including these images in a discussion of pornography is problematic, as different cultures depicted sex for its spiritual power far beyond simple prurience. Sex, as the source of life, possesses a special magic for audiences everywhere.

Mass-produced pornography began with the invention of the woodblock printing press in China in the seventh century and with the invention of the moveable-print press in Germany in the mid-fifteenth century. The Marquis de Sade was imprisoned for his sexual activities and his pornographic writings in late eighteenth-century France and gave his name to practices we now call sadism.

Numerous books and scholarly treatises have been generated on what happened next. For our purposes, modern internet porn was born out of peep shows, "loops," pornographic films, and "gentlemen's" print magazines led by the ubiquitous *Playboy* whose heyday was the 1950s to the 1980s. With the invention of the internet, porn was among the pioneering content on the web, and its creators were early adopters of cutting-edge technologies, most recently for virtual reality headsets. Porn has largely abandoned its old analog haunts and moved—lock, stock, and padded restraints—to the web.

All this fevered porn production and consumption in every time and place begs the central question: what do users of pornography get from it, other than masturbatory relief, obviously? Most could easily get that on their own without porn. They may revel in the forbidden-ness of certain acts. They may try to participate vicariously in acts they are curious about but dare not try. They may enjoy the voyeur's pure pleasure in *watching*. In human sexuality, the term "scopophilia" describes the sexual pleasure that a person derives from looking at prurient objects of eroticism, such as pornography. Users may project themselves into one or another of the participants and try to imagine themselves performing acts that are forbidden or unattainable in their real lives.

An interesting thing about porn is how specific so much of it is. It seems everyone has that one particular kink that really works magic for them. A big recent trend in porn is incest, real or (usually) simulated. It's easy to create: take a standard sex scene and label it to indicate it's a brother and sister. Suddenly, it's sexier! But it gets more specific than that. Various users seem to like incest with a particular class of relative (stepbrother! auntie!), someone who is a certain ethnicity, a certain height or weight or hair color. Or wearing a certain article of clothing, with each partner a different combination of dominant and submissive. The variations appear to be endless, with something for everyone.

Those who like porn say it is an easy way to find sexual release without the emotional and financial complications of maintaining a relationship, or even casual or anonymous in-person sex. They say it helps them relax and find relief when their human partner is not in the mood, or unable to respond due to illness. Some perfectly healthy couples say it spices up their romantic interludes together.

Through the years there have been many attempts to suppress, criminalize, or ban pornography. It has been criticized as something that creates unrealistic expectations for real-life sex, or something that desensitizes and dehumanizes users, or something that makes them jaded about regular sex and craving ever kinkier forms to get the same *frisson*. Research has shown that the average age of first exposure to porn on the internet age is eleven—too young by any standard. Some feminists have criticized porn as objectifying women, promoting violence against women, and exploiting poor women. (Although others say it is empowering to women who are not forced into it.) Employers find that productivity is compromised by the many audience members who watch porn in the office during working hours. Neil Parish, a Tory (conservative) member of the British Parliament, resigned after he was caught watching porn videos at his seat in the House of Commons *while the lawmaking body was in session.*

And, of course, religious leaders have criticized porn as prompting sinful thoughts and spurring users to commit sinful actions. Many religions specifically forbid it.

However legitimate these criticisms may be, pornography appears to meet a basic need in people of nearly all sexual persuasions in all cultures. It seems there will always be an audience for erotica, and so too forces that will oppose and try to ban it.

THE AUDIENCE IN THE PERFORMING SPACE

Many factors affect how an audience receives and interprets its experience. People who tried to watch plays on their laptops or phones during the COVID-19 epidemic found it to be a disconcerting experience. It wasn't the fault of the device; if they were forced to watch a TikTok clip in a football stadium or a YouTube video in a concert hall, they'd likely find it just as odd.

To paraphrase Marshall McLuhan, the venue is also the message.

For most of history, theatre was an outdoor pastime. Classical Greek theatres were open-air, with the audience seated all around the stage. The notion of a "fourth wall" is therefore a relatively recent development. The classical Greek theatres were outdoor performance spaces that, like the Theatre of Dionysos, were usually built into the side of a hill. Today they would be classed as amphitheatres, and despite the developments in theatre technology and design, this style is still sometimes used to marvelous effect in places like the ninety-five-hundred-seat Red Rocks Amphitheatre in Colorado or the eleven-thousand-seat Muny in St. Louis.

Over the past twenty-five hundred years of Western audiencing experience, performing spaces have settled into what is widely considered the preferred configuration, with a stage or other raised performing space facing rows of seats. But there are other traditions and many experiments with other configurations, even within that tradition. The main alternate arrangements are

In-the-round theatres in which the audience completely surrounds the performing space like a mini arena or stadium;

Thrust stages that push the performing space into the audience, which surrounds the stage on three sides; and

Black box stages that consist of empty spaces with moveable risers that can be configured in many different ways to suit the special needs of particular productions, especially experimental ones.

Perhaps the most historic American in-the-round theatre was off-Broadway's Circle in the Square, originally founded by Theodore Mann, José Quintero, Jason Wingreen, Emily Stevens, and Aileen Cramer in 1951 in a former nightclub at 5 Sheridan Square in New York's Greenwich Village. The troupe kept its name and recreated the distinctive configuration when it moved several blocks east to 159 Bleecker Street in 1960. When Circle in the Square expanded uptown and built a Broadway-size space on West 50th Street, its founders again recreated the in-the-round arrangement, but on a larger scale.

The Bleecker Street stage no longer exists, but the Broadway incarnation remains very much in use, preferred for smaller and experimental plays and musicals. Arena Stage in Washington, DC, is among the theatres that maintain both an in-the-round space and a traditional proscenium. Producers Lee Guber and Shelly Gross operated the Westbury Music Fair on Long Island and the Valley Forge Music Fair in Pennsylvania (among others) as in-the-round performance spaces for musicals and concerts.

In-the-round stages allow the audience to see everything that is happening all at once. The downside is that actors must make entrances and exits through the audience, or via "voms," specially designed portals in the midst of the front audience area. Another problem is that actors cannot face all directions at the same time, so they either must keep turning and turning to let the audience see them, or must deliver a key part of their performance with their back to half the house. This is also annoying to audiences who did not pay to see the nape of their favorite star's neck. Because moving scenery on and off is a challenge as well, many in-the-round shows use minimal designs or scenery that can be reconfigured differently for each location. In a 2010 in-the-round revival of *The Miracle Worker* at Broadway's Circle in the Square Theatre, set designer Derek McLane lifted set furniture on wires so they hung over the actors' heads in scenes where the furniture wasn't being used. The arrangement was very uncomfortable for the audience, waiting for something to accidentally break loose and fall on the actors. It must have been a bit of a sweat for the actors as well.

In thrust configurations, the playing area typically juts out into what ordinarily would be the front orchestra section. The audience sits on three sides. Unlike the in-the-round stage, the back of the thrust is connected to the backstage area so actors (and scenery) can make their entrances from more or less traditional wings. The downside of thrust stages is similar to that of in-the-round stages: an obscured or partial view of the action. A considerable part of the audience must watch the show from the side and see the actors in profile most of the time.

Shakespeare's Globe Theatre in London could be classified as a thrust-type stage, but more formal and recent examples include the Olivier Theatre at the Royal National Theatre in London, the Guthrie Theater in Minneapolis, and the Festival Theatre in Stratford, Ontario. The Vivian Beaumont Theater at Lincoln Center struggled with its original thrust design for decades until finally the configuration and acoustics were worked out and the theatre took its rightful place as a first-class Broadway house.

An interesting note: one of the most dramatic reconfigurations of a Broadway theatre occurred during the run of the 2014 musical *Rocky*, based on the film about a broken-down boxer who works his way up to a championship bout. Most of the show was played in traditional proscenium style, but in preparation for the climactic act 2 match, director Alex Timbers and designer Christopher Barreca had the audience in the front orchestra section vacate their seats. A full-size boxing ring then rolled off the stage propelled by hydraulic lifts and thrust itself out over the first dozen or so rows. The big boxing battle was then played out with the cheering audience on three sides.

Punches, sweat, and stage blood were flying everywhere, just like a real match. It was one of the great coups-de-theatre of the season. Too bad the show had a comparatively short run, and only 180 audiences got to take part.

Moving on to larger performing spaces, a stadium is designed to hold many more people than even a large theatre. The Romans introduced the massive circular stadium seating style exemplified in the 50,000-seat Colosseum, and that style persists today in the 107,000-capacity Michigan Stadium in Ann Arbor and the 132,000-capacity Narendra Modi Stadium in Ahmedabad, India, not to mention the Indianapolis Motor Speedway which can accommodate 257,325.

There is nothing "virtual" about these audiencing places, except perhaps the modern jumbotrons that give close-ups of activities happening right before the audience's eyes. Amphitheatres and stadia were the closest thing to "mass media" the classical civilizations had: a lot of people sitting in the same place together, watching the same activities.

With the movement to ban circus exploitation of animals, especially elephants, traditional big-top tented circuses, which once crisscrossed continents around the world, may become a thing of the past. But their history as audience-pleasing entities shouldn't be forgotten. The ancient Circus Maximus in Rome (along with the Circus Flaminius, Circus Maxentius, and other similar arenas) was a place for equestrian and gladiatorial displays. How popular were they? As its name suggests, Circus Maximus is believed to have seated 250,000 spectators.

Modern circuses got their start in eighteenth-century London as horse shows, at a time when horses and horse-drawn vehicles of many kinds formed the basis of overland transportation. Audience interest in showy horses was as keen as the modern interest in showy automobiles. Englishman Philip Astley was the early king of these horse shows, and he built arenas to accommodate them in London and across Europe.

The size of the young United States inspired the creation of touring circuses to entertain cities and towns across the North American continent. To make circuses portable, which is to say easily transported, assembled, and disassembled, American

Joshuah Purdy Brown created the big-top circus tent. This had the added advantage of vastly expanding the number of places his circus could perform. It didn't need an existing arena; it could display its wonders to paying customers anyplace there was a big field.

P. T. Barnum, the showman most closely associated with circuses, began his career in a stand-alone building in Manhattan—Barnum's American Museum (1841–1865). In this period, circuses began to augment their horse shows with animal acts of many kinds, plus acrobats, clowns, "freaks," good-looking performers in tight spangled costumes, and myriad grotesque side shows. Modern audiences spoiled by the instant hyper-stimulation of images on television, movies, and the internet have become blasé about and jaded by such gaudy marvels. But for simple farm and tenement folk who spent their days toiling in factories, or trudging behind mule-drawn plows, or feeding crying babies for years on end, circuses offered a glimpse into a world of unimagined spectacle and wonder.

Only in 1881 did Barnum ally himself with James Anthony Bailey in a traveling circus, which was eventually bought by a rival, the Ringling Brothers Circus, to create what billed itself as "The Greatest Show on Earth": Ringling Bros., Barnum & Bailey Circus, which persisted into the twenty-first century, though it largely eschewed tents after the late 1950s and returned to playing mainly large arenas.

Circuses found special favor in Communist countries, as an entertainment form beloved by the proletariat. The Russians were the first country in the world to host a state-run circus starting in 1929, still popular today as the Great Moscow State Circus. The immense Shanghai Circus World remains one of the primary attractions for residents and visitors to that Chinese city.

Smaller circuses in the United States allow audiences to get closer to the action (and often returned to performing under a big-top tent), including the New York–based Big Apple Circus, the Circus Oz in Australia, the Pickle Family Circus out of San Francisco, and the Cirque du Soleil based in Quebec. These and others helped redefine circuses in the late twentieth and early twenty-first centuries and helped keep the flame of these entertainments alive.

Rodeos

Some audience events involve learning skills, measuring one-self, and primal thrills. Take rodeos, for example. The various events, such as steer roping, team roping, and barrel racing, display skills that are required for ranch work. Events like bronco riding and bull riding give audience members the adrenaline rush of danger, while they measure in their minds how well they might do in such situations. Fans who watch sports on TV at home or in sports bars similarly project themselves into the action, though at a technological remove, to such a degree that they cheer (or verbally abuse) participants and referees as if the participants could actually hear them.

And then there's the phenomenon of "body English"—audience members leaning or gesturing as an attempt to influence the player's or ball's trajectory. This happens when the audience's imagined projection of themselves into the action is almost total. The same can be seen in horror movies where audience members may shout, "Don't go in there!" Or in rom-coms when audience members urge the would-be lovers to "Kiss him!" or "Kiss her!," as if the shadows on the screen could hear them.

Drive-ins

America's love affair with cars blossomed in the 1950s with all sorts of activities you could do without ever leaving your vehicle. It was the era of drive-up burger joints, drive-up banks, and drive-up milk stores. So why not find a way to enjoy the audience experience from behind the wheel of your land yacht?

After some early experiments, the first regular drive-in movie theatre lit up its screen in Pennsauken, New Jersey, in 1933. But drive-ins as a cultural phenomenon began to burgeon after World War II, combining the best aspects of cinemas and amphitheatres. By the mid-1950s, more than four thousand drive-ins lit up the night across North America.

It was a family-friendly and predominantly suburban institution. Many who grew up during that period remember lying on blankets in the back of the station wagon, with Mom and Dad in the front seat. You paid at the gate and pulled into a spot in what seemed like a big parking lot with a huge screen at one end. Posts next to each spot held small speakers that you would hook onto your window to hear the soundtrack. Then you'd lean back to enjoy a family movie. You could even bring your own snacks from home, though the drive-in operators tried to lure people out of their cars with hilarious commercials inspiring customers (especially kids) to march over to the lucrative snack bars.

Not a few families got their start at drive-ins, as young people began to discover that they were ideal make-out spots, offering a semiprivate place to snuggle up to your sweetheart during scary monster movies.

There were plenty of cons to drive-in cinemas as well. They were swell during warm months, but the outdoor theatres were not so comfy during the winter. You had a nice view of the screen on a clear evening, but inclement weather impeded your view, and afternoon matinees were problematic. Drive-in movie lots also took up a lot of increasingly valuable real estate.

It wasn't long before the cons began to outweigh the pros. By the late 1980s, barely two hundred drive-ins remained in business. The institution has enjoyed a modest rebound in the twenty-first century, riding a wave of retro nostalgia, plus some boutique accoutrements (like sound that plays through the car's own sound system instead of the scratchy, low-fi traditional speakers) that justify a premium ticket price.

Moving Indoors

As we've seen, most theatres around the premodern world traditionally told their stories under the bright sun. The London theatres of Shakespeare's time were mostly performed in roofless playhouses, including the Bard's beloved "wooden O," the Globe. Performances were typically at about two or three in the afternoon, for two reasons.

Reason number one was lighting. Centuries before electric lights were invented, the only way to light the interior of a building was with candles, torches, or other open flames. These were too dangerous for theatres that were mostly built of wood with straw floor covering and thatching, and their illumination could not be focused to make a spotlight. Homes and businesses that used those lighting sources frequently went up in flames with no fire brigades to put them out. In 1666, a great blaze in London consumed most of the city's center. As it was, the Globe was destroyed by fire after all, when a prop cannon misfired during a performance of *Henry VIII* in 1613, starting a blaze that consumed the historic playhouse. Happily, it was rebuilt in the 1990s and has resumed operation.

Reason number two was the neighborhood. Theatres for the general public were long considered déclassé and even sinful, and thus were often relegated to lands beyond the walls of the great cities, including the rue des Mathurins in France and the south bank of the Thames opposite London. Shakespeare's Globe, for instance, was surrounded by taverns, whorehouses, and bear-baiting pits. The area was infested with pickpockets and what today would be called muggers. Going to that neighborhood during the day was bad enough. Audience members, especially women, often attended disguised and/or masked. Going at night would have been even more dangerous.

However, theatres open to the sky were also open to the weather, which cut severely into receipts. Indoor performances were limited to special presentations for royalty and the wealthy. These had small audiences who could afford precautions. It is from these theatres that the practicability and popularity of indoor performance began to grow.

As theatre spaces moved indoors and became formalized with the performance space to one side, facing an audience arrayed in rows, the arrangement came to contain what we've previously described as a fourth wall—the invisible boundary between the world of the play and the world of the audience as discussed in chapter 2. The stage developed into a kind of box with walls on three sides and the fourth side facing the audience, which allowed the audience to spy all the things the performers did and said—and judge them.

The fourth wall is usually demarcated by a frame arching over the stage, known as the proscenium. The word is based on the Greek word for a raised performing platform, a *proskenion*. But the practice was formalized as a frame for the action only in late sixteenth and early seventeenth-century Italy.

However, after those problems were overcome by technological advances, some audiences were still attracted to outdoor performing spaces. High up among those still attracting audiences are the Delacorte Theater in New York's Central Park, and Regent's Park Open Air Theatre in London, both of which feature Shakespeare performances.

One of the grandest outdoor theatres in North America is The Municipal Theatre Association of St. Louis, better known to regulars as The Muny. Built in 1916, its eleven thousand seats also make it the largest regularly used legitimate theatre in the United States and comparable to the ancient Theatre of Epidaurus in Greece. Built into a massive hillside in St. Louis's Forest Park, the outdoor theatre has maintained a steady program of summertime stage musicals in the heart of the country.

The Jones Beach Theater on Long Island, New York, more recently rechristened for a sponsor as Northwell Health at Jones Beach Theater, has a highly unusual configuration, originally conceived by master urban planner Robert Moses himself. The outdoor theatre, which opened in June 1952 and was originally known as the New Jones Beach Marine Stadium, was built in October 1949 as part of the Jones Beach State Park. It is located on the bay side of a barrier beach island. The audience sits in amphitheatre-style tiers on Jones Beach Island proper, next to a capacious parking lot and refreshment stand. The theatre was built with eighty-two hundred seats, but later renovations expanded that number to fifteen thousand. The stage is situated on a small island in the placid Zach's Bay, separated from the seats by a narrow waterway.

From 1952 to the early 1980s, the Jones Beach Theater hosted operettas and extravagant stagings of Broadway musical revivals. Productions that featured scenes with boats, such as *Show Boat* and *The King and I*, were able to use the waterway for actual watercraft to make an entrance. Comparatively low prices and the presence of Guy Lombardo and his big band as the house orchestra drew suburbanites from across Long Island. Rain was always a problem, but the family atmosphere in the peak years of the baby boom afforded many youngsters their first taste of stage musicals. Since the 1980s, programming at the theatre has focused on rock concerts. The waterway is now bridged over, connecting the stage island with the audience section.

Box Seats

More public displays are the reason legitimate theatres, especially the older ones, were built with what are known as box seats. Modern audiences expect these seats to be the best in the theatre. But they are disappointed and confused to learn that even though box seats are close to the stage, they offer far from the best view. Often a considerable part of the stage is obscured by the proscenium arch or by scenery.

So why are box seats considered to be so prestigious? It's because they were built not so much so the people in them could see, but so they could *be seen*. In the bygone era when people dressed in their finest to attend the theatre, they sat in the boxes so the rest of the audience could view and admire them. Before photography, royalty and heads of state would display themselves there to give their subjects a rare glimpse of their majesty in the flesh.

That was then. Today, boxes are often regarded by theatres as a nuisance. Some still sell tickets to the box seats, often as "limited view." Others just use them to hold extra lighting equipment or speakers.

Sound and Light

The opportunities for audiencing on television and the internet and other virtual spaces may have become seemingly endless, but even in the old-school analog world, forums and formats for audiencing have been limited only by imagination and budget. Fireworks displays, aquarium feeding shows, Super Bowl half-time games, Olympics opening ceremonies, USO shows, and giant New Year's Eve celebrations at national gathering places all draw huge and enthusiastic audiences curious to see something big, loud, and fun and feel a part of something bigger than themselves.

One of the more interesting examples is the *son et lumière* ("sound and light") shows that are presented, usually after dark, at historical landmarks as various as the Red Fort in India, Parliament Hill in Canada, and Park of the Reserve in Peru. Invented by Frenchman Paul Robert-Houdin, who produced the first recorded such display at the Château de Chambord in France in 1952, *son et lumière* shows reach an international peak at the Great Pyramids at Giza in Egypt, where the story of the pharaohs and their majestic tombs is told nightly, projected onto the pyramids themselves, with the starry night at the edge of the Sahara as a backdrop. Audiences learn about history as they try to imagine themselves in this very same setting forty-five hundred years ago.

Nightclubs and Cabarets

Cabarets and nightclubs represent another cherished and unique entertainment form, one that blossomed and were booming by the twentieth century, but that have retreated in recent years. There are still some around. Almost every city has some form of nightclub life. But they are no longer the cultural force they once were.

These venues developed separately from theatre, although there was always some crossover. More sophisticated urban audiences in Europe, America, and eastern Asia were looking for places where they could drink and be entertained in a more intimate setting than the large theatres. As their name suggests, the clubs also sometimes had membership requirements, making them more exclusive and therefore more desirable.

Performance style varied widely, but by the late nineteenth and early twentieth centuries, clubs had established a template: a host would greet the audience and warm up the crowd with humorous patter. He would then introduce the performers, who would sing or tell jokes, or do whatever their specialty happened to be. Cabarets were closer to theatres; nightclubs were more intimate.

There was usually a star or two backed by an orchestra and often a small corps of dancers. Prominent cabaret demimondes sprang up in New York, Berlin (think *Cabaret*), Paris (think *Moulin Rouge!*), London, Warsaw, Amsterdam, Vienna, and many other cities. They offered audiences a chance to see these talents perform live and—this is key—up close. They made audiences feel that they were part of an inner circle, almost like family, experiencing songs, stories, and jokes that were personal, from the star to you.

Changing audience tastes plus the rising cost of doing business forced the clubs to make do with fewer and fewer personnel, until many began to content themselves with just a singer and a pianist, or a single comedian. But many talented people on the stages and in the wings got their start or found a second career in cabarets, including Barbra Streisand, Josephine Baker, the writing team of Betty Comden and Adolph Green, Barbara Cook, Kaye Ballard, Nina Simone, Eartha Kitt, Peggy Lee, Ann and Liz Callaway, Mike Nichols and Elaine May, Ben Bagley, Sylvia Syms, the McGuire Sisters, Jane Connell, Julius Monk, Gerard Alessandrini, and hundreds more.

But beyond the famous acts listed above, the spirit of the genre was captured by a lesser-known New York performer of the 1990s, Starla Smith. Smith would appear onstage dressed attractively, in all black, accompanied by a pile of small, flat boxes. Smith would then tell her tiny audiences the sad stories of her unhappy love life, and would often begin weeping, or singing a sad or funny torch song about the misery of love with titles like "Love Stinks the Most" and "I Mooned the Moon." She would wait until the heart of someone in the audience broke and the person shouted, "Don't cry, Starla, it will be all right!" or "I love you, Starla!"

Smith would say, "Oh, thank you, thank you! Have a pie."

And sure enough, she would reach for the stack of boxes and pull out a pie, usually a fruit-filled one she had baked herself, and hand it to the sympathetic audience member.

And then she'd sing her heart out again.

Picture Palaces

Even traditional theatres had something special to offer audiences. In the 1910s to the 1930s, theatre owners concluded that one way to attract audiences was to extend the fantasy world of the films into the theatres themselves. It was an era of theatres aptly described as movie palaces (in the UK, picture palaces).

The era began as a way to attract upper-class audiences to the cinema, which had been born in the nickelodeon era and was perceived as entertainment for the lower classes who couldn't even afford to see vaudeville, let alone legitimate theatre. Architect Thomas W. Lamb was responsible for some of the earliest of these palaces. Once his million-dollar Strand Theatre opened in 1914 at the corner of 47th Street and Broadway in the midst of the Times Square theatre district, the gentry started to see movies as a respectable part of the entertainment landscape.

Others soon jumped on the bandwagon and the Western world was soon dotted with magnificent, soaring, temples of fantasy, borrowing themes from Moroccan, Aztec, Egyptian, Babylonian, Gothic, Hawaiian, Rococo, Baroque, and every other extreme style—the more exotic the better.

Among the leaders in this movement was Roxy Rothafel, who managed various legitimate theatres and movie houses in New York City and where he developed his own concept that movie theatres should be palaces, designed to sweep audiences into an opulent fantasy world as compelling as the movies they were there to see. His greatest achievements were the Roxy Theatre at 153 West 50th Street between Sixth and Seventh Avenues, and its sister pleasure dome, Radio City Music Hall, which still stands.

These theatres were designed to make an upper-class audience feel pampered and comfortable. But as the style spread across the North American continent and to Europe (which had its own tradition of magnificent opera houses), these super cinemas also began to attract a working-class audience, who found them a source of jaw-dropping grandeur in their humdrum lives. These mansions of entertainment continued to stand in towns everywhere, even after the advent of the Great Depression in the late 1920s. Audiences able to scrape together 25 cents could, for an afternoon or an evening, immerse themselves in luxury.

Many of these theatres proved to be white elephants, however: difficult to fill and expensive to maintain. In the 1940s, and as television began siphoning away their audiences, many fell to wrecking balls in a sad mass destruction of theatres that continued into the 1970s.

Few buildings inspire the love that theatres do. Fans may be sorry to see a favorite restaurant close or an elegant old apartment building come down, but few architectural treasures inspire the urge to rescue like a threatened theatre. A common compulsion moved civic-minded theatre lovers in communities across the nation. And these weren't just pie-in-the-sky campaigns. The death of theatre often means the death of a neighborhood. Community leaders began banding together to save not just their theatres but the hearts of their downtowns. Theatres reflect economic power. Saving them traditionally takes three steps. Step one is the raising of money, the obtaining of deeds, the designation of landmark status. Step two is restoring the palaces to their original magnificence. Step three is the hardest part: figuring out how to fill the stages with attractions that would fill the seats. Some were landmarked and repurposed as legitimate theatres or multiuse concert halls. Many were also multiplexed.

The movie industry found that few towns could fill a one thousand to two thousand–seat theatre for a single movie for more than a week or two. But they discovered that those towns could support a cluster of fifty to four hundred–seat cinemas that could cycle in (and out) their attractions as often as needed. Some towns built multiplexes from the ground up, but most tried to repurpose their old movie palaces by dividing them up.

The balcony was closed off from the orchestra and a wall was erected down the center to create two small cinema boxes. The orchestra was usually divided into two or even three screening rooms. Beautiful decorations were painted over or covered with plywood and plaster.

A handful of these palaces survived or have been restored, notably the Emporia Granada Theatre in Emporia, Kansas; the Fox Theatre in Atlanta, Georgia; the Majestic Theatre in San Antonio, Texas; the Al. [sic] Ringling Theatre in Baraboo, Wisconsin; the Kings Theatre in Flatbush, New York; the Historic Fox Theatre in Hutchinson, Kansas; and the Beacon Theatre in Manhattan. Audiences visiting these Xanadus can still enjoy the sense that they are special because they are doing something special in a magically special place.

Reconfigured Spaces

Standard Broadway theatres have sometimes been reconfigured for special productions that took an approach opposite that of theatre-in-the-round. Instead of surrounding the action with the audience, they surrounded the audience with the action. When director Harold Prince wanted to move his 1974 revival of *Candide* to Broadway, he needed a space to match the in-the-round staging of its off-Broadway premiere at the Chelsea Theatre Center of Brooklyn. He found it in Manhattan's Broadway Theatre, which had already been massively reconfigured for the short-run musical *Dude*. Most of the action occurred in the center of what had been the orchestra section, with other scenes being played out on stairs, ramps, and platforms that had been built into what used to be the balcony, boxes, and even parts of the stage.

Similar reconfigurations were allowed in New York for the long-running original 1982 production of *Cats*, which turned the Winter Garden into a giant trash-filled alley for the singing and dancing Jellicle Cats. The Imperial Theatre was massively revamped for the 2016 production of *Natasha, Pierre & the Great Comet of 1812*, which had previously been performed in a specially designed tent called Kazino when the show was done in the Manhattan meatpacking district, and in a vacant lot next door to the Imperial.

What was the point of these expensive changes? Directors and playwrights believed that by fragmenting the playing space and dispersing it around the theatre, it had the effect of moving the play closer to the audience, the better to immerse them in the storytelling.

These principles are also being applied to theatres being built in the twenty-first century. On Broadway, for instance, the Stephen Sondheim Theatre, which opened in 2010, was built on the site of an older venue, Henry Miller's Theatre. But it did not follow the design of its predecessor. The new performing space kept the facade of the older theatre, but inside, the stage was relocated below ground level so that the audience space could have a sharper rake and the seats could be spread out, both side to side and front to back for today's larger audience members. It is now one of the most comfortable theatres on Broadway as well as being the most "green," in that it cools and heats and recycles water in a much more environmentally friendly way.

But the Sondheim still follows the basic historical audience-facing-proscenium design. On the other hand, The Shed, a new flexible space, opened in 2019 on the far West Side of Manhattan as part of the Hudson Yards urban renewal project. It is designed so that the stage and the seating can be reconfigured for any sort of play, musical, concert, art exhibition, dance recital, or any other sort of performance that can be imagined now or in the future. And all of this sits under a retractable roof that can open the audience to the stars or protect it from the rain.

As for the future, producer Dalton Dale has announced plans for a new $150 million theatre to be built in the Times Square area, with the descriptive working title of the Immersive Arts Complex. The modular space will allow configuration as both a traditional proscenium theatre or as a multifloor, multiroom performance space to accommodate immersive experiences like Sleep No More. "The Immersive Arts Complex is a vision of where theatre will be moving," he told Forbes magazine. "It is a renaissance of stage entertainment and will make it a necessity to a whole new generation of audiences."

Such experiments are not exclusive to the United States by any means. The celebrated fifteen hundred–seat Schaubühne in Berlin consists of seventy-six adjustable platforms that can be raised or lowered in various configurations by hydraulic lifts to create any number of audience spaces. This truly multipurpose venue can even be divided into three separate spaces for different functions.

As far as other traditions are concerned, Japanese Kabuki uses a specially designed stage and performance space developed in the 1600s and is based on the even earlier classical Noh theatre. The L-shaped stage accommodates a central performing area with a small-roofed space (*yuka*) for musicians on the audience-right side. Actors enter from the sides, but may also enter and perform on a raised ramp (*hanamachi*) that runs diagonally through the audience. Some productions use a *mawari butai*, a turntable that can be used for scene changes. An elevator device called a *suppon* allows characters to appear in the midst of the audience.

The *wayang kulit* or shadow puppet theatre of Indonesia (also practiced elsewhere in Asia) uses intricately built puppets, traditionally made of buffalo hide. But instead of performing like traditional puppets, they perform behind a huge white cloth screen upon which their shadows are projected by a bright light. Audiences used to sit on just one side of the screen to watch the shadows grow or shrink or move about, as operated by the skilled puppeteers. But in recent decades, audiences are allowed to sit in two groups, on either side of the screen. One side, the *wayang* side, gets to watch the shadows; the other side, the *dalang* side, gets to watch the beautifully decorated and articulated puppets themselves, as well as the nimble puppeteers as they manipulate them with bamboo sticks.

The Perpetual Palimpsest

Many legitimate performance spaces were built in the early decades of the twentieth century and remain in use in the twenty-first. Numerous opera houses, especially in Europe, were built even earlier. They were designed to present entertainment in an era before electronic amplification. And while many have now been wired for sound and advanced lighting effects, they remain what they once were: giant musical instruments of a sort, with the stage as the mouthpiece and the auditorium as a vast hornlike bell to project natural acoustic sound to the back of the balconies. Even the bas-relief designs and the cloth tapestries on many walls are there to look pretty, yes, but they have an acoustic purpose: to soften and mellow the sound. Those designs may not be necessary anymore, but they still have a subtle effect on what the audience members hear, and how they hear it.

The proscenium arch was designed to focus the audience's attention on the action, like the frame around a painting, and to make it easier to hide and then reveal scenery. Despite huge advances in mechanized scenery, most theatres, even newly built ones, still use a proscenium to present plays, concerts, and other entertainment forms. Similarly, while video game systems and virtual reality hardware are experimenting with three-dimensional projections, most games and filmed entertainment are still played on TV screens, a 1920s invention. Technological advances still are flavored by analog styles of presentation. We still say we will "tape" a show we want to watch, and "dial" a phone number, even though tapes and dials are basically extinct.

Older modes of presentation provide a perpetual palimpsest for the audience experience.

TECHNOLOGY

Developments in technology during the past two centuries have radically affected the audience. The importance we place on seeing and hearing is reflected in the fact that we developed technology to create images as early as humanity's cave-dwelling days, when we figured out how to draw. Advances in photography, film, and videography over the past two hundred years merely extended those tools and methods.

Recording sound took a bit longer. Sheet music gave us a way to play music so it could be recreated in live performance. But it wasn't until the late nineteenth century that the phonograph (whose name literally means "sound writing") enabled us to record sound directly. For most of humankind's history, there was only one way to hear something: directly, in proximity to the original source of the sound. With the advent of recording, with its amplification and electrification of sound, we had to use a separate word, "acoustic," to describe what once was the only way to experience sound.

Recordings were magnificent inventions that massively extended the way audiences were able to appreciate sight and sound. But they affected only two of our five senses. It's interesting that we've never come up with comparable technologies to record and replay smell, taste, and touch. Perhaps it's the complexity of how stimuli reach our sense organs in those cases.

Light and sound are both wave forms. Sound can be propagated through air (or other material media like water); light can be propagated through air or even a vacuum. The other senses require more direct contact with the thing being sensed, or bits thereof. Similarly, dreams and memories can be described, but the emotions they produce cannot be recorded directly. Perhaps someday they will (see the final chapter in this book, "What's Next?").

Audiencing has been enhanced in a thousand different other ways over the past century and a half, through developmental leaps in every phase of technology. Advances in lighting technology alone revolutionized the audience experience. The advent of gaslight allowed audiences to move indoors and for performances to take place, with relative safety, in the evening. The invention of electrical lighting made theatergoing even safer and more pleasurable, as it produced no smoke or smell.

But two of the least showy developments may have conferred the greatest advantages and expanded the comfort of live audiences everywhere.

The first game-changing innovation: window screens. Before screens were invented, audiences in theatres had two options in warm climates and in summertime everywhere: trying to watch shows in a cloud of flies, mosquitoes, midges, moths, spiders, and even birds (especially after dark) . . . or shutting the windows and sweltering in stifling heat and airlessness.

In 1861, relief was delivered by the food processing manufacturers Gilbert, Bennet & Co., who were selling wire mesh sieves and found they could also be custom-cut for windows. These screens were first used in coal-fired railway cars to keep out hot cinders, but by the turn of the twentieth century they were being sold for homes and businesses.

The second game-changing innovation was air-conditioning. For decades, the theatrical season followed the social season, which followed the climatic seasons. Social interaction in cities ground to a halt during the torrid summer months as those who could afford to attend theatre fled to the beaches or the mountains. Imagine being a performer trying to dance under hot lights in the dog days of summer, and imagine being in the audience, which used to dress up to go to the theatre, trying to watch them as the mercury crept toward 100°F. Also, subtract screens to keep out summer bugs and you can clearly see why most shows and concerts took a break during the summers and resumed, when the white clothes were tucked away, in the fall. Some shows braved the months named for Roman emperors, but most went into hibernation or retreated entirely.

Then along came Willis Haviland Carrier, a genius clearly robbed of the Nobel Prize (he was never even considered). Asked to solve the problems extreme heat and humidity were causing at a printing plant in 1902 Brooklyn, New York, Carrier applied concepts of mechanical heat transfer and created a machine that could cool air. He began mass-producing his invention in 1933 with the founding of the Carrier Air Conditioning Company of America. As of 2022, more than 80 percent of American households have air-conditioning systems. But before air conditioners were affordable by middle-class households, they could be found primarily in businesses. They were quickly embraced by theatres, concert halls, and cinemas, which avidly advertised on their marquees (in signs with special typefaces glistening with pretend icicles) that they were "air cooled" or "air conditioned" refuges from the summer heat.

The development of air-conditioning and window screens also made urban theatre a year-round experience. Starting in the 1940s, hit shows began to run around the calendar. The ability to house actors and audiences in comfort meant that long runs began to creep up, from the 2,212 performances of *Oklahoma!* in 1943, the 3,242 performances of *Fiddler on the Roof* in 1964, the 6,137 performances of *A Chorus Line* in 1975, the 7,485 performances of *Cats* in 1982, to the 13,981 performances of *The Phantom of the Opera* as of its closing in early 2023.

The Sound of Near Silence

The intimacy created by the camera and its ability to provide audiences with close-up views of actors' faces has had another unintended effect. People no longer like to sit above orchestra level in live theatres. Theatre owners have had to rename the balcony as the "mezzanine" or even the "rear mezzanine" to disguise the fact that it's the spurned balcony. Some theatres have simply closed off their unsellable second balconies. Audiences like to sit close so they can "really see" the actors, since so much of their performance is in their face, where traditionally it was expressed through their entire body.

Sound designers are driven to distraction for the same reason. There was a time when actors were trained to project their voices into the back row. Audiences trained by electronic media found this artificial. They wanted a more "realistic" form of acting, which includes even whispers that must be heard by everyone. This requires that actors' voices become amplified, which increasingly means personal microphones. An increasing number of shows required that microphones be not just hidden around the stage, but worn by actors, powered by battery packs hidden in their costumes.

Master Broadway sound designer Tony Meola, in his 2006 essay "Finding Pianissimo," writes about how difficult it has become, in live theatre especially, to make a sound that is deliberately quiet:

> I try very hard not to use a process called compression. You might not recognize the term, but if you listen to recorded rock music or popular music, you've heard it. Compression takes the highest of the highs and compresses them down so there's not much difference between the very quiet parts and the very loud parts. They do that so you can hear everything all the time at a specific volume setting. . . . Radio stations compress so you don't have to keep adjusting your volume. But that's not the way you were meant to hear sound. You're meant to hear loud sounds fortissimo [very loud] and soft sounds pianissimo [very quiet].

Just as audiences have been trained by movies and TV to see actors' faces close-up, they have also been trained to hear everything at high volume. However, Meola says there are some places where audiences still appreciate the beauty and drama of quiet sounds.

I am a classically trained musician. I love to go to the symphony. I am reminded what pianissimo is at the symphony. I almost never hear pianissimo in the theatre anymore. People complain that they can't hear. But they're hearing fine. What they are hearing is *quiet sounds*. On most modern musicals we never get below a mezzo forte [medium loud]. But when your quietest is a mezzo forte, fortissimo isn't loud enough and you get charged [by the director] with making it louder to make it more exciting.

Meola, who designed sound for *The Lion King, Wicked,* and other hit musicals, says he is also challenged to make the show sound roughly the same for audiences in all parts of the theatre.

The audience is always foremost in my planning. I spend technical rehearsals and previews sitting all around the theatre to make sure that I've covered it. The first place I go is the critics' seats and adjust the balance, if necessary. Then I move from corner to corner until I get the best balance of sound I can from every seat. Contrary to what you probably think, the balcony is the easiest place to adjust the sound. The hardest places are the most expensive seats. They are right down in front and you can't put a speaker between the performer and the audience. I try to put speakers all around the proscenium and balance them so it sounds like it's coming from the stage. But you get up [in] the balcony and there's plenty of places to put them: on the ceiling, on the balcony rail, on the sides.

Despite his efforts and the efforts of his colleagues, audiences still often find themselves complaining "Wow, why is it so loud? It's hurting my ears!" or "Why are they mumbling? I'm missing every other word!" Sometimes you get both of these reactions at the same theatre, depending on seat location, actor technique, and the individual audience member's power of hearing.

For their part, actors who are used to working in theatre exclusively find they must dial down their performances to keep from seeming hammy on the screen. Similarly, TV and film actors who attempt stints on the stage find that they have difficulty projecting their performance across the proscenium because their sly little smile, their flirtatious sotto voce, their soft, weary sigh, and their quizzical raised eyebrow are not discernable past the fifth row. They need to adjust their whole technique.

Translation Software

Recent developments have allowed automatic translation for audiences who speak a different language from that of the actors. Like many technological advances, these were science fiction until not that long ago.

Opera companies were among the first to offer supertitles for performances in other languages. The translations appear on a narrow screen above the stage. These are not to be confused with intertitles (for silent films) or subtitles (used by international films since the earliest days of the movies).

Simultaneous interpretation has long been a necessity in the world of diplomacy when the diplomats speak different languages but clear and accurate translation is crucial, with all the nuances kept intact. But such translation has only gradually spread to the performing arts. Signing for the deaf has become an accepted and regular feature for politicians, and some live shows on Broadway and elsewhere offer special signed performances for hearing-impaired audiences. Timing is crucial for these skilled signers, who need to keep up with a show that is often moving at an allegro pace.

Some performances offer translations from and into various languages via headsets. These work well for performances that always stay the same, like films, or basically the same, like live stage shows. But they are more problematic when the material is being extemporized or ad-libbed. Any hearing person who watches a speech, a news report, or a comedy scene with screened real-time subtitles knows how incredibly inaccurate they can sometimes be. Cell phone apps like iTranslate and Google Translate are mainly used for translating documents, but doubtless these will become available for live performances before long.

Beepers and Cell Phones

Not all technological developments have improved the audience experience. Though we think of our portable devices as the cutting edge of communications technology, we are still barely at the dawn of an era of interconnectivity of the human race whose implications are just beginning to be imagined. The bygone beepers and today's cell phones in an audience setting are often just a damned nuisance.

Though beepers, aka pagers, were invented in 1921, they were used mainly by police until the 1980s, when they caught on with doctors, firefighters, and inevitably, drug dealers. They offered an advantage over telephones. You could see who was calling you and reply—or not—at your leisure instead of right then. Emergency service personnel would carry them everywhere they went so they could be summoned if they were urgently needed. The beeping or buzzing would alert them that they needed to get to a telephone tout de suite. Among the places owners brought them included theatres and concert halls. These owners felt that their need to answer emergencies conferred on them an elevated status that trumped other people's need to enjoy the show undisturbed. But their fellow audience members didn't always agree, and simply assumed, rightly or wrongly, that they were entitled jerks who just wanted to show off how important they were, never mind the irritation they might cause to others.

Beepers became a plague. Audiences everywhere wished they would go away forever. It turned out to be a classic "be careful what you wish for" situation, because after their heyday in the 1980s and early 1990s, beepers quickly went extinct . . . only to be replaced by something infinitely better and worse: cell phones.

Cells don't just beep; they ring, sing, chirp, and play dippy electronic ringtones. They also talk, take photos and videos, and light up a dark theatre with bright display screens. On July 2, 2015, nineteen-year-old Nick Silvestri was attending a performance of the Broadway show *Hand to God* when he realized his cell battery was running low. Looking at the stage, he noticed the realistic church basement set featured what looked like a working electrical outlet. So he did what certainly any of us would do: he climbed up on the stage and plugged his charger into the outlet on the set. Friends, mainly girls, had been lighting up his phone with social calls all day, the college lacrosse player later explained. "What would you do?"

After members of the audience began shouting, he said, "about five security guards came running down. So I hopped off the stage. They were pretty mad. They said, 'What were you thinking?' I said, 'Hey, buddy, what's the problem?'"

Unfortunately for him, the outlet was just a prop.

Audience members like Silvestri are accustomed to carrying and using their portable devices everywhere, almost an extension of their arms. They're used to taking photos and videos wherever they want, even when instructed that such activities are not allowed, or actually against the law. Buying tickets, especially expensive ones, make them feel entitled, and they don't let things like laws and courtesy to performers impede them.

It's true that many concerts allow or even encourage taking photos with cell phones (sometimes people even hold up tablets). As a result, they think movies and plays should do the same. So they blithely text, flash lit screens, and sometimes even take calls while the people around them—others who also have paid for tickets—try to focus on the performance. You even find people using their cell phones during religious ceremonies.

Theatres and cinemas usually begin performances with an announcement to turn off all phones. But theatre managers don't want to enforce these rules too stringently for fear that a resistant audience member might make a ruckus that is more disruptive than the original infraction. And they have good reason to worry. The problem reached its pathetic extreme in 2014 when retired police SWAT commander Curtis Reeves and Chad Oulson separately took their wives to see a matinee showing of the Afghan War movie *Lone Survivor* at a Tampa, Florida, area cinema. Oulson, who was sitting in the row in front of Reeves, kept texting during the film. Bothered by the light from the phone, Reeves asked him to stop. Oulson refused, and reportedly threw popcorn at Reeves, verbally abused him, and then reached for him. Reeves, who claimed to have felt threatened by his fellow audience member, drew a .380 handgun and fired, killing Oulson.

Reeves was later charged with second-degree murder and aggravated battery. At trial, he was acquitted. A miscarriage of justice in a gun-loving state? Perhaps. But audience members who have sat quietly seething while a thoughtless fellow audience member sends photos, takes videos, or even engages in a phone conversation during a show, concert, film, or religious ceremony and then gets belligerent about it may feel that, on some level, justice was served!

Audience Members with Disabilities

Great strides have been made in recent years toward making all sorts of public facilities more accessible to audiences with various disabilities. Adding ramps and special seating for wheelchair-using people is only the most noticeable of these.

Infrared listening system (ILS) headsets have been available on Broadway for people with hearing challenges since 1979. Generally distributed free before performances to anyone who asks, the system, designed by Sound Associates, allows audience members to hear amplified sound over a wireless headset. Many theatres, concert halls, and cinemas throughout North America, Europe, and elsewhere now offer ILS or similar systems. As a result, America's legitimate theatres were ahead of the curve when the Americans with Disabilities Act guidelines, passed in 2010, required that "an assistive listening system" must be provided anyplace that uses audio amplification.

In addition to those with a hearing disability, ILS has also been embraced by those with normal hearing who have difficulty with some theatres' acoustics, and for plays that feature characters with strong accents. In recent years, as the technology improved, hearing-impaired theatergoers have been able to receive this enhanced sound over their own hearing aids.

Furthermore, the not-for-profit Theatre Development Fund (TDF) organizes special sign-language performances for theatergoers who are deaf and use American Sign Language as their primary means of communication. For those who don't use ASL, TDF has helped theatres install and schedule special performances with open caption (OC) equipment that displays electronic text, not just of the script, but descriptions of what the characters are singing or saying. TDF is best known to the general public as host of the TKTS discount tickets booths. But the organization has been an industry leader more broadly in finding ways to serve audiences with various disabilities. TDF Accessibility Memberships are free. Lisa Carling, director of TDF accessibility programs, says she has a simple goal: "To be as inclusive as possible, welcoming audiences with disabilities. We want them to have a fair chance of enjoying the show just like anyone else."

There's also new technology for the visually challenged. People are living longer but their eyes are succumbing to cataracts, glaucoma, macular degeneration, et cetera. For them, TDF hosts special performances of many shows that have trained "describers" who verbalize what is happening on the stage. Their narration is conveyed through a receiver and a single earpiece, so the vision-impaired theatergoers can still hear the dialogue and music with their other ear. It's similar to what you can enable on smart TVs.

One of the subtler challenges faced by those who promote theatre accessibility is what to do about audiences, particularly younger audiences, who are on the autism spectrum or deal with other developmental cognitive disabilities. TDF's Carling says their biggest expansion of programs for the disabled in the past decade has been in this area. Working with a show's creators and technicians to create these specially scheduled performances, TDF's experts lower the brightness and loudness of the show and they train the ushers and other house staff to allow the audiences to move around the theatre and to "vocalize" during performances. The theatres also set aside spaces outside the auditorium to which audience members can retreat if the performance becomes too intense for them.

Though accommodations like these are steps in the right direction, much still needs to be done to allow audiences with various disabilities and challenges to become full members of the audience, not just at home, but everywhere.

Images

In the 2020s, we have, if anything, an overabundance of choices for our audiencing experience. In streamed television alone, we have hundreds of choices at any one time, yet people complain that there is "nothing good on."

How different it was, just over one hundred years ago. With a few exceptions, like the enjoyment of paintings and drawings, all audiencing experience was live. If you wanted to see a particular play or musician or dance, you had to go see it in person—or had to figure out a way to perform it yourself.

Then, starting in the nineteenth century and proliferating in the twentieth, things began to change. Technology drove a massive expansion in audiencing options. It was dizzying to the people who lived through it. It seemed that every few years, something new came along, and audiences had to grow and adapt.

Painting, which can be traced back to cave walls, such as ones at Laas Gaal in Somalia, Lubang Jeriji Saléh in Borneo, and Lascaux in France are among humankind's first ways of recording one of the senses. Artists throughout human history tried to capture lifelike images through the tip of their paintbrushes or whatever tool they were using.

How lifelike? Many marble statues from the classical period in Europe are still considered to be among the most accurate and most beautiful ever created by humankind. There is the legend of fifth-century rival painters Zeuxis and Parrhasius to see who could capture nature more perfectly. Zeuxis claimed his still life of grapes was so realistic that birds would fly down to peck at what they thought was juicy fruit. Not to be outdone, Parrhasius asked Zeuxis to pass through a curtained doorway to see a painting he had done. When Zeuxis tried to brush aside the curtains and enter, he found the doorway was just an utterly convincing painting. Whether that story was merely a fable, it tells us the effect the painters were striving for, even in ancient Greece.

That goal continued for most of the next twenty-three centuries. Audiences for paintings wanted to see the world and the people in it recorded as accurately as possible. They were satisfied with the feats of white magic that turned dabs of color into recognizable images of their children, pretty vistas, or the world around them.

Then, suddenly, in the early nineteenth century, new ways were found to record images. After some early experiments with silver iodide and its ability to darken on exposure to light, French inventor Joseph Nicéphore Niépce produced the first permanent photograph in 1826. Now people could get a precise image that would have shamed Parrhasius. And they didn't have to sit for days to get a portrait.

But did that mean photography brought about the end of painting? Of course not. Painters had always brought something of themselves to their work, developing unique and individualized styles. But now that style became the most important thing. Painters began adding impressions, abstraction, interpretation. They began giving the audience something they couldn't get from photographs. Photographers were both freed and trapped by their literalism. They, too, began adding interpretation to compete with painters. Literal and painstakingly realistic paintings now became a style known as trompe l'oeil, meaning to "fool the eye."

But the speed, relative inexpensiveness, and precise accuracy gave photos a special and immediate quality. People whose houses catch fire often stay too long trying to save their family photos. If photos are lost, owners often lament their loss almost as if they had lost the subjects of the photos themselves. A bit of their loved ones' spirit inhabits the photo, like a benevolent ghost.

Much later, the invention of cell phone photography would prove to be a boon to amateur and professional photographers alike—though it was a disaster for Kodak and other film companies.

Motion Pictures

But we're getting ahead of ourselves. People loved their pictures but wanted to try the novelty of seeing them move. "Race Horse," a brief clip of a horse galloping, was shot by an Englishman, Eadweard Muybridge, in 1878. Audiences got to see some of these early short films in indoor arcades known as nickelodeons (the inspiration for the children's network of the 1990s), which took their name from the five-cent price of admission. Inside, you could watch short features primitively made to move by turning a crank that flipped still pictures fast enough so the persistence-of-vision phenomenon kicked in and the pictures appeared to move. The hand-cranked machines came to be called nickelodeons themselves. Soon there was a run on nickel coins so eager new audiences could see short features with titles like *Village Fire Brigade, A Mother's Sin,* and *Great Lion Hunt.*

Many of the working-class people who frequented the nickelodeons did so because they were so much cheaper than other forms of entertainment. But as the films grew in quality, people from all walks of life began to enjoy them, setting the stage, as it were, for cinema and the longer features that the new technology made possible.

Shooting first in Westchester County, New York, the nascent film industry soon decamped to Hollywood, where the sun shone every day. Pictures could now move, so why couldn't they talk, too? Finding ways to synchronize sound and image in film took the industry the better part of twenty years, but in 1927 the first commercially released "talkie," *The Jazz Singer*, rolled out in cinemas.

Within the span of 101 years, humankind went from oil painting through to photography, telephones, photographs, moving photographs, and on to talking and moving photographs in its quest to record and preserve sights and sounds just as they are being experienced by the eye and ear.

To quote *Sunset Boulevard*, humankind found "new ways to dream." That film and musical, about a former silent film star coping with an industry that embraced talkies, was a poster child for the human cost of these proliferating changes, as was the classic *Singin' in the Rain*.

Radio and Recorded Music

In parallel with the development of motion pictures was the development of recorded music. The first known crude sound recording was made by French inventor Édouard-Léon Scott de Martinville in 1860. But American inventor Thomas Edison developed the first phonograph seventeen years later, a tinfoil-covered cylinder that could be mass-produced and distributed.

Until then, music around the house was provided by a piano in the parlor, or a fiddle and guitar on the porch. Sheet music was the way music was distributed beyond the walls of theatres. As the twentieth century dawned, audiences every-where suddenly found themselves able to hear the greatest art-ists of the opera house and the concert hall in their own living rooms. Radio was developed in the 1890s by Italian Guglielmo Marconi, who was seeking to create a wireless telegraph. The first experimental radio broadcasts vibrated the airwaves start-ing in 1906. By the 1920s, recorded music and radio had joined forces to create the world's first mass medium. The Era of the Ear had begun.

Music was always an important part of radio, but it was soon matched by the spoken word. There was a time when, if you wanted to hear a vaudeville comedian, you had to go to a vaudeville theatre. With the explosion of radio, you now could hear these stars performing their acts in your own home. Within just a few years, audiences could listen to *The $64 Ques-tion*, *The Adventures of Sam Spade*, *Amos 'n' Andy*, *The Shadow*, *Little Orphan Annie*, the *Pepsodent Show*, a plethora of soap operas, and a hundred other shows that created what became known as the "theatre of the mind": listeners had only pure language (along with periodic sound effects) to stimulate their imaginations. A rattled sheet of metal conjured up thunder, which prompted audiences to picture lightning, rain, and a dark mood. The sound of knuckles knocking on a piece of wood made them envision a door with a mysterious visitor waiting to be admitted. Who could it be? Is the visitor romantic? Dangerous? Do they have a terrible message to deliver? Or great news? It was all in the mind's ear.

Audiences became immersed in the lives of fictional characters on the soap operas, whose travails sometimes became more real to them than those of their own families. In 1938, a Halloween Eve dramatization of H. G. Wells's novel *The War of the Worlds* on the anthology show *The Mercury Theatre on the Air* was so realistic that some listeners believed they were hearing news coverage of an actual Martian invasion, which resulted in a panic.

Radio came into its own during the Great Depression. It offered a bounty of free entertainment for those who could afford a radio and electricity to run it. It also helped boost music of all kinds, and music in turn helped boost radio. The Big Band era budded and blossomed on the radio, but two game changers came along in the late 1940s and mid-1950s. The first was Broadway cast albums. During the 1930s, show music and the equivalent of the Top 40 were virtually synonymous. Songwriters like Richard Rodgers (then with Lorenz Hart as lyricist), Cole Porter, the Gershwin brothers, Harold Arlen, and their contemporaries wrote songs for librettos that are difficult to revive today because they were so wispy and inconsequential. But the songs were masterworks that were quickly "covered" by the major recording artists of the day. It wasn't until the success of *Oklahoma!* in 1943 that producers thought to bring the original cast into the studio to record the songs from the show, often with the Broadway pit orchestra and conductor to give audiences an idea of what the show was like.

The earliest cast recordings were released on collections of slatelike 78 rpm (revolutions per minute) discs. Columbia Records producer Goddard Lieberson, who came from the company's classical records division, developed the 33⅓ rpm LP (long-playing) so that movements in classical symphonies didn't have to be interrupted to flip the disc. The format also proved ideal for the average length of Broadway scores (with some editing), and cast albums took off. For a while they were the most popular recording format. They did so well that in 1956, Lieberson's Columbia put up the entire $400,000 financing for the musical *My Fair Lady*, just to get exclusive right to the cast recording. The show became (for a time) the longest running in Broadway history and the cast album became (for a time) the best-selling recording.

Audiences in the New York area, and those with access to touring theatres across the Americas and beyond, could see Broadway musicals live if they had the price of a ticket. But the overwhelming majority of fans experienced Broadway through original cast albums. Kids, teens, and even grown-ups spent many an evening "dancing around the living room" as they say in *A Chorus Line*, singing along with the tunes, picturing themselves in the roles, conducting the orchestra, and imagining the staging in their heads—literally theatre of the mind.

About the same time as *My Fair Lady*, the second "killer app" for recorded music erupted: rock 'n' roll, which took advantage of the LP format and eclipsed the popularity of show music, providing a format to showcase the Beatles, the Rolling Stones, Pink Floyd, the Eagles, Michael Jackson, Billy Joel, Garth Brooks, Shania Twain, Madonna, and hundreds more. Audiences who never saw any of these artists in concert know every word of their songs. Each succeeding generation of audiences has continued to revel in the sounds of these albums, a radio format called the "Music of Your Life." Ask those audiences and they will tell you they built an important part of their identities through the music they came of age with.

Long after audiences moved on from vinyl LPs (though they've enjoyed a modest renaissance in recent years), recording artists have continued to release LP-length "albums" on cassettes, eight-tracks, CDs, DVDs, and now fully digital files that can be played on devices the size of your thumb. Or on your cell phone, which is now also used for video, email, photography, internet access, as a calculator, watching movies, buying tickets, Zooming, getting driving directions, checking your pulse, ordering groceries, and a thousand other tasks in addition to calling your mom on Mother's Day.

Television

As rich and varied as it was, the Era of the Ear lasted barely thirty years, roughly from 1920 to 1950. Radio had a big advantage when radio talked and movies didn't. But when movies began to talk in the late 1920s and television began to do both in the late 1940s, the Era of the Ear was quickly followed by the Era of the Eye.

Audiences avidly made the transition, first gathering to watch TV at a neighbor's house, then buying their own. The big-case radios that once enjoyed pride of place in the family room were moved aside to make room for the big-case/tiny-screen black-and-white televisions. Screens soon got bigger, added color, and expanded their audience enormously. Several of the most successful radio shows, like *Abbott & Costello*, *The Lone Ranger*, *Truth or Consequences*, *Dragnet*, *Burns and Allen*, and *The Ed Sullivan Show*, got costumes and sets and made the transition to television. In 1950, televisions were in 9 percent of American homes, which added up to 3.8 million households. By 1978, the number of TV households had grown to 72.9 million, which represented a stunning 98 percent of American homes. And many of those homes had multiple TVs in different rooms. In 1940, there had been none; four decades later TVs were virtually everywhere.

Audiences who once would go to vaudeville or the theatre a few times per year, now had top entertainment of all kinds pouring into their laps in an electronic waterfall. At the same time, however, television arguably narrowed the imaginations of the audience by showing everything so literally. Writer Peggy Noonan says, "TV gives everyone an image, but radio gives birth to a million images in a million brains." The same is true about classic novels that are made into movies: when audiences read a book, they imagine what the characters look like and sound like, and imagine the world in which they live. Once as story has been preserved in the amber of film, all the possible images collapse into one: the vision of the director and the actors. The audience member is dreaming someone else's dream. Television represented a gain, but also a loss.

Television came through the airwaves via an antenna on the roof or "rabbit ears" antennae on the TV itself. All this amazing content was funded by commercials—lots and lots of commercials. But to the audience, it was completely free!

And then came paid cable TV. Cable originally advertised itself as commercial-free. If you paid for the service you didn't have to watch commercials, of course! That soon went out the window. But satellite TV came in through the roof. Today, people find themselves paying for services like HBO, Netflix, Disney+, and a host of other copycat "pluses." So now you not only have to pay for the service, you also have to watch commercials, and then you have to pay extra for premium content. They have convinced you to pay three times for something that used to be free.

These gigantic, globe-girdling industries grew out of the simple fact that humankind found ways of recording sound and visual images. It says something about our priorities regarding our five senses that no budding Edison ever figured out how to record taste, smell, or touch, as mentioned previously.

Networks

Although radio made it possible to communicate with a mass audience, "mass" in the early days of the medium meant, potentially, everyone within a radius of about a hundred miles of a single station. Stupendous by traditional audience standards, the reach quickly began to seem, if anything, too cramped. Creating programming was expensive, and radio stations in smaller markets didn't always have the sponsor revenue to compete with those in large cities.

The solution quickly presented itself: networks.

In one of the great innovations of the new broadcasting era, the National Broadcasting Company (NBC) was formed in 1926, giving stations across the country access to the best programming on the air, and giving the network's organizers access to income in multiples of small checks from north, south, east, and west. Stars no longer had to travel from city to city to be heard by many; all they had to do was plop in front of a single microphone. The idea was so immediately successful that NBC divided into two networks, designated Red and Blue.

Competition arose in 1927 with William S. Paley's creation of the Columbia Broadcasting System (CBS), but the Red and Blue networks grew so powerful that the newly formed Federal Communications Commission (FCC) ordered the breakup of the company. The Blue Network became the American Broadcasting Company (ABC). Smaller networks came and went, including the Mutual Broadcasting System and, later, the DuMont Television Network, but NBC, CBS, and ABC dominated both radio and, eventually, television until the 1990s.

It's easy to focus on the personalities and the immense amount of money and power that flowed from the advent of national broadcasting networks. But something even bigger was at work. For the first time, people in Des Moines and Tulsa and Montpelier and Tampa and Coeur d'Alene could hear and see the same comedian, the same drama, the same music, the same news broadcast as people in Chicago, Los Angeles, and New York. And at the same moment.

Think of the first step on the moon, the Super Bowls, the attack on the World Trade Center, Lucille Ball in the candy factory, The Beatles on *The Ed Sullivan Show*, the assassination of President Kennedy, *Saturday Night Live*, *The Tonight Show with Johnny Carson*, Mary Martin flying out the Darlings' window in *Peter Pan*, the election of Barack Obama, the storming of the Capitol in Washington, the fall of the Berlin Wall. For the first time in history, there could be a national, even global, culture. And for the first time, nearly all humankind had the potential to hear the same words and see the same images at the same time, and at the moment they were happening. The global audience was born.

The Internet

Then, of course, came the medium that combined all the others, the internet. It may not have been "live" like in-person concerts and theatre, but the audience was able to express the interactivity of a phone call with the reach of a network.

Author Peter Hirshberg addresses the significance of this development in his essay "First the Media, Then Us: How the Internet Changed the Fundamental Nature of the Communication and Its Relationship with the Audience." He writes:

> We maintain deeply intimate relationships with our connected devices. Within minutes of waking up, most of us reach for a smartphone. We go on to check them one hundred and fifty or more times throughout the day, spending all but two waking hours with a mobile device nearby. As these devices become omnipresent, more and more data about our lives is nearly permanently stored on servers and made searchable by others (including private corporations and government agencies).

This continual immediate access to worldwide communication and information is changing how we think and act in more ways than we perhaps realize. Hirshberg observes,

> This idea that everything we do can be measured, quantified, and stored is a fundamental shift in the human condition. For thousands of years we've had the notion of accountability to an all-seeing, all-knowing God. He kept tabs on us, for our own salvation. It's one of the things that made religion effective. Now, in just a few thousand days, we've deployed the actual all-seeing, all-knowing network here on earth—for purposes less lofty than His, and perhaps even more effective.

This new era, when all devices and even objects will be connected and responsive with the ability to collect and emit data, he calls "The Internet of Things."

> Here is a big number we will contend with, and soon. There will likely be one trillion Internet-connected devices in about 15 years. Nothing on earth will grow faster than this medium or the number of connected devices and the data they emit. Most of these devices will not be people, of course, but the impact of a trillion devices emitting signals and telling stories on our mediated world cannot be overstated.

Empowering the Audience

Word of mouth has always been the most powerful tool for audiences to get information about shows or movies or bands or teams they might like. Advertising, while demonstrably potent, is always suspect, since it is paid for by the subject. Getting a thumbs-up from a friend whose taste you share, who has spent hard-earned money and scarce free time, will almost always carry greater weight than a commercial.

But word of mouth is not something businesses can directly control. So they use other means, like advertising, sponsorships, or putting their logos on the fences at a tennis match or painting them on the side of a race car. Millions of dollars are spent to spread the word about their products, as anyone knows who has spent a few hours watching commercial television, listening to commercial radio, or battling pop-ups every time they open a website.

Nevertheless, even desirable target audiences retain many ways to assert their control. The advent of electronic media not only allowed producers to track what audiences wanted to see, it also gave audiences power to shape what they were shown.

For many years, the gold standard in American audience tracking was the Nielsen Ratings (Nielsen Media Research). Nielsen began tracking radio audiences in the late 1930s and 1940s and expanded into television ratings in 1950. The company chose statistically representative households and required member families to write down what they were watching in a Nielsen diary.

Though the system depended on the diaries being strictly accurate, it left considerable room for subjects to skip entries, or to record things they thought they "should" be watching, rather than what they actually were watching. Nielsen Media strove to account for these blips and their work was considered accurate enough for the company's reports to be followed religiously by the American television industry for much of the next fifty-six years. During that time people began watching television in many ways other than switching it on when the show was on. People began recording shows to watch later, or watching on the internet, and later, on their phones and other digital platforms. People also began watching in locations other than their living rooms, leaving them far from the Nielsen diaries.

Nielsen repeatedly updated their data-collection parameters in an attempt to keep track, but accurate ratings became harder and harder to guarantee. Meanwhile, social media like You-Tube, Twitter, Facebook, and Instagram began using supremely detailed (and invasive) software that tracked not only what audiences were watching, but how they discussed them and what they bought online. If you went to a website to shop for underwear for your significant other, you would find, to your chagrin, that your feed would suddenly be inundated with underwear ads.

The audience's opinions, viewing preferences and buying habits began to be consulted in ways the troubadours of old couldn't possibly imagine. The music industry tracking followed much the same development, starting in the 1950s with the advent of Top 40 music sales tracking, which evolved into a format based strictly on music sales rather than the taste of deejays and radio station managers.

The invention of the internet has empowered audiences in an even more proactive way. Message boards, chat rooms, instant news, and the ability to share MP3 files have transformed what the audiences sees, what it knows about it, and how its opinions are shared.

The Advent of Zoom

In early March of 2020, few people outside the tech industry had heard of a media company called Zoom Video Communications. But within a month or two, Zoom had become central to educating children, conducting business meetings, keeping in touch with friends and family members, and allowing entertainment folk to keep up with each other and with their audiences. Here was an amazing new way to empower the audience.

The impetus was the explosion of the COVID-19 pandemic, which drove people into quarantine, and eventually got them to wear masks and take vaccines—well, most of them anyway. Zoom allows multiuser meetings and conferences via laptops or handheld devices. Large groups could be accommodated, led by an emcee/organizer. Everybody could hear what the others were saying, though the emcee could turn off individuals' sound as needed. You could see the person you were conferring with, pass them messages, share your screen with them, and so on.

The point is, Zoom not only gave people quarantined during the COVID-19 pandemic a way to stay in touch with groups, it also gave them new ways to approximate the audience experience, but virtually. The comments section during a Zoom session or during a live video feed create not just a virtual audience but one that shares interests, understands technology, and has money to buy or update computer equipment. The Zoom app, which had been getting a few dozen new subscribers a day, was suddenly overwhelmed by thousands of people trying to download it because they needed it so urgently.

Several other companies had launched before the pandemic began or shortly thereafter, including Webex Meetings, Microsoft Teams, Lark, Google Workspace, and RingCentral. But "Zoom" started to be used as a generic term. Zoom helped save many businesses, helped school-age kids maintain their grades and classroom contact, and helped ordinary people hear and see (but not yet touch) their quarantined loved ones. On one day in March 2020, at the very dawn of the COVID-19 period, some 2.13 million people downloaded the app in a single day. At the beginning of March, the number of daily meeting participants on Zoom stood at ten million. By the end of April 2020, the number had grown to three hundred million daily meeting participants.

At first used almost exclusively for business meetings, Zoom kept growing even as the pandemic was fading. Audiences began creating theatre and music segments for sharing on Zoom. Concerts, whole plays, and even musicals were written, produced, and performed remotely, even by people locked away in their basements and attics. They were on the web, but they were produced and performed live—on Zoom, though with an audience that could come from anywhere, as long as they had downloaded Zoom software.

Zoom audiences could see who was speaking and could reply to them as well, limited only by the reach of their Wi-Fi. Several things changed in society, thanks to Zoom and similar software. These audiences began to enjoy working from home, sometimes in their pajamas and underwear, though these couldn't usually be seen. These audiences also began drinking more and weighing more, but they were happy to do it in exchange for not having to endure a long commute.

Changing Expectations

If you've ever watched old movies and noticed how exaggerated the acting is, or revivals of classic plays and seen how talky they can be, or sat through an opera and wondered why they're singing so loudly, or perused clips of sports games from a century ago and thought how scrawny or tubby even the top athletes once were, you've probably realized how much audience expectations have changed over the years.

Before movies and television, most people's experience with actors took place in a live theatre setting. People lucky enough to have seats in the front orchestra could see the actors' facial expressions easily, but they were only a small percentage of the audience. Most people sat further back or in the mezzanine or balcony—the "cheap seats"—and what they could see was limited. The same was true of what they could hear. Actors were trained in a vocal technique called projection that enabled them to push their voices to the back of the house.

Nevertheless, it helped the audience if the performers were simply *big* and *loud*. The booming power of the opera voice, the musical comedy "belt," and the symphony orchestra were developed in the era before microphones.

The exaggerated gestures of François Delsarte's nineteenth-century Delsarte System of broadly gestural acting poses were designed to communicate emotions that could be seen from a distance. The hyperbolic facial features of stars like Jimmy Durante (his big nose), Eddie Cantor (his "banjo eyes"), Joe E. Brown (his broad mouth), even Groucho Marx with his obviously painted-on greasepaint moustache and eyebrows, helped make them visible and memorable to audiences sitting in the second balcony.

Modern audiences who wonder why opera singers sing so loudly, why silent film acting and facial expressions seem so ridiculous, and why performers from early movies are so grotesque looking can point a quivering finger of blame on the same thing: they were never meant to be heard or seen so closely. "We had faces then," the character of Norma Desmond memorably states in the movie *Sunset Boulevard*. But the close-ups she was so ready for also killed the audience's need for them.

As discussed in chapter 6, the miking of stage shows allowed actors greater nuance in their vocal performances and created an expectation in audiences of a more intimate kind of performance. It also changed the way actors used their bodies. But the technological advances since World War II have changed a lot about how audiences experience many varieties of performance.

As each new technology was introduced (movies, radio, TV) over the course of the late nineteenth and early to mid-twentieth centuries, those inside and outside show business predicted that each one would bring about the death of legitimate theatre. And indeed, some forms did die. Vaudeville did not survive the 1930s; most situation comedies and variety shows transferred from the stage to radio to TV in the 1950s.

But, like opera, live theatre, especially musicals, managed to survive and even to boom from time to time. Musicals, however, hold greater appeal to a broader audience. That's because musicals differ from opera in form and intention. The emphasis in opera is more on the music. The music tends to be more formal in style, and the target audience tends to be more elite. Musicals emphasize the story and the characters, with music being used as a way of illuminating them. Musicals also are freer in their use of contemporary music, even when telling historical stories. The Broadway "sound" has emerged as something of a hybrid style created by the tension between popular musical and classical style, especially opera. The intended audience is more middle class, and therefore musicals have always been quick to absorb whatever musical style was popular among middle-class people.

Musicals have always been a bastard form, combining elements of high culture like ballet and orchestral music with populist elements like satire, burlesque, melodrama, and vaudeville. Just as Americans like their beer lite and their bread white, Americans turned around during the peak popularity of opera and created a populist opera form that softened the edges and absorbed these other forms.

As mentioned, the Broadway sound is the product of tension between operatic classical music and popular music of the time. In the nineteenth century it drew on the music of minstrel shows and operetta. In the early part of the twentieth century, the tension was between classical and jazz, which produced the work of George Gershwin, Irving Berlin, and their contemporaries. In the 1940s and 1950s, it was the big band sound. In the 1960s (*Hair*) and onward, it was rock, and even rap (*In the Heights, Hamilton*). In staging, it uses a similar tension between ballet and popular dance.

Labeling one thing an opera and another thing a musical often has to do with the proportion of opera and pop in the mix. With high opera standing at one extreme, stage performance forms shade to comic opera, opera bouffe, operetta, musical drama, musical comedy, rock musicals, and finally rock and rap concerts, the latter two being purely pop.

But musicals absorb much more than pop music. They represent the acme of Wagner's notion of a *Gesamtkunstwerk*—a master artwork that includes all the other arts: music, dance, drama, literature, painting and sculpture (sets), clothing design, lighting design, and more recently, film and video. Musicals can be thought of as storytelling operas that incorporate pop music. It's a flexible category, which occupies a lot of ecological niches in popular entertainment, and therefore thrives despite economic challenges such as extremely high ticket prices.

While musicals have continued to evolve at a Darwinian rate, operas have changed less so. That evolution has been studied and analyzed extensively in books by authors like Ethan Mordden, Ken Bloom, Stanley Green, Peter Filichia, and others. But those studies focus mainly on what happened from about 1890 on. The period from 1866 to 1890 has been much less examined. And the period before that even less so.

Along with that evolution, musicals have tended to absorb and replace all the other forms that influenced them. While operetta, burletta, vaudeville, burlesque, and the others all had their day in the theatrical sun, all survive today on stage almost exclusively as parts of musicals. Broadway's Tony Awards (and other New York and regional awards) recognize plays and musicals as the two main branches of legitimate theatre. All other categories have melted into insignificance and irrelevance, like the black-and-white film category for the Oscars. The only significant exception is opera, which has managed to survive mainly in a backward-looking form. The rare new modern opera tends to sound more like a musical than like *Siegfried*.

Jazz has been called the only uniquely American art form, but musical comedy certainly is too. The film *42nd Street* calls "musical comedy . . . the grandest words in the English language," and these words certainly reflect an art form that has not only survived but prevailed (apologies to William Faulkner).

But instead of becoming more like movies and TV, which was the initial urge, live theatre has survived by becoming less like those competing media and emphasizing what the others can't do. In *Scapino*, for instance, Jim Dale delighted audiences by running out into the audience on the backs of people's seats as he fled from pursuers. By the 1970s and 1980s, the very artifice, imagination, and live-ness of theatre began to make it more appealing to audiences grown tired of experiencing so much of their lives vicariously.

Breaking the fourth wall, making entrances from the back of the theatre, or even playing scenes in the aisles at arm's length from the actors—that's something theatre could offer that other media could not.

That's one of the most important reasons for the rediscovery of elemental audiencing experiences. Audiences loved what they were watching and wanted a more intense version of the same experience. It accounts for the popularity of extreme sports, of paintball, of New Vaudeville, of New Burlesque, the resurgence of Broadway, and other in-person, live activities. People can listen to their favorite bands play all their hits with studio-balance perfection, but they want to see them live. They can watch their favorite teams in color close-up any day of the week, but they want to go to the stadium and see them compete in person. They can even watch a movie on a huge plasma TV at home—but nothing beats seeing a big movie on a full-size or IMAX screen surrounded by a crowd gasping along with them.

Audiences get tired of just watching other people doing things on a screen, even with computerized special effects, even if it is in 3D virtual reality. They want to get out and see it happen live in front of them—or get out and do it themselves.

Technology Transforms Audiencing

There was a time in the nineteenth and early twentieth centuries when theatre and classical concerts ruled the entertainment world. When movies arrived, theatre folk feared they would crowd out live theatre. They were partly right. Audiences thronged to the silent and then talkies, which helped kill theatre forms like traditional vaudeville and burlesque.

But then along came radio and analog television, which were free (except for commercials) and could be watched by audiences "in the convenience of your home" and began to crowd out movies.

Then along came streaming services and the internet, which began to crowd out movies.

And who knows what's coming next?

In each case, the only reason the entertainment forms survived is because they evolved, and played to their strengths, and thereby kept a slice of the audience.

Theatre focused on musicals, which just never seemed to come across on television quite as well. Radio stopped trying to do scripted shows and settled on mainly music and talk, both of which came across better on radio.

Movies surrendered serials, newsreels, and short light comedies to analog TV, but tried a series of innovations including 3D and big-screen formats like Cinemascope and IMAX. During the 1940s and 1950s, the movies kept audiences in their seats with lush musicals like the ones from the Freed Unit at MGM,

Enjoying the Chinese Film Festival in 3D, Cinema Gaumont Champs-Elysees, Paris, France.
Directphoto Collection / Alamy Stock Photo

which rolled out masterpieces like *Singin' in the Rain* and *An American in Paris*. In recent years, cinema owners have tried to lure in the fans with huge stuffed reclining chairs complete with cupholders.

Analog TV kept game shows, news, and sports and gave up big-budget costume drama and science fiction to streaming services.

And then came the format that trumped them all.

Those who grew up with TV, movies, radio, television, recorded music, and all the other technological advances were convinced, like Will Parker in *Oklahoma!*, that things had "gone about as fur as they can go." Science fiction movies imagined all kinds of spaceships, faster-than-light travel, matter transfer, humanoid robots, et cetera. But few before William Gibson predicted the most society-changing technology of all—the internet.

This communication system used telephone lines to transmit not just voices, but images, data, whatever anyone wanted to see or hear. Nearly all human knowledge, and all the recordings that had been so painstakingly gathered and preserved, suddenly became available virtually anywhere to anyone.

All the services we now take for granted—Twitter, Facebook, Instagram, Netflix, Disney+, Hulu, Twitter, and the latest, Zoom and its imitators that were barely imagined just a few decades ago, now are central to human discourse around the world. And those who once again sit back and think we've "gone about as fur as [we] can go" are going to be in "fur" a big surprise in the decades to come.

It seems we're always on the threshold of Shakespeare's "brave new world."

7

GROUP BEHAVIOR

Ancient Greek audiences attending the City Dionysia would spend a whole day at the theatre, watching three full-length plays in a row, plus comedic skits. The Elizabethan audiences watching the plays of Shakespeare, Marlowe, and their contemporaries oohed, aahed, hissed, wept, guffawed, and shouted back at the players as they cracked hazelnuts and cockle shells. These audiences were supremely engaged and reactive ones. They got a lot from what was happening on the stage. But what did they get from each other—from being members of an audience? What were the group dynamics?

An audience is a highly specialized mob. Some of the same social dynamics are at work. Like a mob, the participants often find themselves doing things in a group that they wouldn't have done on their own.

There is a show business maxim to the effect that "Individual audience reactions are always wrong; collective audience reactions are always right." In practice, it means that if you ask one person for their opinion about your show, it will likely be useless or dead wrong. But if you stand at the back of the theatre and listen to how the audience responds as a group, pro or con, they are right.

This is the theory behind collective opinion-sharing websites like Quora, Yelp, Reddit, Yahoo Answers, and many others. But it's not a new concept. To quote Aristotle's *Poetics* once again, "It is possible that the many, though not individually good men, yet when they come together may be better, not individually but collectively."

People behave differently when they are part of an audience. With a live audience, they find themselves in the dark, close to strangers with whom they have a sudden bond. It's very intimate. They create consensus from observing the reactions of fellow audience members and participating with them. They often laugh out loud more than when they are alone. They will shout encouragement at live performers (though I've seen many people also shout back to their TVs). They watch or listen to others for cues about what is funny or sad, or when to clap.

If you talk to any of one hundred individuals, you will get a variety of opinions on any said topic, and in how they express those opinions. But, when those same people are part of an audience, their outward responses are surprisingly uniform. They generally tend to laugh in the same places, be quiet in the same places, applaud in the same places, and get restless in the same places. They start to act like a unit, almost in unison.

Have you ever been in an audience where you don't quite get a joke—but then hear the people around you laughing uproariously, and, after a moment of thought, you finally get it, just in time to join the general laughter? If you were by yourself, you might just have let it go. Of course, there are those sweet times when you get the joke first, and the rest of the audience chimes in with laughter a moment later. That's a nice win.

Then there is adrenaline. It's exciting to watch an action movie at home on your wide-screen TV. But there is a reason so many people throng the stands at a sports game. You get even more pumped in a stadium. You're with a group, and all of you have the same goal: to help your favorite team win by cheering or shouting advice. During an action-packed movie or play, you amplify excitement and suspense through the collective experience.

Etiquette

There have been a million pieces written on theatre audience etiquette. I've written one or two myself. These are the usual main points:

- Arrive early or at least on time.
- Be silent and, better yet, switch off all electronic devices, including cell phones, pagers, and even watch alarms. Doctors and lawyers, this applies to you, too. If that serious of a problem could crop up, you probably shouldn't be out on the town anyway. Influencers, you can post your review on social media at intermission or after the show.
- How should you dress? Be comfortable but have respect for the artists who can see you just as easily as you can see them. You're not at home.
- If your child is able to sit still and be quiet for an hour-long video, she or he is ready to be taken to see a live show. But not before.
- Even if the venue allows photography, which most do not, don't use flash. It's distracting to the performers and leaves the same blue dot in their field of vision as it does yours. If they then trip and fall and hurt themselves, it's your fault.
- At a musical, once the orchestra starts to play live music, it's time to be quiet and listen.
- Hold off on talking or singing along with the show, even humming, unless it's a pop concert.
- Stay till the bows are over, even if you are in a rush. It's part of the show. On the other hand, you can leave during the play-out music of a musical, because that's what it's for. But it's nice to stay and give the orchestra its own hand.

What all these rules boil down to is this: Remember you're not the only one at the theatre. You spent a lot of money on a ticket? So did the person next to you. Your right to swing your arm ends at the tip of your neighbor's nose. The Golden Rule of being in a live audience is the same as the Golden Rule for the world at large: Do unto your fellow audience members and the people who work at the theatre as you would have them do unto you. If everyone does these few simple things, they will have fun and so will you.

But not everyone agrees with these rules, or, indeed, many rules at all. On the flip side of these perennial think pieces are reflections that aren't about what not to do, but rather how audience members should feel free to enjoy and indeed express themselves at the theatre.

Theatre blogger Howard Sherman believes that guidelines such as the ones listed above are too restrictive, or worse. In a piece titled "Stop Telling Audiences How to Behave—Let's Encourage People to Enjoy Themselves at the Theatre," Sherman writes:

> These handy reference guides range from the condescending to the witty. . . . But the problem with these pieces, while likely cathartic for the writers and those who read them, is that by being placed on the arts pages, they are highly unlikely to reach their target audiences: the casual or even rare theatre-goer who may well have been dragged along against their will.
>
> In all likelihood, the perpetrators don't reserve their self-centered, everyone-else-be-damned discourtesy for live arts events. One imagines they're also cheering on their football team in houses of worship and during important business meetings.
>
> Will they ever learn? Hard to say. But if they don't, at least they'll continue to provide fodder for arts journalists and fans who are shocked to find such behavior at the theatre. But it was ever thus: when I would usher and house manage in the early 1980s, it wasn't uncommon to find audience members with transistor radios surreptitiously listening to sporting events during Chekhov, often erupting in uncontrollable, though slightly muted, cheers. All that has changed is the technology.
>
> [In 2018], also at Lincoln Center Theater, at a performance of the revival of *My Fair Lady*, another theatergoer took it upon himself to inform a theater artist about proper behavior at the theater. Appearing in script form on a Twitter thread, the exchange was described:

Condescending Theatergoer: Well, I didn't know this show had so many laughs—you were certainly enjoying yourself. (Passive aggressive shaming me for laughing—at the jokes.)

Me: Yup, it's a great show!

CT: Oh yeah, I've seen it a million times. I like old-fashioned musicals. (Emphasis on Old Fashioned: He doesn't like *Hamilton*.)

Me: So do I, this is one of my favorites! (My cheer is throwing him.)

CT: I like shows where YOU CAN UNDERSTAND ALL THE WORDS. (Haaaaaaaa. Aight, let's get into it.)

Me: SO DO I! What show ARE YOU REFERRING TO?

The ultimately chastened Condescending Theatergoer had actually entered into this conversation with . . . Lin-Manuel Miranda, the creator of *Hamilton*, who apparently put the fool in his proper place without ever being anything less than polite.

Miranda concluded his Twitter thread by counseling his millions of Twitter followers: "The lesson here, if there is any: there is always the type of theatergoer that defines themselves by excluding others. You could write musicals, and they'll still try to make you feel like you don't belong. Don't you dare let 'em. You love theater? You belong. Welcome."

Virtual Crowds

Virtual crowds were well established before COVID-19, but became more commonplace during the quarantine when it was the only kind of crowd in which you could safely take part.

Since the early days of online user groups, people with similar interests tended to gravitate together in virtual spaces to share information. You could stay in touch with long-lost cousins on Facebook, ask for recommendations for restaurants on Twitter, communicate with your government reps on their personal websites, learn about history on podcasts, or watch your niece give a piano recital on YouTube.

YouTube created the option to share opinions on a performance with real-time streaming commentary running beside the live video window. At last: an environment outside of a sports bar where people could talk during a performance and no one minded.

With the advent of Zoom and other video conferencing software, audiences can meet, face-to-screen-to-face with friends, family, teachers, students, business coworkers, lecturers, or seminar professors anywhere on earth with no one hogging your armrest, stinking up your cubicle with their nasty lunch, or kicking your seat. It's true that people may talk over one another (unless muted by the host). Their phone may jingle, interrupting their talk. But if worse comes to worst, you can claim a technical glitch and log out without seeming rude.

It's not a perfect substitute for the real thing, but you can see their face and hear their voice, which is better than nothing.

Fandom

Audiences rarely just happen to wander into a performance. They take part because they want to learn something, because they heard the performance or game or display is really great, or because they are *fans*. Short for "fanatic," the word denotes a person who admires a celebrity, a sports team, a type of entertainment, or something else to an extreme degree.

Fandom is powerful. Fans follow your career. They listen and watch your every move. They debate your latest efforts and defend you against naysayers. They cheer your successes, or sometimes just cheer your presence. Think of the fans screaming for Frank Sinatra, Elvis Presley, the Beatles, Michael Jackson, or their successors.

They aren't usually just aficionados of sports or musical theatre in general; they're fans of a particular team or player or show or star or songwriter. Fandom grows and changes as a fanbase grows or diminishes with time in cases such as *Super Mario*, *Babylon 5*, Spanish-language soap operas, pro wrestling, the Boston Red Sox, film noir, Benny Goodman, Jay-Z, Harry

Potter, Rudolph Valentino, soccer teams, Mel Brooks movies, Drake, the Ritz Brothers, and K-pop.

Because fans are self-chosen, they are predisposed to like what they see and hear. They can either be intensely forgiving of your stumbles because they are just happy to be seeing you, or they become hypercritical because they know what they expect—and woe betide you if you fail to deliver.

Being a part of these audiences gives people a way of establishing a group identity that is different from an ethnic or generational one. Wearing the T-shirt or the team jersey helps give them a sense of belonging to that group. There is safety and security in numbers. When they're with their fellow fans, in person or virtually, they are no longer just crazy nerds; they are part of a manageable self-contained world, filled with sympathetic characters who grow and change with time but stay essentially the same inside. And the fan feels they are one of them.

Sometimes fans hold a star back. A lot of artists can't understand why people want to hear a song they've heard many times in the past or can hear for free by slapping on their iPods. The "old stuff" becomes a kind of enemy to the "new stuff." It's frustrating for artists because they want to grow, and growth usually means change. But audiences like the familiar. It helps them remember a time in their lives when they first fell in love with the song or the show or whatever, and accepting "new stuff" can get harder.

Six-time Grammy Award–winning singer and songwriter James Taylor had a number 1 hit with his 1971 song "Fire and Rain," but quickly found that no matter what other songs he would write, fans wanted to hear that tune every time he did a concert. In his 1985 song "That's Why I'm Here," he shook his head lyrically about the phenomenon, saying "Perfect strangers can call you by name. / Pay good money to hear 'Fire and Rain' / again and again and again."

Similarly, some performers become so identified with a single role that they either can't do anything else, or they have trouble getting hired to do anything else. Nineteenth-century actor William Gillette played detective Sherlock Holmes in the play of the same title an estimated thirteen hundred times in his life. Vaudeville performers would do the same act, sometimes for decades. Actor Leonard Nimoy, who became typecast playing the uber-logical alien Spock on the *Star Trek* TV series, wrote an autobiography titled *I Am Not Spock* in 1975. But then, twenty years later, after he came to terms with how special and rare it was to create a character who so deeply affected so many people, he followed up the memoir with a sequel, *I Am Spock*. P.S.: In the series, Spock is asked for his first name and replies, "You couldn't pronounce it." One of the series's fans made up a full name for him, "S'Chn T'Gai Spock," which was later accepted as canon by the series's creators.

This phenomenon accounts for why long-running TV shows continue to do so well in syndication, playing the same reruns of *The Jeffersons* or *M*A*S*H* or *Friends*. Yes, they may attract appreciative new audiences, but often they are watched by their original audiences who find comfort in watching favorite episodes over and over until they know the dialogue by heart. It's the same as rereading a favorite book or replaying a beloved music album. These fans come to regard the characters as old friends they really like and watching the reruns is like paying them a visit.

In the world of cosplay, fans spend time and money building amazingly detailed costumes to make themselves look like the objects of their affections. The documentary film *Into the Wasteland* chronicled a convention of fans of the Mad Max movies. Attendees flew in from all corners of the world to gather at the Australian location where the film was shot, dressed like the postapocalyptic characters, for a chance to meet actors from the film who played secondary and even tertiary roles. The actors were bemused but grateful; the fans were over the moon.

Fandom sometimes goes further. Valeria Lukyanova, a fan of Mattel's Barbie dolls, underwent an extensive series of plastic surgeries to resemble the toy. Several others have done this as well. Lukyanova became a darling of tabloid media, which christened her the Human Barbie.

For some fans of fictional works, the characters become as real or realer than the "real" people in their life. Soap operas have a special hold on their audience in this way, and fans sometimes get more emotionally involved with the vicissitudes of the characters in "my stories" than they do with their actual families and friends.

And sometimes it goes even further. In 2022, the *New York Times* reported that "thousands" of Japanese "fictosexuals" have entered into romantic relationships of various kinds . . . with fictional characters. The *Times* story focuses on Akihiko Kondo, a thirty-eight-year-old businessman who took part in an unofficial ceremony to marry Hatsune Miku, "a turquoise-haired, computer-synthesized pop singer who has toured with Lady Gaga and starred in video games." Kondo had a life-size doll made of his "wife." He eats meals with her, talks with her, and even takes her on romantic getaways. He knows it's odd and he realizes that most people think he will grow out of it, but he also said such a wife has advantages over a human partner: "She's always there for him, she'll never betray him, and he'll never have to see her get ill or die."

Phenomena like this aren't limited to Japan, either. The more skilled that image-makers become at creating "real" fictional images, the more audiences everywhere will perceive them as really real.

A History of Applause

Sometimes, when audiences hear very rhythmic music in a performance, they start to clap along. Maybe one or two people start it, but eventually pretty much everyone joins in. Why? When you go to see the Rockettes at Radio City Music Hall in New York and the precision core of dancers at some point begins high-kicking in a uniform kick line, they always get a huge hand. How come?

When introducing the star attraction at an event, the emcee will proclaim their name, which naturally gets cheers and a hand. But then the emcee will say something to the effect of "I can't hear you!" or "I'm sure you can do better than that!" or some other way of bumping up the response. And the audience always consents and comes back with louder cheers and a bigger hand.

If you stop and think about it, banging your hands together seems a very odd way of showing approval.

And yet, so accustomed to the thunder of applause have we become, so natural it seems to clap for friends, family, or entertainers, we barely think about it. Babies clap their hands, though not necessarily to indicate approval. It seems natural and universal, like breathing or laughing.

But it's not. Applause is a learned behavior that we absorb from our culture by osmosis. Nobody teaches it to us. It has complex rules and a long history.

The clapping of hands and stomping of feet is believed by anthropologists to have begun back in the primitive days of sitting around a campfire. The Bible makes a specific mention of it in the Old Testament's Book of Kings, believed to have been written in the sixth century BC: "And he brought forth the king's son, and put the crown upon him, and gave him the testimony; and they made him king, and anointed him; and they clapped their hands, and said, God save the king" (1 Kings 11:12).

There is no documentation of the ancient Greeks applauding during their Dionysia celebrations, though they were known to make a great deal of noise including cheering, woofing, and drumming their feet, whether approving or disapproving of a particular show, and applause definitely makes noise.

The Romans, on the other hand (so to speak), did leave documentation of clapping as a way to show approval. In fact, they gave us the root of the word "applause": *applaudere*, to strike upon or clap. Playscripts of works by the comedy writer Plautus often included a final speech that ended with "Valete et plaudite!," Latin for "Goodbye and applause." The Romans had several ways of indicating approval: snapping fingers, traditional clapping, flapping a handkerchief or the hem of their toga, and waving their thumbs in the air above their heads.

Over the intervening centuries more detailed applauding behaviors developed. It became bad form to applaud in the middle of a performance, unless the performer has said something designed to get a hand ("It's great to be back in Rome, the greatest city in the world!") or following the execution of a particularly difficult or impressive trick or solo performance.

Performers sometime do such an extraordinary job on a song or other piece of business that the audience will not stop clapping. This is known as "stopping the show." Audiences sometimes stop the show at the end of a concert to extract an encore (French for "again")—either an additional piece or a repeat of the one they've just triumphantly concluded.

During the Renaissance, the institution of the claque was developed; a group of people were paid to sit in a theatre or concert hall and applaud wildly for whomever had hired them, "sweetening" the reaction to impress critics or to stroke the performer's ego. Sometimes a rival performer hired rival claques who made a great deal of unnecessary disapproving noise and likely didn't fool anyone.

Political leaders often get this kind of applause from people who support their programs, or who depend on them for employment. An extreme example is the American State of the Union address, in which the current president sets forth his or her programs, punctuated sometimes dozens of times with applause, deserved or not. The opposing party typically withholds applause in a very deliberate and pointed way.

Among other special types of applause: Nightclubs of the mid-twentieth century would supply patrons with small wooden hammers to tap on their tables. Audiences at rock concerts indicate the intensity of their approval with lighters or, more recently, cell phones on flashlight setting. Fans at sports stadiums have various chants for various teams, and blow plastic stadium horns where they are allowed; these horns, called vuvuzelas in Latin American countries, are a buzzing staple at international soccer matches. Snapping fingers in place of applause, once the province of hep beatniks, is now having something of a renaissance among millennials.

On the other hand, the "slow clap" is the act of clapping your hands slowly, usually to show sarcasm or humorous disapproval. The "golf clap" is a variation of the slow clap, performed by lightly clapping the fingers of one hand against the palm of the other, or clapping the fingers together very softly so it looks like your hands are moving but no actual sound is produced, to show indifference or disdain, although it is sometimes used

The crowd at the 2010 FIFA World Cup, Cape Town, South Africa.
Ulrich Doering / Alamy Stock Photo

unironically to show polite or quiet appreciation. It's named for the type of applause you hear at golf tournaments where the audience does not want to disturb the golfer's concentration but wants to show appreciation. (If instead you want to amplify the sound of your applause, just cup your hands slightly and it comes out considerably louder.)

At live theatre and concerts, the audience is expected to applaud after the finale. Even though when watching television and movies it's considered ridiculous to applaud because the performers are not there to hear it, the interesting thing is that some people still do it—they can't help themselves?

Actors crave applause, and consider it part of their pay, along with their salaries, of course. In the title song of the Tony Award–winning 1970 musical *Applause*, lyricist Lee Adams called it "the sound that says 'love'," writing, "Nothing I know brings on the glow / Like sweet applause."

Like Plautus, William Shakespeare sometimes even ended his plays with a specific request for applause. At the finale of *A*

Midsummer Night's Dream, Puck breaks the fourth wall to exhort the audience to forgive the players for their silly comedy, imagine it was all just a bad dream, and "give me your hands":

> *Gentles, do not reprehend:*
> *If you pardon, we will mend:*
> *And, as I am an honest Puck,*
> *If we have unearned luck*
> *Now to 'scape the serpent's tongue,*
> *We will make amends ere long;*
> *Else the Puck a liar call;*
> *So, good night unto you all.*
> *Give me your hands, if we be friends,*
> *And Robin shall restore amends.*

When There Was No Applause

Arthur Miller's landmark American drama *Death of a Salesman* serves this purpose. It invites us to mourn for a lost way of life and feel pity for a man who clings so desperately to things that are ultimately empty, especially his obsession with being "well-liked." The drama affords us the opportunity to mourn for these lost things in ourselves. It is said that on the first performance of the play the audience did not applaud. They sat there in stunned silence, unable to put their hands together for something that understood their conflicts so completely, that articulated something too painful for them to articulate themselves, and thereby had so skillfully eviscerated their hearts.

The Real Gravy

Shakespeare is certainly not alone in his desire for a bigger hand. In a 1925 *Saturday Evening Post* essay, veteran actor Walter De Leon describes tricks the various vaudeville acts would pull to bump up the applause:

The artifices of less-talented performers for stealing bows and applause were many. Leaving one hand in sight on the proscenium arch when exiting; standing on the stage with an innocently inquiring expression as though asking the audience, "Do you really want another song from modest little me?" Tricky manipulations of the spotlight; bringing a musical instrument on for a bow to suggest that if the applause was strengthened a trifle, a beautiful saxophone solo would be the reward; changing hats or—comedy—coats for each bow, thus stringing them out till the wardrobe was exhausted—these were but the more obvious stalls to enable the perpetrators to bow numerous bends at the close of their acts. Such doings went into the manager's report, willy-nilly, as six bows. It read well, but actors and managers knew that it was not the real gravy, the expressive term used in referring to a sincere, spontaneous, long sustained volume of enthusiastically genuine applause.

Different audiences applaud differently in different places, and even on different nights of the week. This was most noticeable in the days of vaudeville, when an act had to make slight adjustments in their performance as they moved from town to town.

De Leon analyzed the phenomenon, based on close observation over many years in show business:

> There are certain well-known good audiences and certain tough ones. Detroit is soft for comedy acts, either classy or hokum, but tough for highbrow musical turns. Youngstown— try to make him laugh there, that's all! A comedian playing Baltimore will sometimes insert a suggestion of the risqué when he would not think of pulling the line in Minneapolis.
>
> But the vaudevillian knows that from every theatre he plays a report of his act goes into the main office of the circuit. This report states how his act was received by the audience, whether it was liked muchly, or not so much, and the quantity and quality of the applause it elicited. Keen and Cutting [a sample vaudeville act] may get a bad report from New Orleans. The office, however, knows that New Orleans does not usually go crazy over that type of act. So its lack of success

there is discounted. At the end of the season, if Keen and Cutting have a high percentage of good reports to their credit, it is fairly certain that the office will re-route them the following season.

There is a maxim in show business: "Leave 'em laughing." The principle varies depending on the type of act, but, according to De Leon, the principle of how to end a performance remains the same.

Finishes fall naturally into five groups or types—the dancing finish, the singing finish, the effect finish, the surprise finish, and the trick finish. There is no law against combining two or more of them into one period and for them all, the orchestra almost invariably plays fast and forte.

"Go into your dance!" is a cynical bit of advice often heard, similar in significance to the "louder—and funnier!" that was shouted at [actor] Louis Mann from one corner of the room during a speech he was making at an actors banquet. Many a performer, struggling with an unresponsive audience, consoles himself with the reflection, "I'll get 'em when I go into my dance at the finish."

He knows that an audience which is sitting on its hands, as the phrase is, will warm up and applaud dancing when nothing else will stir it from its lethargy. Why? Your guess is as good as anyone's. Human nature perhaps.

Certain it is that the rhythmic movements of more or less graceful limbs attached to a body of more or less beauty, when accompanied by more or less musical noises, has a universal appeal. Neither intelligence, education nor culture is any bar to an appreciation of dancing. Former President Woodrow Wilson, who counted vaudeville among his valuable relaxations, was known to actors playing Washington as a great audience for a song and dance act.

A dance at the finish—it need not be a routine of difficult steps, provided it is well done and well sold—is the surest method known of releasing the appreciation of the actor's worth and transforming it into tangible applause. These finishes depend somewhat upon the setting an act uses, whether it be a full-stage turn—one using all or most of the available stage space—or an act "in one." "One" is that strip of stage extending from the footlights to a drop curtain hung directly behind the tormenters. Tormentors? Oh, they are the stationary wings that jut out from both sides of the stage to frame the picture of the stage setting proper.

The full stage act has the advantage of a curtain to close in on it. The very descent of a curtain prompts applause, and if it descends on a pretty picture, an effective grouping or a stage full of lively stepping dancers, it constitutes a climax. But the act "in one" has got to get off the stage. He may dance off, or he may finish his dance near the entrance on one side, wait until the applause starts—if ever—and bow off.

More concretely, the always-effective split may be used for the finish of a dance in full stage. The shapely-limbed danseuse pirouettes dizzily, leaps blithely and carefree in the general direction of the roof and lands on the stage in a perfect split, smilingly. Curtain!

There is one measure of audience approval that rises above mere applause. For many years, standing ovations at professional theatres were considered a very special accolade reserved for only the best performances. But over the past few decades they have become more or less standard. There has been a lot of theorizing about why this is. The best explanation I've heard is that audiences pay so much for tickets that they convince themselves that the performance was worthy of a "standing O." It's a way of validating their decision to pay so much. Whether or not that is right, if every show is going to get a standing ovation, perhaps we need to find something new to indicate extraordinary approval.

In the meantime, put your hands together, folks. Applause is here to stay.

A History of Booing

If we are going to discuss applause, we need to deal with its antithesis: the rich history of audiences expressing disapproval.

Just as there are a hundred ways to cheer for something, audiences have developed many techniques to express their disapproval. There is, of course, the time-honored boo. Hisses, jeers, catcalls, and simple roars of unhappiness also have helped to do the job. Describing audiences in the days of the City Diony-sia, Scott Schwertly of Ethos3 writes, "The crowd would partici-pate to vote on which tragedy they liked best, using shouts and whistles for plays that stunk. It was considered a civic duty to participate, so we can perhaps thank our great-great-great-great grandparents when we are booed today."

Hooting was apparently preferred in the Middle Ages, but in the nineteenth century, unhappy audiences began imitating the sound of farm cattle, not with a "moo" but with a "boo," which replaced the relatively pleasant humming "em" sound with the explosive "buh" sound, leading into the low-growing "ooh." Not a squeaked "ooh," but one as coarse and basso as you can manage. All things considered, there are few activities more satisfying to an unhappy and abused audience than the opportu-nity to boo lustily, with cupped hands and deep diaphragmatic breath support.

Throwing things at a disfavored actor was also once very much in vogue. In 63 CE, the Roman emperor Vespasian was pelted with turnips during a speech. Preferred missiles in the days of vaudeville included rotten tomatoes, other juicy fruit, and rotten eggs, though it's hard to imagine that someone going to a performance for which they paid good money would just happen to be carrying spoiled produce with them. Such dem-onstrations needed to be planned. But the planning seemed worthwhile because the repulsive ordnance not only hurt, but spattered and smelled bad. The disapproval *lingered.*

In modern times, the boo has become something of a nuclear option for decorous audiences. You don't boo unless the show is really bad. Television and internet audiences don't have to worry about booing what they don't like. They have their own "nuclear option": changing the channel.

Critic John Simon published a monograph on the subject in the June 24, 1968, issue of *New York* magazine titled "The Boo Taboo." It is richly worthwhile reading in its entirety, but among his most salient points, he writes that audiences who like a performance have established a kind of "dictatorship" over those who don't:

> It is the dictatorship of the assenters over the voices of dissent, of the applauders and cheerers over the booers and hissers, and its effect on our performing arts is to encourage the status quo, however mediocre or lamentable it may be. There is an urgent or, if I may say so, crying need for the voices of protest to be given equal rights and equal time.

Simon analyzes the various reasons audiences applaud:

> There are, obviously, those who applaud because they genuinely like the play, opera, concert, recital or ballet. Their judgment may be questioned, but their motives cannot. What about the others, the fellow-grovelers? There are those who applaud because it is the thing to do. There are those who believe, without any real feelings or opinions about what they have just witnessed, that applause shows discernment, connoisseurship, culture. There are others (and I proceed in an ascending order of sinisterness) who clap to show off: as if the loudness of their palms equaled the weightiness of their opinions. This group excels not only at the manual thunderclap but also at vocal bombardment. They erupt into promiscuous roars of *Bravo*, and even *Bravi* and *Brava*, to display either their knowledge of Italian, or their deftness in distinguishing the number and sex of the performers.

Simon continues his attack on mindless approbation, saying,

> No better, however, are those who applaud because others are doing it, or because they have read favorable reviews, or because they firmly believe that whatever is put on at the Met, Philharmonic or Carnegie Hall, or at a large Broadway theatre, is guaranteed to be good. Things do not change much; back in 1885 [playwright George Bernard] Shaw observed: "In every average audience there is a certain proportion of persons who make a point of getting as much as possible for their money— who will encore, if possible, until they have had a ballad for every penny in their shilling."

At a Metropolitan Opera performance of *Carmen*, which Simon did not like, largely owing to the performance of tenor Richard Tucker as Don José, Simon cut through the undeserved applause with a series of heartfelt "Phooeys." He recalls,

> The reaction was instantaneous. From several boxes around the one I sat in came frantic retaliation—mostly of the 'Shut up!' or 'How dare you?' or 'Go home!' variety. One middle-aged woman intoned lachrymosely, 'He has given you years of beauty!' When the lights went on [Met general manager] Rudolph Bing, who was sitting a couple of boxes away, had already dispatched his Pinkerton men after me, right into the box. But I walked out, ignoring their reprimands. In the corridor, I was set upon by a mob of some twenty or thirty people berating me and following me almost to the bar with their objurgations and insults. The gist of it was that this sort of thing wasn't tolerated here, and if I was a foreign guest, I should behave or get the hell back wherever I came from.

P.S.: Simon survived, and his point is well-taken. If it is OK to cheer and applaud a good performance, it should be equally acceptable to exercise one's right to boo and hiss. Though it seems that, in this case, his fellow audience members were, in effect, booing his booing.

Opera diva Maria Callas inspired fervent fans and equally fervent antifans among her 1950s audience. Her supporters loved her power and majesty. Her detractors felt her voice was not pretty enough for the grand music she was singing. They attacked her for her looks, her temper, her style of dressing, even her weight, which seesawed throughout her long career.

After a 1959 performance of *La Traviata*, as she was being showered with congratulatory bouquets at the curtain call, one hater rose from the audience and flung a bouquet of onions and radishes at her feet. (It wasn't the first time she received such an insult; sometimes the displeased audience members threw turnips as well.) Callas picked them up with her flowers, remained composed, pressed the vegetables to her breast and thanked the person who had thrown them, provoking "thunderous applause" from the rest of the audience.

Opera singer Maria Callas accepting audience accolades, Munich Concert Hall in Germany, 1962.
Photofest

But Callas was devastated. "When I got home, I screamed and cried for hours, and experienced a panic at each curtain call for weeks after."

Booing is more accepted in the looser worlds of pop and rock performances. Among many examples, Machine Gun Kelly was notoriously booed off the stage at the Louder Than Life Festival in Louisville, Kentucky, in September 2021, after he flipped off fans unhappy with his stylistic transition from hip-hop to punk rock. MGK then got into an actual fight with some audience members offstage. The battle continued at the subsequent After-shock concert in Sacramento, California, when unhappy fans started throwing bottles at him. When he again displayed his middle finger, the boos again rang out.

It may be hard to believe that a beloved Broadway star like Gertrude Lawrence could ever be booed by anyone, especially not when playing Anna Leonowens in the original 1952 run of

The King and I, a role tailored to her talents. But Lawrence was secretly suffering from the cancer that would shortly kill her and it affected the quality of her performance so noticeably that the usually circumspect Oscar Hammerstein II drafted a letter upbraiding her for slacking off. Lawrence was roundly booed at curtain calls more than once but soldiered on like a trouper. By late summer she finally withdrew, and by September 7, she was dead.

I once had the misfortune to attend a suburban theatre performance of *A Funny Thing Happened on the Way to the Forum*, featuring a third-string TV and nightclub comedian in the leading role of Pseudolus. The curtain rose on Pseudolus introducing the setting and main characters in the song "Comedy Tonight." It quickly became apparent that this actor had not bothered to take the important step of memorizing the script. So he attempted to ad-lib his way through Stephen Sondheim's devilishly and wittily rhymed lyrics—these were necessary to get right because they not only set the farcical tone of the musical, but included important information that set the scene for everything that followed. But the actor decided that since he didn't know the actual words, he would just make something up as he went along.

Try to imagine the result. You can't. It went on for more than two hours.

The rest of the cast did their professional best to help both him and the audience navigate the twists and turns of the plot. But by the end of the performance most of the audience had taken a powder. I don't know why the others stayed, but I wanted to see just how bad it was going to get. I was richly rewarded for my patience.

For the benefit of the few of us who were left, the star delivered what he apparently thought was a self-exculpatory curtain speech that must go down in history as one of the most appalling ever addressed to an audience by an actor. First of all, he blamed the late arrival of the bus carrying the cast to the theatre owing to what he perceived as the mental deficiency of the driver who was African American, though that is not the profoundly offensive term the actor used. The actor then went on to say that he had trouble concentrating during the show because the women in wheelchairs down front kept allowing their legs to flop open, revealing their private parts.

Though there were only a few dozen people left in the audience at that point, we produced the lustiest booing I have heard in my professional career.

Bad Behavior

In that case, audience hostility was clearly warranted. Unfortunately, there is also a long history of audience members failing to follow rules, interrupting performances, stealing the spotlight, and generally misbehaving in indefensible ways.

One of the earliest recorded instances, and one that changed theatergoing permanently, involved English master actor David Garrick (1717–1779) who tried throughout his distinguished career to raise the professionalism of and respect for the live theatre. Garrick (the namesake of London's Garrick Club for theatre folk) was so popular that one commentator wrote that he "engrossed the minds of men to such a degree . . . that there existed in England a fourth estate, King, Lords, and Commons, and Drury-Lane play-house."

One tradition Garrick detested was allowing audience members to sit on the stage. That's right: it was long considered OK for aristocrats and those who paid top price for tickets, to take a chair and sit in the performing space while the actors were working. Upset by talking, eating, scratching, and, in the case of some female audience members, showing off their legs during performances, he took the extraordinary step of banning from the stage anyone not actually working on the production. He reorganized the backstage area of his theatre so audience members could no longer enter through the stage door.

Only Garrick had the popularity and power to do this, and other theatres soon followed suit.

Nonetheless, audience members today still talk, eat, sing along with, and otherwise disrupt performances. Movie theatres allow the consumption of popcorn and other quiet edibles. Sports stadia, where silence is less valued, allow all sorts of snacks. Broadway theatres allowed eating and drinking in the lobby and concession areas but banned food and drinks at the seats for many years until the development of spill-proof "sippy cups." But I personally have witnessed people at Broadway shows scarfing smelly lunches from plastic clamshell salad bar containers, with no intervention from ushers.

Sports seem to inspire their own brand of misbehavior. Apart from verbal attacks on the players, people in the stands have been known to throw bottles and other trash onto the field when they are unhappy with the players' performance. On the other hand, in 1969, a seventeen-year-old named Morganna Cottrell ran out onto Crosley Field during a Cincinnati Reds game and planted a smooch on center-fielder Pete Rose. She became a darling of the media, which dubbed her "Morgana, the Kissing Bandit." Among many other similar incidents, two women, Julia Rose and Lauren Summer, earned indefinite bans from Major League Baseball games because they flashed their breasts on live TV during Game Five of the 2019 World Series. And streakers—audience members who run naked in public during an event—have enlivened everything from ball games to the Academy Awards ceremony.

Speaking of the Oscars, there was the notorious incident of actor Will Smith rising from his seat in the audience at the 2022 Oscars and slapping comedian Chris Rock when he took offense at a joke Rock made about Smith's wife, Jada Pinkett Smith. Though the action brought about swift condemnation and censure of Smith, it also left comedians in general afraid that a precedent had been established—that it was now OK for audiences to attack if they felt personally insulted in some way. Sheryl Underwood, cohost of TV's *The Talk*, said on her show, "I'm going to say this as a comic, I am afraid now to get on a stage, because in my third show, when everyone's been drinking, if you don't like my joke, do you now believe that you can get up and slap me?"

Cell phones have inspired their own whole category of audience misbehavior. Though using phones is banned in most performing venues, some owners insist on taking calls, texting, photographing, and even videoing during live performances.

During a 2015 production of *Hamlet* in which he was playing the title character, actor Benedict Cumberbatch had to beg fans to stop recording his performance. "It's mortifying," he said, saying there is "nothing less supportive or enjoyable."

The recent Broadway revival of the play *Take Me Out* was the scene of some truly egregious audience behavior. The story of a star baseball player who comes out as gay, the play includes a scene in a shower in which many of the actors, notably leading man Jesse Williams, appear fully nude. The production went to extraordinary lengths to keep ticket holders from using their cell phones to take photos and post them on the internet. As audience members entered the theatre, they were required to hand over their phones to be locked inside of small pouches made by the Yondr company. The pouches were unlocked and phones returned at the end of the performance. However, the theatre relied on the honor system in asking audience members to hand over their phones—and several apparently lacked honor. Shortly after the opening of the show, photos of Mr. Williams in the buff began popping up on the web.

Broadway diva Patti LuPone has become famous for stopping performances to upbraid audience members for bad behavior. In one noteworthy incident during the run of *Gypsy*, she stepped out of character during the volcanic final number, "Rose's Turn," to tear someone a new orifice for recording her on a cell phone. And LuPone wasn't done. At a subsequent performance of her *Shows for Days* at New York's Lincoln Center, she left the stage and snatched a cell phone out of the hands of an audience member who was texting during her performance.

But LuPone got some blowback in May 2022 when she appeared at the Schoenfeld Theatre as part of a Q&A sponsored by the American Theatre Wing after a performance of her hit revival of *Company*. Noticing that one woman in the audience was not wearing an anti-COVID-19 mask, as was required by the theatre, Lupone stopped the forum and demanded the woman cover her nose with her mask, saying, "That is the rule. If you don't follow the rule, get the [expletive] out. I'm serious. . . . Who do you think you are if you do not respect the people sitting around you?"

The offender clapped back, shouting, "I pay your salary."

Not all audience misbehavior is as dramatic as what I've described here. Overall, audiences sit in relative silence, but when attention wavers, you start to hear coughs. People shift in their seats or stretch. Or sneak peeks at their watches or even, rudely, their phones.

Some audiences talk back during stage plays—and sometimes during movies as well. They shout encouragement or advice or warnings: "Look out!" They have become so immersed in the experience that they feel part of it, and they want both the actor and the character to know it.

If a familiar song comes up, some audiences sit in respectful silence, or tap their feet, or mouth the words, or hum, or even sing along. Sometimes audiences are moved to rise from their seats and dance. This behavior is greatly encouraged at pop concerts, strongly discouraged at plays, and absolutely forbidden at classical concerts and operas.

What do all these responses have in common? Affirmation. Different social languages of affirmation for that particular audience experience. In some cases, wild cheering is affirmation; in others, respectful silence is. It's the audience's way of collaborating with the performers and with each other.

Specialization of the Audience

There have always been multiple audiences. Shakespeare's Globe, where so many of his classic dramas premiered, was located in the same neighborhood as bear-baiting pits, and sometimes drew the same avid watchers. But with the proliferation of technology in the late nineteenth and early twentieth centuries, audiences began to diversify and splinter as never before. Performers evolved new ways of entertaining the crowd, and the crowd developed new tastes in entertainment. And with that evolution in taste has come an evolution and specialization of audience behavior.

Talking during most live performances is considered offensive and distracting. After all, people don't pay for tickets to

A rapper and fans, Huntsville, Alabama.
Jeffrey Isaac Greenberg 10+ / Alamy Stock Photo

listen to you yakking. They want to hear what's being performed on the stage. Perhaps people do it because they are indeed rude jerks. But perhaps they also do it because they're used to watching television at home where conversation is considered acceptable during a viewing. With today's DVR technology, if you miss something said in a show, you can always just rewind and watch it again. People have grown so used to it, their behavior spills over into live performances.

But even in live performances there are different expectations depending on the medium. At an opera or a symphony, you are expected to be absolutely silent and sit still. However, at a rock or rap concert you are expected to cheer and scream and sing along and even dance in the aisles.

It's the same with sports. If you're watching golf you are expected to keep mum. Even the commentators whisper. But at soccer or baseball or football games, you're encouraged to cheer and stamp your feet and chant and do the wave. Golfers can't concentrate unless it's completely silent; ballplayers can't concentrate and do their best unless they hear the crowd roaring their support. Bowlers become furious if they hear anything but the sound of the neighbor's ball rolling down the lane. But football players seem like they can't do their best unless they have a raucous corps of cheerleaders chanting for their success.

For many years, fans of the Atlanta Braves baseball team did something called the "tomahawk chop" to encourage heightened efforts on the field. That's regarded as racially insensitive today, though it's still often done. But nothing has been deemed offensive (yet) about fans of the Green Bay Packers wearing hats that look like giant wedges of cheese on their heads. All baseball games everywhere stop for a mini-intermission called a seventh-inning stretch—not halfway through the typical nine innings, but seven-ninths of the way through the game. Audiences aren't told to perform these rituals; they just do them because it's an expected part of being a fan.

A baseball crowd leaping for a fly ball in a stadium.
SuperStock / Alamy Stock Photo

If you throw objects onto the baseball field or the football field, you can be hustled out of the stadium or even arrested. But if you're a skater, you look forward to the audience throwing stuffed toy animals onto the ice. And if you're an opera diva or ballet dancer, you feel let down if people don't throw bouquets onto your stage. If you attend the annual Comic Con, where those who love comic books, cartoons, and animated video games get to meet the people who make them, it's good manners to come dressed as your favorite character. And the more elaborate and handmade the better. Don't look for that at your typical dentist convention.

Fans of hockey, basketball, and other sports like to attend games wearing the jersey of their favorite player. But big tennis matches take it a step further. No one would be caught dead wearing a jersey with their favorite competitor's name on it . . . but fans do come fully dressed in tennis whites, as if they are going to be called down to the field at any minute to jump in for a match or two.

At the annual Boston Science Fiction Marathon, the audience will sometimes burst into chants of "Wheat Chex!" and "Rice Chex!" in tribute to a funny clip from a TV show screened decades earlier.

This specialized behavior comes to a peak among the fans of *The Rocky Horror Picture Show*. Members of the show's cult—not too strong a word in this case—don't just come dressed as the characters in the movie; they recite a fan-crowdsourced meta-text, inserting cheeky remarks during slight pauses in the dialogue.

These things are not required of the audience; they just happen spontaneously by those "in the know."

These specialties reflect another aspect of audience participation: fandom and the stimulation of group identity. When you meet someone new and start to get to know them, it's always a pleasure to discover something you have in common. You both love Moby Grape? Amazing! You both collect Disney female villain figurines? Sweet! You both mourn the cancellation of *Police Squad!*? Righteous! You are both devoted followers of Delta State baseball and their mascot, the Fighting Okra? Who'd a thunk?

The bigger and more fervent the fandom, the more it tends to splinter into smaller and smaller sub-fandoms. For example, science fiction movie fans are divided into adherents of *Star Wars* and *Star Trek*. Even among the Trekkers, there are those who like only the original TV series, and others who prefer *Star Trek: The Next Generation*, and the spinoffs of spinoffs. And don't start talking to *Star Wars* fans about the original trilogy versus the prequel and sequel trilogies. Then there is yet a third group of sci-fi fans who turn up their noses at both those fan groups. And then there are the audiences for *The Twilight Zone* versus *The Outer Limits* versus *Black Mirror*.

And that's just science fiction. Many fans of folk singer (and Nobel Prize winner) Bob Dylan revere his early acoustic work and despise his later electronic recordings—and vice versa. There seems to be no room for compromise. Audiences may not know much about how these artworks are made, but they know what they like.

Fandom has another side. Sometimes fans turn on their favorites and spit on them with the same intensity they once lavished in adoration. Sometimes, as with Bill Cosby or Fatty Arbuckle, it's for crimes like sexual assault or other social transgressions. Reasons for fan rejection are as varied as voicing unpopular political opinions, making racist or homophobic statements, cheating, revelations of off-camera emotional, physical, or sexual abuse, et cetera.

These transgressions, real or perceived, have led to the "canceling" of dozens if not hundreds of former fan favorites as diverse as Ellen DeGeneres, Woody Allen, the Dixie Chicks, J. K. Rowling, the 1919 Chicago White Sox, DaBaby, Dave Chappelle, Pete Rose, Mel Gibson, Louis C.K., Martha Stewart, Sinéad O'Connor, Laura Ingalls Wilder—even good ol' Dr. Seuss.

Some of these outcasts managed to work their way back into fans' good graces, like Robert Downey Jr., who was popular in his youth, then fell into disfavor owing to legal problems and drug abuse. But he managed to enjoy a fan resurgence with the *Iron Man* films. Such second chances are rare and come about only because the celebrity shows genuine regret and repentance, stays clean, works to undo the damage they did, demonstrates humility, works hard, serves jail time, or convinces both the audience and power brokers in their industry that they have turned over a new leaf.

Rarer still are performers like Betty White and the Rolling Stones, who avoided cancellation altogether and stayed in audience favor for virtually their entire lives. What's their secret? Brains, talent, strong family and industry support—and, in some cases, a truckload of luck.

Sometimes audiences also turn on their former favorites because their time has passed, or because the audience perceives that they have said all they have to say. It's a rare artist who accepts that their fifteen minutes of fame are over and surrenders the spotlight willingly and gracefully.

Playwright Tennessee Williams gave the world masterpieces like *The Glass Menagerie, A Streetcar Named Desire, Cat on a Hot Tin Roof* and others from the mid-1940s to the early 1960s. But after that, he seemed to be repeating himself, and audiences turned away from plays like *The Red Devil Battery Sign* and *The Seven Descents of Myrtle*. Williams kept writing until his death, haunted by the sense that critics and the audience had deserted him. For their part, however, audiences felt that he had deserted them as well. Similar fates befell playwrights as disparate as Arthur Miller and Neil Simon. They kept writing after their formerly adulatory audiences had moved on. Pop musicians know this phenomenon all too well. First, they're on top of the world, then their audiences age out or abandon them. Then, if they're lucky, they come back as "Oldies" bands.

On the other hand, the phenomenon of fickle audiences also accounts for so-called one-hit wonders—bands, filmmakers, writers, and actors who enjoy a single success but never grab the gold ring again. These include the Irish band Dexy's Midnight Runners with their hit, "Come on Eileen," Bobby "Boris" Pickett and the Crypt-Kickers with their Halloween novelty song "Monster Mash," and dozens if not hundreds more.

Irritainment

Even in traditional online reviews from experts, some readers skim or completely skip the "official" piece to get down to the Comments sections to follow the often-contentious debate among fellow members of the audience. Such debates are often a mixed blessing, to say the least, especially when they devolve into name-calling or when politics is dragged in. Flame wars and trolling have become perverse entertainment forms of their own—call it "irritainment."

One person may express a controversial opinion. Rather than address the point of the person's opinion or simply express a contrary opinion, another poster will counter that the first opinion is "wrong." Without a *Robert's Rules of Order* to organize debate, the opinions quickly devolve into acrimony and ad hominem name-calling. Other commenters pile on, agreeing or disagreeing. The tongue-in-cheek "Godwin's Law" states that "as an online discussion grows longer (regardless of topic or scope), the probability of a comparison involving Nazis or Adolf Hitler approaches 1." In recent years, such debates also often devolve into left–right donnybrooks.

Those who are swinging rhetorical fists are usually outnumbered by lurkers, another name for the audiences who follow these battles without taking part. Whatever side they're on, they may watch from the sidelines for several reasons: 1) They learn from these contretemps so they can understand both sides of the issue. 2) They already have chosen a side and want to pick up some talking points for when they engage in these arguments themselves. 3) They enjoy the blood sport the same way they might enjoy a boxing match or rubbernecking at a car accident. Sometimes these lurkers will post a meme of a person eating popcorn to indicate that they are watching the proceedings like a movie, and possibly to shame the participants into lowering the temperature. This is the essence of irritainment.

A notable outgrowth of irritainment is a practice known as "ragefarming," in which people post information in discussion

forums that is *deliberately wrong*, often to mislead readers, especially on political subjects, but also sometimes simply to trigger
and enrage them into giving entertainingly furious rebuttals.
Just for evil fun.

Other online audiences take their thirst for woe a step further. "Doomscrolling" is the practice of spending hours online
looking for stories about things going wrong, people behaving
badly, and just all-around bad news in a quest to confirm the
belief that the world is indeed going to hell in a handbasket, or
just to see someone having a worse day than you are having so
you don't feel so bad about your own sorry life. Company, in
this case, loves misery.

There have been instances where the audience has risen up
and destroyed things they didn't like, or given life to things they
did, such as uncanceling canceled TV shows including *Brooklyn
Nine-Nine* and *Family Guy*. *Firefly* didn't get a new series but
did get a big-screen movie. CBS brought back the series *Jericho*,
which featured a character who famously used the word "nuts"
in the season-one finale, after the fans in the audience sent forty
thousand pounds of nuts to network executives. *Mystery Science
Theatre 3000* fans organized a GoFundMe campaign to bring the
series back for one reunion episode. Fans wound up donating
enough money to produce a full thirteen-episode season.

The 2006 movie *Snakes on a Plane* offers an extreme example.
It was originally announced as a tongue-in-cheek action film
starring Samuel L. Jackson, an actor known for using profanity with special relish in several of his film roles. In the case of
Snakes, he played a federal agent who finds himself aboard an
airplane that turns out to be slithering with venomous snakes as
part of a complex (and ridiculous) mob scheme to whack a stool
pigeon being escorted by Jackson.

When word got out to the public that Jackson was going to
star in a film of that title, his fans were absolutely delighted.
Knowing nothing more than the star and the title, a pair of fans
made a mock trailer for the film. Their parody included Jackson delivering the line "I have had it with these motherfucking
snakes on this motherfucking plane!"

Online fans were thrown into such a frenzy over this cheesy line that the studio, New Line Cinema, actually had the director go back into production and shoot a scene where the real Samuel L. Jackson actually delivered the line, which then became part of the final film as released. P.S.: The movie, with reshoots, cost $30 million but earned $60 million.

This ability to circumvent marketing and influence the creative outcome of a project amounts to a revolution in the power of audiences.

Fickle Audiences

Audiences can also be fickle. Sometimes they just can't get enough of a particular show or song or star—but then suddenly they *do* get enough, and the popularity crashes. The audience moves on.

Cats was one of the most popular Broadway musicals of the late twentieth century. The Andrew Lloyd Webber musical set to poems by T. S. Eliot ran 8,949 performances in London and 7,485 performances on Broadway, becoming for a time, Broadway's longest-running production. The show, which featured dancers costumed as cats, tells the story of a group of special "Jellicle" cats who are preparing for a supernatural event. The show was so popular and seemingly immortal that its advertising slogan was "Now and Forever."

But in 2019, after numerous attempts to adapt the show for film and video, Universal released a feature film version, directed by Tom Hooper, which used advanced CGI to create the cat "costumes." Not only was the film a massive failure among both critics and audiences—losing between $71 million and $114 million and registering just 19 percent on Rotten Tomatoes's Tomatometer—audiences seemed put off, if not thoroughly creeped out, by the sight of the cat-costumed actors. Many nonfans speaking on social media claimed they also *never* liked the stage show either. Which was odd, considering that so many people in so many countries had paid so much for so long to see it, and seemed to love it.

Hummels, little sculptures of cherubic German children doing cute things, were internationally popular in the years after World War II, when returning soldiers brought the figures home with them. They were little symbols of prewar innocence. Originally created by German nun Sister Maria Innocentia Hummel in the 1930s as illustrations on postcards, they were turned into porcelain figures and became massively collectible on several continents. Sales reached their peak in the 1970s, but the figurines gradually declined in popularity as the original fandom aged. Some of the figurines are still treasured by those who have an emotional attachment to them, but their resale value is now negligible in all but a few cases. The company that manufactured them declared bankruptcy in 2017.

If it's a celebrity, a drop in popularity can be caused by committing a crime or saying something controversial and offensive. Sometimes it's just because the performer loses their looks, or has a string of failures, or simply burns out and leaves the business, only to be forgotten by their former fans. Ironically, many plays and films have been fashioned out of this phenomenon, most memorably the ironically titled *A Star Is Born*.

It's not just an American or a Western phenomenon. Parveen Babi (1954–2005) quickly rose to become one of the superstars of India's Bollywood, appearing in more than a dozen films in varying genres, including *Deewar* (1975) and *The Burning Train* (1980). In 1976, she appeared on the cover of *Time* magazine and became one of the highest-paid performers in her business. But she developed physical and mental health problems, and the work dried up. She died broke and alone in her home; the death undiscovered for two days because no one came to visit her in that time.

What causes people to turn their backs? There are so many options for audiences in all the arts, and only so many hours in the day to take them in. No one can keep track of everything. But for performers, feeling the love of an audience is a powerful thing. The adulation of a truly mass audience is an agonizing thing to give up, or to lose, or to have taken away.

Extreme Audiencing

One aspect of audiencing that has stayed more or less consistent throughout human history everywhere in the world is the length of time that people want to watch a show. One to three hours is pretty standard. The ancient Greeks wrote plays that lasted about that long, so did the Japanese in the Middle Ages, so did Shakespeare, and so did those who wrote operas, minstrel shows, movies, comedy shows, rock concerts, and just about every other form. There are plenty of outliers, and attention spans seem to be getting shorter. Look at the popularity of Tik-Tok videos that last a minute or less.

But in recent years, audiences have also gone in the opposite direction, engaging in mega watchathon binges lasting all evening, all day, all night, or all weekend. Let's call this overall phenomenon Extreme Audiencing, after the concurrent trend of extreme sports, meaning demanding or even dangerous stunts that test the limits of human endurance. Extreme Audiencing is like that too.

The 1969 Woodstock rock festival, billed as "An Aquarian Exposition: 3 Days of Peace & Music" was a pioneer in the music world. Some four hundred thousand audience members overran a farm in Bethel, New York, owned by Max Yasgur, and enjoyed the privilege of watching thirty-two musical acts, including several current and future superstars, in what turned out to be a mini-monsoon. Those who skipped Woodstock or were unable to get there envied the muddy but triumphant survivors. Woodstock became a badge of honor, of hard-coredness.

Altamont, Coachella, Bonaroo, High Sierra, Lollapalooza, and Burning Man are among other multiday concerts/art events that have followed in its slightly stoned footsteps.

In the wake of Woodstock and decades of demographic and technological changes, there is a segment of the audience that just likes to consume mass quantities of various entertainments, like binge-watching *Downton Abbey, Game of Thrones, Girlfriends, Girls, The Marvelous Mrs. Maisel, The Chi, The Mandalorian, East Los High, The Office, Jeopardy!,* or dozens of other shows, including thousands of hours of classic sports games. Instead of

Woodstock Music Festival, 1969.
Collection Christophel / Alamy Stock Photo

waiting for the next weekly episode of a popular series, audiences can now watch a whole season in a weekend. They may have to wait a year for the next season, but then gobble down that whole season in a single weekend again.

If you had told the same audience members that they were going to have to sit and watch a fourteen-hour movie, they would probably say that's ridiculous. But if you tell them there's fourteen one-hour episodes, they happily sit and spend a day cocooned, eyeballing the whole damn series from beginning to end.

Here's a classic example of extreme audiencing: the 24-hour Boston Science Fiction Marathon, which was founded in 1976 by MIT film students, survived blizzards, cinema fires, the Great Recession, and COVID-19 to become the longest-running such gathering in the United States. Every year on Presidents' Day weekend, sci-fi fans gather to watch a collection of twelve to fourteen movies: some revered classics, some cheesy classics, some hi-tech new releases, some "big-bug" movies of the 1950s, some silent-era films, some international films, et cetera. The films are punctuated by classic cartoons, trailers, commercials, trivia contests, filmmaker interviews, and some clips from old and new TV shows. For several years, the organizers showed episodes of old-time *Buck Rogers* and *Flash Gordon* serials between each film, complete with exciting cliff-hangers.

But none of these things can match the biggest wonder of the event: the audience. As fans of classic films, they try to be a classic audience. When an obvious villain enters the screen, an angry hiss rises from the audience. When the good guy/gal enters the screen obviously headed for trouble, the audience calls out warnings to them. When there is a countdown, the audience helps by intoning 5-4-3-2-1 in unison. When a battle erupts, audience members whip out noisemaking toy ray guns and join the fray. They don't like being called nerds. The truth is, they are nerds. But these nerds consider themselves *high-class* nerds. That's the truth too.

Some are *Star Trek* fans, some are *Stargate SG-1* fans, some are *Babylon 5* fans. But some are not interested in any of those TV series. They are interested only in sci-fi movies. A place to celebrate *Mystery Science Theatre 3000, Cinematic Titanic,* and the oeuvres of Georges Méliès, Ray Harryhausen, and Larry Blamire.

The marathon runs (or rather, sits) over the Presidents' Day weekend from noon Sunday to noon Monday. They show more family-friendly films during daylight hours because that's when old-time marathoners bring their spouses and kids, and then leave to come back in the morning. The scarier or R-rated films are shown during the late hours. The sleepiest hours are three to six a.m., when some of the livelier films are shown to help people stay awake. But they pause around six a.m. to open the doors to let the morning sun flood in, fooling the audience's circadian rhythm into thinking they just woke up and have energy for the last six hours of movies.

Longtime producer Garen Daly compares the Marathon to the Lerner and Loewe musical *Brigadoon*, in that a community comes together one day a year, sharing experiences and friendships that developed over decades in some cases. But when the twenty-four hours are over, the satisfied sci-fiers pack their ray guns and disappear into the highland mists of New England, not to reappear again until another year into . . . *the future.*

VIOLENCE

Most people think of an audience as a big, passive blob—just a bovine herd being fed sounds and images, which they absorb and process . . . and then move on. That's false, of course. As we've seen in previous chapters, engaged audience members are processing what they see, leading to stimulation of their emotions, their minds, and often their bodies.

What's the result? Audiences are often moved to action, sometimes before they even go home. News, and even history, has been made in the audience.

Like a Family Sitting Around a Parlor Fire

Perhaps the most dramatic example occurred on April 14, 1865, inside Ford's Theatre in Washington, DC. The assassination of President Abraham Lincoln by actor John Wilkes Booth was witnessed by the actors, several of the stage workers, the orchestra, and the more than one thousand audience members gathered to see the comedy hit *Our American Cousin*.

Confederate General Robert E. Lee had surrendered to Union General Ulysses S. Grant just five days earlier. Who were the people in that audience? What were they thinking when they sat down for a light-hearted Friday evening, just days after the effective end of the American Civil War?

Not everyone was celebrating. Many of the same attitudes in national politics we see today were very much in operation during that period. The slaveholding South had lost the war, and were wildly angry that they were losing their slaves, whom they regarded as their inferiors and their property. White Southerners' whole lifestyle, economy, and self-image were built around this, and they knew whom to blame. Washington, DC, where Ford's Theatre was located, shared a border with Virginia, still a part of the Confederacy. The US capital was full of Southern sympathizers, and one of them was Booth.

Booth came from a theatrical family. Broadway's Booth Theatre is named for his brother, widely regarded as a superior talent. But John Wilkes had the good looks and dashing manner of a later Errol Flynn. He harbored a murderous hatred of Lincoln, whom he blamed for destroying the very idea of America.

The pressures of war and a tragedy-filled personal life had been crushing to Lincoln. But this lifelong theatergoer and inveterate quoter of both Shakespeare and variety shows knew a great way to relax. Go to the theatre to see a comedy! Five days after Appomattox, he did just that, accompanied by the First Lady, Mary Todd Lincoln.

Booth had played at nearly every theatre in Washington and was easily admitted backstage anywhere he went. He knew Lincoln loved theatre, and he hatched a plan to kill the president. Fate presented his chance quickly.

Booth was welcomed to Ford's that night by old backstage friends. He slipped into the passageway leading to the boxes and waited somewhat impatiently until the middle of act 3, when he knew a joke from the old familiar comedy always got a big laugh. He planned to use that laugh to mask the sound of a pistol shot.

What did the sold-out audience at Ford's Theatre see that night? What was it like to be sitting there? Did any audience members try to stop him? In his masterful account, "Backstage at the Lincoln Assassination," Thomas A. Bogar recorded the following:

Curtain time was scheduled for 7:45. A few minutes before 7:30 [manager John B.] Wright ordered the act curtain lowered into place and okayed the opening of the house. . . . Outside, an air of expectation was palpable. The temperature had dropped into the low 50s, an intermittent wind was gusting up 10th Street, and a light drizzle had begun as the last twilight faded. Dark clouds obscured the moon, which had been full only four nights before. Patrons hustling up from Pennsylvania Ave were guided to the theatre by torches of burning tar wedged into barrels and barkers crying, "This way to Ford's!"

Clusters of men stood in the midst around bonfires that exuded thick smoke pungent with pinesap. Occasional cries of "Three cheers for the president!" "Hurrah for old Abe!" wafted through the open door as the festive crowd poured in . . . Word of mouth and effective advertising had negated the traditional theatrical curse of "Black Friday." The dominant color of apparel seemed to be Union blue, with more than a few gold stripes. Excited conversations bubbled up as everyone glanced toward the decorated box at house-right, as yet unoccupied, as they scurried to find whichever seats might afford the best view of it. Seven forty-five, the theatre's normal curtain time, came and went with no presidential party. . . . By 8, the situation had not changed. Backstage, despite reassurances . . . actors in the wings fretted. Those already called to their "places" for act one paced. Though through the heavy act curtain, over the music, they could hear the excited murmur of the crowd. Finally, at 8:15, with still no sign of the evening's most important guests (who were only now leaving the executive mansion), Wright decided that the time was at hand. Announcing, "Clear the stage, ladies and gentlemen," he heard the actors close by in the near darkness offer each other words of encouragement as they completed last minute costume checks and [stage workers] handed them properties. Then, Wright said to dim the house lights to half and bring up the stage lights to full. He rang his little bell to signal to [workers] on the fly rail to raise the opening curtain.

Our American Cousin was underway. About eleven minutes into the performance, a group of figures could be heard entering the back of the house. Everyone knew who had arrived. [Star] Laura Keene, delivered her line, "Well, anybody could see that," and ad-libbed a gesture to the new audience arrivals.

As they shook out the evening's mist from their bonnets and overcoats, little Joseph Hazleton [a boy responsible for the programs] nervously handed them one-sheet playbills (miniatures of the larger versions posted throughout the city).

As the Lincoln party climbed the stairs to get to the . . . box seats, the conductor launched his orchestra into "Hail to the Chief" and the house lights were pushed back up to full.

The audience rose as one, applauding, cheering, waving hats and handkerchiefs as the on-stage actors stood respectfully silent. Many of the others, along with some of the stagehands, crowded around [the stage manager's] desk in the downstage right wings to watch from across the stage. The president paused behind the dress circle patrons, leaning against one of the white columns, his right hand over his heart, and acknowledged the hearty reception by bowing slightly, twice. His face remained a mask of ineffable weariness and sadness, his body stooped from the burden of the past four years.

Catching his eye, Keene curtsied, as the musicians swung into "The Conquering Hero Comes." Mrs. Lincoln curtsied repeatedly in return, smiling uncharacteristically broadly. Even after the presidential party had entered its specially decorated box, the applause continued. . . . After bowing solemnly once more from the front of his box and settling into his chair, the president gestured to [the actors] to continue.

Soon after, the script contained a fairly lame joke about a dog's tail. Lincoln laughed out loud. Though Lincoln often joked in private, most of those in the audience who had any mental image of him knew him only from his grave speeches and his serious photographs. If you look at a collection of presidential portraits, both painting and (later) photographs, it's interesting to note that the pictures never show a smiling president until after World War II. For an audience of the Civil War period, hearing the president—especially *this* president—laugh out loud was a startling and exhilarating experience.

This was the kind of folksy humor that Lincoln loved. Unlike Mary's polite hand-clapping, the president's appreciation of a joke was evident in a burst of hearty laughter. From that point on, every humorous line in the play seemed to "hit" and every

piece of comic business raised the level of warm shared mer-
riment. The cast had the audience in the palm of its hand. . . .
Every now and then an easily identifiable guffaw would erupt
from the presidential box, and the actors thrilled to see, out of
the corner of their eye, that careworn, craggy face wreathed in
a smile.

Lincoln himself must have found the experience of laughing to
be cathartic and sobering. There had been nothing to laugh at for
such a long time.

Yet for other long stretches of time Lincoln seemed lost in a
distant world. "He sat," recalled May Hart, "with his head on
his hand gazing down at the stage, his eyes wide open, but not
seeing. . . . If ever a man's face carried the expression of sadness, his did that night."

As the evening went on the April night grew chilly, which
could be felt inside Ford's. Audience member Amy Wright

noticed from her seat in the fourth row on the opposite side of
the parquet that the president had put his overcoat back on,
and his wife still wore her bonnet. The stage manager's wife
found it comforting that Lincoln spent the [intermission] leaning forward in his box, his elbows on its ledge and his head
in his hands, watching the audience, as if "to ascertain how
many persons there he recognized. He barely moved through
the entire intermission." A young woman near her had similar feelings as she regarded "Father Abraham . . . there like a
father watching what interests his children, for their pleasure
rather than his own." It seemed so sociable, "like one family
sitting around their parlor fire."

James Suydam Knox, also a member of the audience that
night, wrote his own account (spelling and punctuation intact):

My room mate and I were seated on the second row of orchestra seats, just beneath the president's box. The President
entered the theatre at 8 ½ o'ck amid deafening cheers and the
rising of all. Everything was cheerful, and never was our mag-
istrate more enthusiastically welcomed, or more happy. Many

THE ASSASSINATION OF PRESIDENT LINCOLN.

Artist's rendering of John Wilkes Booth on the stage of Ford's Theatre waving a dagger before the horrified audience as Mary Todd Lincoln (in pink dress at top) reaches for her husband, President Abraham Lincoln, moments after Booth shot him.
North Wind Picture Archives / Alamy Stock Photo

pleasant allusions were made to him in the play to which the audience gave deafening responses, while Mr. Lincoln laughed heartily and bowed frequently to the gratified people.

Just after the 3d Act, and before the scenes were shifted, a muffled pistol shot was heard, and a man sprang wildly from the national box, partially tearing down the flag, then shouting "sic semper tyrannis," "The South is avenged!" with brandished dagger rushed across the stage and disappeared.

The whole theatre was paralyzed but two men sprang for the stage, a Mr. Stewart & myself. Both of us were familiar with the play, and suspected the fearful tragedy. We rushed after the murderer and Mr. Stewart being familiar with the passages, reached the rear door, in time to see him spring on his horse and ride off. I became lost amid the scenery and was obliged to return. My roommate had followed me and secured the murderer's hat. The shrill cry of murder from Mrs. Lincoln first aroused the horrified audience, and in an instant the uproar was terrible. The silence of death was broken by shouts of "kill him," "hang him" and strong men wept, and cursed, and tore the seats in the impotence of their anger, while Mrs. Lincoln, on her knees uttered shriek after shriek at the feet of the dying President. Finally the theatre was clear and the President removed. Still greater was the excitement in the city . . . mounted patrols dashed every where, bells tolled the alarm, and excited crowds rushed about the avenues.

In his desire to cross the fourth wall and make himself a part of one of the greatest audience dramas of all time, Knox's observation that his friend had "secured the murderer's hat" is funny . . . and a little bit heartbreaking.

The brief, happy moments of relief and entertainment suddenly ended for the chief executive. If there is any comfort, it's good to know that Lincoln, as an audience member, died laughing.

Theatres of War

Lincoln's murder was not the first and sadly not the last time a theatre saw real-life violence. Areas of the world where war is taking place are called "theatres of war," and the actual theatres within them have never been spared the misery of indiscriminate warfare. But several times in recent years, theatres full of people have been attacked directly, usually when they had taken refuge inside their walls. There have also been times when the audience was the target and attacked during a performance. It's a sad fact about theatres and other venues, that they hem in large numbers of people in a way that leaves them vulnerable to violence—that the flip side of the communion and proximity that audiencing offers is that it makes an attractive target in certain rare but horrific instances.

During the years that France controlled the northern African nations of Algeria and Tunisia as part of its overseas empire, many of the primarily Muslim residents of those lands settled in France proper, seeking a better life. Instead, they found they had become a poverty-stricken underclass living in a secular nation that did not always follow or welcome the strictures of their faith. Tensions were only exacerbated by more recent developments, such as France's involvement in the wars in Syria and Iraq, and satirical cartoons that depicted the prophet Muhammad in the magazine *Charlie Hebdo*, which prompted a terrorist attack on the magazine offices.

Ten months after the *Charlie Hebdo* attack, on November 13, 2015, the Islamic State of Iraq and the Levant (ISIS) launched coordinated suicide bomber attacks in the Paris area, first at a soccer match, then in the cafés, and finally at the Bataclan, a concert hall where some fifteen hundred fans were watching a performance by the rock group Eagles of Death Metal. The jihadists opened fire on the crowd, starting with those gathered around the bar, killing ninety audience members, then took the survivors hostage. Police tried to rush the theatre, only to have one of the jihadists blow himself up with an explosive vest.

The attack was followed by a standoff with authorities that ended when the attackers said they wanted to massacre the hostages in front of the media. Police rushed the remaining jihadists, shooting one and causing another to detonate his vest, killing himself.

It was the worst such atrocity in France since World War II.

Russia's efforts to suppress separatists in the southern region of Chechnya led to a shooting war in 1999 and 2000, followed by an insurgency that lasted much of the next decade. On October 23, 2002, during a sold-out performance of the musical *Nord Ost* at the Moscow Ball-Bearing Plant's Palace of Culture, a group of fifty Chechen terrorists sought to bring the war home to the Russian capital. The terrorists burst into the backstage area, then appeared on stage, firing a machine gun and threatening to blow up the theatre if the Russian leadership didn't immediately withdraw the military from their country.

Approximately eight hundred *Nord Ost* audience members were held hostage for fifty-seven hours. Two were shot to death as the Chechens became impatient for the government to meet their demands. Ultimately, the Russian authorities pumped a narcotic gas into the theatre, rendering everyone inside unconscious. Though the attack was over, an overdose of the gas itself was responsible for killing nearly all the attackers, plus 120 of the very audience members they were trying to save.

But the Russians created an even greater theatre terror of their own during their 2022 war against Ukraine. On March 16, 2022, a series of airstrikes demolished the Donetsk Academic Regional Drama Theatre in the city of Mariupol. The attack was only a small part of the devastation much of that city and country suffered in the war. But the theatre attack stirred special international outrage because it resulted in the deaths of an estimated three hundred civilians, many of them children, who had taken shelter within its walls from the Russian bombing campaign. The attack came despite the fact that the Russian word for *children* was written outside the building in large Cyrillic script: Дети.

The total of the dead was not compiled for several days because it took that long for all the survivors and the dead to be pulled from under the collapsed theatre roof and walls as the bombings continued. About a thousand people survived, though many were wounded.

"Our hearts are broken by what Russia is doing to our people, to our Mariupol," Ukrainian President Volodymyr Zelensky said.

American theatres have not been spared either. As part of the recent plague of random mass shootings, mainly at schools and shopping centers, the Century 16 cinema in Aurora, Colorado, was targeted on July 20, 2012, during a midnight screening of the Batman franchise film *The Dark Knight Rises*. Dressed in combat gear, a disturbed young man named James Holmes entered the theatre, set off tear gas grenades, and opened fire on the audience, killing twelve. Some seventy others were injured by the gunfire and in the panic that followed. That number sounds horrifically high, but it should be remembered that as this book went to press, Aurora was only the *nineteenth* deadliest such mass shooting in modern US history.

Redouble the Uproar

There is a still darker side to audiences too. The power of charismatic performers to move an audience to laughter or tears is matched by their power to awaken evil in their hearts and move them to violence. We're seen how effectively modern social media are able to tap this well of darkness. But audiences have a long history of being transformed.

Unruly audiences have been a problem since the days of the classical Greeks. In his *Republic*, the philosopher Plato complained, "When . . . many of them sit together in assemblies, courts, theatres, army camps, or in any other gathering of a mass of people in public and, with a loud uproar, object excessively to some of the things that are said or done, then approve excessively of others, shouting and clapping; and when, in addition to these people themselves, the rocks and the surrounding space itself echo and redouble the uproar of their praise or blame."

The Astor Place Riot

It's hard to imagine dignified modern audiences getting riled up to a murderous rage over a Shakespeare play, but that's exactly what happened May 10, 1849, in New York's Greenwich Village. It was a class war of a very literal kind. Although Great Britain had been America's archenemy in the Revolution and the War of 1812, the common language and culture between the two countries meant that American entertainment still leaned heavily on British models, even in 1849. But things were starting to change.

The upper class, which was very much Anglo-Saxon, revered the elegant English actor William Charles Macready, while the lower and middle classes, substantially composed of Irish and German immigrants, found a home-grown American champion in Edwin Forrest. Macready's acting style was understated and "English"; Forrest's was bombastic and "American."

The two men started as friends, but their friendship gradually modulated into rivalry. Forrest famously booed Macready from the audience in an Edinburgh production. When Macready toured to New York, patriots in the audience greeted him by heaving a sheep carcass onto the stage. How the sheep was smuggled into the theatre is not recorded.

The carcass is perhaps not surprising, considering that the entertainment world and its audience were very different in the 1840s. A remarkable feature of downtown New York in the early nineteenth century were the young roughnecks who formed themselves into private firefighting companies and operated somewhat like gangs. They owned their own equipment and sometimes battled with each other at the scenes of fires to defend their "territory" while the building burned. Perhaps the most famous of these gang members was a fictional character known as Mose the Fireman, the subject of books, pamphlets, and event plays, based on a real-life person, Mose Humphrey.

The most interesting thing about these gangs, for our purposes, was that they didn't gather at firehouses, which didn't exist as such. Instead, they had pet theatres where they hung out to drink, carouse, and get entertained while waiting for word of the next conflagration. Rumbles and riots between rival "theatre gangs"—because that's what they were—were not uncommon. Many of their theatres were clustered on and around the Manhattan street known as the Bowery, which ran parallel to lower Broadway, where the aristocracy gathered to see their more genteel shows. The two streets, very symbolically, came close to intersecting near the Astor Place Opera House, which is the setting of this story. (The venue is long gone, but it stood just steps from what is today the Public Theatre, an entertainment powerhouse that has produced hits including *Hair*, *A Chorus Line*, and *Hamilton*.)

On that fatal night in 1849, Macready was booked into the Astor Place Opera House to perform the title role in Shakespeare's *Macbeth* for the upper crust. Not to be outdone, Forrest landed a booking in the same role of the same bloody play a few blocks away, attracting his blue-collar fans, known collectively as the Bowery b'hoys and g'hals. They regarded Macready's booking at the Opera House as an insult and a provocation.

The New York City Police Department bosses suspected that trouble was brewing and told the mayor they didn't know if they could handle things by themselves if the crowds got out of hand. So the mayor called out the heavily armed 7th New York Militia Regiment to help "keep the peace." It didn't work out quite that way. Some 350 soldiers, including mounted troops and light artillery (!), reinforced 150 policemen stationed inside the Opera House, and another 100 outside to protect the aristocrats.

Forrest's supporters were outraged by Macready's booking *and* by the show of force against ordinary American citizens. A crowd estimated at ten thousand converged on Astor Place at about 7:30 p.m. and began hurling stones at the Opera House, smashing windows, battling with police, and trying to set the theatre on fire. Macready rushed through his performance and escaped the building in disguise. His audience was besieged inside the theatre.

By 9:15, the situation had turned into a full-on donnybrook, and the military leaders decided they'd had enough. They lined up the soldiers and, after shouted warnings that were tough to hear over the din of the riot, opened fire on the crowd.

In the end, between twenty-two and thirty-one audience members and rioters lost their lives, virtually all of them Forrest supporters, along with some passersby who came down to see what was going on and got caught in the melee. Forty-eight more of the rioters were wounded. Police reported fifty to seventy cops were injured, as were 141 from the militia.

As Macbeth says, "blood will have blood."

Surrender of the Will

Which brings us, in true Godwin's law fashion, to Adolf Hitler (1889–1945), the charismatic German dictator who rose to power in the 1930s, propelled by shame that the nation had fallen into mendicancy in the wake of a humiliating loss in World War I, coupled with the especially severe domestic effects of the worldwide Great Depression.

He was one of several autocrats who rose to power during the period, including Benito Mussolini in Italy, Joseph Stalin in the USSR, Francisco Franco in Spain, and others. All used recently invented mass media to spread their messages and develop cults of personality.

But Hitler was unequaled as a public speaker, with the power to connect with his audiences and hypnotize them with the pure force of his oratory. His speeches were mesmerizing, punctuated with shouts, hoots, gesticulations, and flashing eyes. Shifting abruptly from warm fatherly tones to near sobs, and then suddenly screaming with gargling, *r*-rolling passion, he implored, dared, inflamed, wheedled, mocked, stirred, and provoked outrage. He would practice these techniques in private for hours in front of a mirror and had himself photographed so he could see how he looked to inspire maximum emotional engagement.

The power of Hitler's voice over his followers can't be underestimated. He poked their most sensitive emotional buttons, asserting that Germany had been cheated, abused, and tricked by their adversaries, betrayed by their leaders, and robbed by that perpetual scapegoat, the Jews. Moreover, this was done out of jealousy of German excellence. He asserted that these enemies had deprived Germany of its rightful place in the world—not just as the equal to but, indeed, as the superior of all other nations. He sought to turn German shame to pride, and their pride to action.

Hitler's oratory reached its apotheosis in a series of mass rallies held from 1933 to 1938 on a vast parade ground in the Bavarian city of Nuremberg. The sinister majesty of the rallies is remembered today principally because of the way the 1934 iteration was captured on film by master movie propagandist Leni Riefenstahl in her *Triumph des Willens* (Triumph of the Will).

Everything at the rallies was colossal—engineered to imply massive power and strength. Red swastika'd banners and flags towered over the crowd, Wagnerian orchestral music blasted

Some of the 48,000 boys and 5,000 girls who attended a Nazi Party Congress rally in Nuremberg cheering and saluting Adolf Hitler's speech, 1937.
Hulton Archive / Getty Images

through loudspeakers, fireworks filled the sky. But most awe-inspiring/terrifying of all was the rank upon rank of hundreds of thousands of soldiers, all wearing identical uniforms, all marching in perfect unison, all chanting "Heil Hitler" with a single voice, seemingly invulnerable, unstoppable, and over-whelmingly *right*.

And then, as one high Nazi Party official after another whipped the crowd into hysteria, out came the Führer ("leader") himself, Hitler, to stoke the audience to a frenzy of pride at their ancestry, anger at those perceived to be their opponents and betrayers, and determination to do something about it. To *make them pay.*

The thousands of onlookers who attended were either swept away or horrified. Those who watched newsreels or Riefens-tahl's film of the events were intended to become either super-charged with pride (if they were Aryans as Hitler defined the blond-haired, blue-eyed Teutonic "master race") or intimidated (if they were anyone else).

Riefenstahl's film would have been better titled *Surrender of the Will*, because the goal was to annihilate dissent and surrender the audience's will to the inevitable success of the party, as reflected in its favorite slogan, "Ein Volk, ein Reich, ein Führer" (One People, One Empire, One Leader). In his book *A Concise History of Nazi Germany: 1919–1945*, historian Joseph W. Bendersky writes that the watchcry "left an indelible mark on the minds of most Germans who lived through the Nazi years. It appeared on countless posters and in publications; it was heard constantly in radio broadcasts and speeches." The audience learned that to get back on the winning team, they had to shut up and follow orders.

The crafters of these rallies, especially Hitler and his propaganda minister Joseph Goebbels, knew exactly what the prideful German audience wanted to hear. Their efforts were resoundingly successful and wound up leading their nation in a triumphant goose-stepping march down the garden path to catastrophe and disgrace.

Propaganda

Goebbels is credited (blamed?) for the primary law of propaganda: "Repeat a lie often enough and it becomes the truth."

His techniques were eagerly embraced by totalitarian governments everywhere, which seized control of mass media to indoctrinate "the masses." Look at how the dynastic leaders of North Korea keep their starving and desperate people in line by telling them over and over again how great life is there, and how other countries are itching to invade and destroy their shabby paradise.

Writing for the BBC, Tom Stafford took a close look at these audience-manipulating techniques. Repetition makes a fact seem true, regardless of whether it is or not. Understanding this effect can help you avoid falling for propaganda, says psychologist Tom Stafford, who asked,

Even if a lie sounds plausible, why would you set what you know aside just because you heard the lie repeatedly? Recently, a team led by Lisa Fazio of Vanderbilt University set out to test how the "illusion of truth effect" interacts with our prior knowledge. Would it affect our existing knowledge? They used paired true and un-true statements, but also split their items according to how likely participants were to know the truth. . . . To cover all bases, the researchers performed one study in which the participants were asked to rate how true each statement seemed on a six-point scale, and one where they just categorized each fact as "true" or "false." Repetition pushed the average item up the six-point scale, and increased the odds that a statement would be categorized as true. For statements that were actually fact or fiction, known or unknown, repetition made them all seem more believable.

The good news is that they also found that the biggest influence on whether a statement was judged to be true was . . . whether it actually was true. With or without repetition, people were still more likely to believe the facts as opposed to the lies. This shows something fundamental about how we update our beliefs—repetition has a power to make things sound truer, even when we know differently, but it doesn't always override that knowledge.

We can all bring to bear more extensive powers of reasoning, but we need to recognize they are a limited resource. Our minds are prey to the illusion of truth effect because our instinct is to use short-cuts in judging how plausible something is. Often this works. Sometimes it is misleading. Once we know about the effect we can guard against it. Part of this is double-checking why we believe what we do—if something sounds plausible is it because it really is true, or have we just been told that repeatedly?

During the Russian war on Ukraine, many of these techniques were very much in evidence. First, Russian dictator Vladimir Putin suppressed all media not controlled by his government, and silenced, jailed, or murdered any journalists who questioned the official reason for the war. All outside media were banned or jammed, the internet was censored, and even social media were cut off or severely limited.

The Russian audience, following the progress of the war on Putin-controlled media, were shown only one reality: that Ukraine was run by Nazis (despite the fact that its leader was a Jew whose family had been decimated by real Nazis), that Ukraine was a threat to Russia (despite being so much smaller and less powerful), that Ukrainians would be easy to beat, and finally that Ukraine wasn't even a real country and didn't deserve to be independent. They were told these things day after day.

And Russians, who are not a stupid people by any means, by and large started to believe these things. Putin's propaganda machine played into the audience's fears of being hated by the rest of the world, of being invaded and conquered once again (as had happened with the Mongols, the French, and the Germans, among others), and mainly of not being adequately respected by the world for the greatness they saw in themselves.

They were easy prey.

That's not an exclusively Russian problem. Audiences around the world have fallen for the same tired bag of tricks again and again. The English were told by their imperial government in the eighteenth and nineteenth centuries that their civilization was superior to all others, and therefore destined to rule the world. So it was perfectly OK to sail to the other side of the globe and conquer and take control of any country they liked.

Americans who wanted Donald Trump to be president kept being told by their targeted media that the 2020 election had been "stolen" even though repeated recounts, including those by his own supporters, showed that it hadn't been. Trump supporters kept insisting that he really *was* president. They stuck stubbornly to the oft-disproved falsehood—because they wanted it to be true and kept hearing that it was true, never mind the source.

Many Americans were told, and therefore believed, that getting vaccinated for COVID-19 was a way of taking away their rights (unlike death or being on a respirator, apparently), or implanting mind-altering microscopic devices, or actually killing them. They heard it on their news or read it on their favored parts of the internet again and again, so it must have been true. Americans fought for their freedom and love it, and they pride themselves on seeing through propaganda that bamboozles so many others. But without adequate information, they tried to peer through what they believed to be a fog of lies and wound up seeing only a chimera.

Which brings up an interesting question about the Ukraine war. Were we in the West the ones being propagandized by *our* government? By writing this historical account in this book, am I participating in this propaganda? Let's consider: Journalists from around the world were reporting the same things. Other history books freely published are saying the same things. And that I am even bringing up this question—questioning the reality of what we in the West were told about it—should tell you something. But perhaps I'm just playing a deep game.

As Euripides told his audience twenty-four centuries ago, "Question everything."

Fireside Chats

While Hitler was rousing his nation to blood and glory in response to the Depression, another master of mass communication was responding in quite a different way on the other side of the world. Soon after taking office in early 1933, US President Franklin Roosevelt began a series of what came to be known as Fireside Chats with the American people. These conversations were broadcast over the dominant mass medium of the time, radio, and were used to communicate directly with the electorate, explaining his plans for mobilizing the power of the federal government to ameliorate the economic crisis facing the nation. Roosevelt had tested the power of these chats starting in 1929 when he was still governor of the state of New York. They were designed to circumvent the news media of the day, which the Democrat felt were arrayed against him.

In practice, the chats gave him a platform from which he could ask voters to pressure recalcitrant members of Congress to support his plans. Along the way, they provided soothing reassurance and encouragement to the nervous and despairing public. His patrician tones, reasonable arguments, and straightforward delivery convinced his audience that someone capable was in charge. The term "fireside chat" emerged from the sense that they were all sitting next to Roosevelt in a firelit sitting room of their imaginations. He addressed listeners as "My friends." It gave them the feeling that the captain of the good ship *USA* knew how to steer them out of the hurricane and was asking for their help in doing so.

FDR gave fewer than three dozen national fireside chats during the twelve years of his presidency, which modulated from talking about the Depression to the progress of World War II. But their influence made them one of the most memorable aspects of Roosevelt's presidency.

Novelist Saul Bellow was quoted by Doris Kearns Goodwin in her book *No Ordinary Times* describing his experience with one of the chats as he was walking on the Chicago Midway one evening:

> Drivers had pulled over, parking bumper to bumper, and turned on their radios to hear Roosevelt. They had rolled down the windows and opened the car doors. Everywhere the same voice, its odd Eastern accent, which in anyone else would have irritated Midwesterners. You could follow without missing a single word as you strolled by. You felt joined to these unknown drivers, men and women smoking their cigarettes in silence, not so much considering the President's words as affirming the rightness of his tone and taking assurance from it.

War

No movie, play, or anything else can convey the full experience of war to an audience, but many have tried. Some do it by showing the violence of war. Some do it by glorifying the aims of war and contenting themselves with that. Others do it by protesting war. Many are combinations of all three.

Sophocles's *Ajax* and Euripides's *The Trojan Women* are among the surviving classical dramas about the spiritual cost of war. Aristophanes found comedy in the situation in his *Lysistrata*, about Greek women so sick of their men marching off to war that they stage a sex strike.

As has been discussed, conflict is the essence of drama, and war is conflict writ large. So it has been a perennial subject of plays, operas, melodramas, movies, TV shows, video games, and every other kind of entertainment.

Harriet Beecher Stowe's *Uncle Tom's Cabin*, which presented a vivid picture of the evils of slavery in mid-nineteenth-century America, wasn't a book about war. But it was widely read and widely adapted to the stage in the years leading up to the Civil War, enabling (white) audiences with little direct experience of slavery to see that it was far from the benevolent institution that plantation owners tried to paint it. It changed a lot of minds and spurred many of those audiences to action.

When Lincoln finally met Stowe in person during the war, legend asserts that he greeted her, saying "So you are the little woman who wrote the book that started this great war."

There have been thousands, probably tens of thousands, of stories about various wars told in different media. The American Civil War was portrayed in *Gone with the Wind*, World War I in *Journey's End*, World War II in *Saving Private Ryan*, *A Bridge Too Far*, and too many others to count. Charlie Chaplin, the Three Stooges, and Mel Brooks all tried to rob Adolf Hitler of his fearsomeness by poking fun at him.

During the Vietnam War, for the first time, audiences got to see real war in real time without the filter of fiction while watching the news on their TV screens each night. Like *Uncle Tom's Cabin*, it roused them to action, but this time against war. Bringing a taste of the horror of war into their living rooms changed the way audiences thought of war.

In 1939, when World War II was already under way in Europe and the Far East but the United States didn't yet have "boots on the ground," Dalton Trumbo wrote a novel titled *Johnny Got His Gun*, which horrified the people who were able to finish it. Trumbo adapted and updated it as a movie in 1971 to suit another war, the one in Vietnam, and it lost none of its power. It's the story of an America soldier grotesquely wounded in battle, losing not just his arms and legs, but also his nose, ears, mouth, and eyes. Yet medical science is able to keep him alive. His heart continues to pump and his brain continues to think, though it's now trapped in a body with no senses—a kind of living death.

Living inside his mind throughout the book and film gave audiences a grim sense of the kind of suffering war can bring.

It was Aeschylus who said that humans "suffer into truth."

The Cradle Will Rock

"Agitprop" is short for agitation and propaganda, a theatre movement developed in Soviet Russia after the communist revolution to inculcate the social aims of the revolution throughout the new conquered—er, "liberated"—countryside. Theatre was seen as an ideal tool for this purpose, since it dramatized scenarios like capitalistic bosses oppressing and exploiting workers, which evoked powerful emotional responses in the working-class audience. The movement spread to Germany and later to other European nations, as well as to China after the revolution of 1949. Musicals were found to be particularly effective at touching the hearts of audiences because they were seen to be so innocent and heartfelt, as well as filled with color, music, and attractive young dancers. *The Threepenny Opera, Happy End, The City of Mahagonny* and the so-called Chinese tractor operas and ballets—the *yang ban xi* (model works)—notably *Taking Tiger Mountain by Strategy* and *The Red Detachment of Women* were especially well-known and widely performed examples.

Elements of agitprop found their way to the United States as well, resonating with audiences in the grip of the Great Depression of the 1930s and finding new adherents in the socially conscious plays of the 1960s and beyond. Its tactics still crop up from time to time in plays, TV shows, and movies that want to connect audiences viscerally with a given social issue.

Two of the most dramatic (and spontaneous) politically significant audience-participation events in American theatre history occurred in the mid-1930s, fueled by restless anger in the audience about the dire effects of the Great Depression. The worldwide economic collapse had numerous interlocking causes, though many felt at the time that it was inherent in the capitalistic system. Communist theory predicted that revolution would follow just such a collapse, and it was widely believed that the final catastrophe of that economic system was at hand.

In this environment, Clifford Odets's 1935 agitprop drama, *Waiting for Lefty*, targeted corrupt unions that conspired with capitalist business owners to keep employees quiet. In the play, a union of taxi drivers is on the verge of a strike. As the corrupt union boss tries to dissuade them, the drivers demand to see their own elected representative, Lefty. When it is eventually revealed that Lefty has been murdered, apparently by the owners, the drivers are driven over the edge and furiously begin to chant, "Strike! Strike! Strike!"

At the play's January 6, 1935, premiere, the audience took up the chant, which continued through no less than twenty-eight curtain calls. Similar audience participation continued through much of the New York run and productions around the United States.

In his review of the first performance, critic Harold Clurman writes,

> The first scene of *Lefty* had not played two minutes when a shock of delighted recognition struck the audience like a tidal wave. Deep laughter, hot assent, a kind of joyous fervor seemed to sweep the audience toward the stage. The actors no longer performed; they were being carried along as if by an exultancy of communication such as I had never witnessed in the theatre before. Audience and actors had become one.

A similar scene played out on the stage and in the audience just two years later, at the opening night of Marc Blitzstein's musical *The Cradle Will Rock. Cradle* was created under the auspices of the Federal Theatre Project, one of the national programs in the Works Progress Administration (WPA) designed to get American workers—in this case, theatre folk—back to work during the Depression. Once again, as part of the anticapitalist atmosphere of the time, Blitzstein assembled a piece designed to attack the abuses of the existing economic situation. Produced by John Houseman and directed by Orson Welles, the musical followed the efforts of a union organizer named Larry Foreman who tries to stir up the workers against fat-cat Mr. Mister, who controls all major businesses (along with the media and even the churches) in the mythical Steeltown, USA.

Getting wind of the show's provocative content, the WPA not only attempted to cancel the production, it got the actors' union to withdraw permission for its members (including Howard Da Silva, John Adair, Olive Stanton, and Will Geer) to appear on stage. As a result, the Maxine Elliott Theatre on West 39th street in Manhattan, where it was to have played, was padlocked.

Undeterred, Blitzstein's supporters rented the Venice Theatre on Seventh Avenue at West 58th Street, about a mile away. Audience members who gathered outside the Elliott memorably marched uptown to the Venice, gathering people off the street on the way to join them in what felt like a glorious parade for freedom. When the burgeoning crowd arrived at the Venice, they found the composer sitting on stage with a piano, performing the score himself. He was joined by Stanton, but other members of the cast, appearing on their own time, rose from their seats in the house to perform their roles in defiance of the ban. Breathless coverage of the scene led to commercial producers taking over the show and presenting it in a full production at a regular Broadway house. It ran 131 performances. But the sanctioned production could scarcely match the excitement of that pugnacious opening night.

Direct Action

Social change in repressive societies is very difficult. The call for direct-action revolution is very appealing to idealists, but often leads to greater repression. Communist theory predicted proletarian revolutions in industrialized countries, but, in reality, only largely agrarian countries like early twentieth-century Russia, China, and Vietnam underwent communist revolutions from within. Industrialized nations like the UK, France, and the United States resisted violent revolution, but underwent systemic changes that adopted certain socialized programs such as Social Security and National Health that changed their societies incrementally.

What was the engine of this change? To a great extent, the arts. Dramatizing the suffering of workers changed hearts and minds in a way that led to changes from within. International sanctions helped South Africa end its policy of apartheid. But it was writers like Athol Fugard and theatre companies like the Market Theatre of Johannesburg that helped prepare South African audiences for the coming abolition of apartheid and acceptance of a more equitable order.

In Nigeria, the Afrobeat music of Fela Aníkúlápó Kuti helped give voice to the protests of the downtrodden audience members against the military dictatorship in that country.

In the United States, writers including Zora Neale Hurston, James Baldwin, Lorraine Hansberry, Richard Wright, Langston Hughes, Toni Morrison, Alice Childress, and others fought for and won a place in American letters for Black people and their struggles by telling compelling stories. They made audiences of all colors hear new stories that hadn't been told before by the people who lived them.

LeRoi Jones, who later changed his name to Amiri Baraka, wrote plays that confronted the (mainly white) audience in powerful ways with plays like *The Slave* and *Dutchman*. More than passing laws or cracking heads, these plays changed the minds of the audience in fundamental and enduring ways and helped dramatize their plight to audiences so caught up in white privilege they had no clear idea what the civil rights upheaval of that period was all about.

But the work of these and other artists were not just directed to the white community. A body of Black music and the other arts that had been growing since the nineteenth century began to fully flower in the 1960s. This celebration of Black power and Black pride came to a head with the Harlem Cultural Festival

(1967–1974), but especially the landmark 1969 edition (the same summer as Woodstock), which featured acts from the spectrum of Black talent. The festival's very existence and the variety and vitality of the acts presented made a profound impression on its largely Black audience. Its subtext was, "Our culture is as good or better than anybody else's. We have an equal place in this world and this nation and we deserve to assert it." In its own way, it was a revolution.

Grand Guignol

Not all theatres were designed to politicize audiences, delight them, or lull them. Some, like Le Théâtre du Grand-Guignol in Paris (1897–1962), were designed to shock and horrify them— and the more extreme and bloody the show, the better.

Located in Pigalle, the city's nightlife district, the theatre was founded by Oscar Méténier and later run by André Antoine, who sought to push the boundaries of what naturalistic the-atre—and the human stomach—could endure. Audiences could expect to see beheadings, blindings, stabbings, strangulations, impalements, asphyxiations, dismemberments, and disfigure-ments, all created by a demented team of master makeup and special effects artists. As horror writer Stephen King later did so masterfully, the creators of shows at the Grand Guignol didn't try to jolt audiences with scary monsters. Instead, they used people and situations audiences usually considered comfortable and trustworthy—children, doctors, spouses, and friends—and revealed their darkest dark sides.

"There were audience members who could not physically handle the brutality of the actions taking place on stage," writes Richard Hand and Michael Wilson in their book *Grand-Guignol: The French Theatre of Horror*. "Frequently, the 'special effects' would be too realistic and often an audience member would faint or vomit during performances. [The producer] used the goriness to his advantage by hiring doctors to be at perfor-mances as a marketing ploy."

However, there were other audience members who found the proceedings not just exciting and fun but actually arousing. The theatre maintained semi-private boxes that hung beneath the balcony, where these peculiarly ardent audience members could pursue their enjoyment of the repulsive proceedings unobserved.

Though largely forgotten today, the Grand Guignol served as the model for the entire genre of horror films and slasher films of the past half century. Audiences, it seems, still get their jollies from stories that are anything but jolly.

Some of the creepiest and most malevolent characters in literature have become stars among their fans, from Dracula to Freddy Krueger. Why do some audiences like to witness things that would traumatize them in real life?

Media personality and horror film historian Jay Michaels has a theory, expressed for this book in July 2022:

> Our minds, or more particularly, our imaginations are far more vast than we think. The worry of getting to work on time can grow into something so nightmarish within our imagination. We need to assuage this by facing creations as horrifying. Mythology stems from that. As we strive to rationalize something as simple as rain and lightning we created a siren, medusa, or cyclops. The same can be said about horror films. We assuage millennia old terrors in our DNA by confronting Freddy, Jason, Michael, Chucky and Pennywise.

In his book *Danse Macabre*, Stephen King says people use horror to measure their own ability to withstand horror. "That was pretty scary, but I was able to handle it! I'm pretty tough!" Michaels agrees.

> Yes. If we can stand Dracula, now it's time to tackle Frankenstein. If we conquered the Werewolf, now it's time to battle the Mummy. In this way, subconsciously, we say to ourselves "If I can tackle my office one more day" . . . "If I can pass this class," et cetera. When you think about it, that's why horror movies get more gory, more frightening, more interactive, or

CGI laden, and push the envelope in terms of plots. Because we want to win one more challenge. Ironically, the world is starting to realize the value of horror films. That's why they're winning Academy Awards and great Shakespearean actors are playing superheroes.

There is the famous, though perhaps apocryphal, story of Auguste and Louis Lumière's 1895 movie short, *Arrival of a Train at La Ciotat,* that consists of little more than forty-nine seconds of a steam train pulling into a station and people disembarking while others gather to board. The film was presented as part of the Lumière Brothers' *actualités* series—microdocumentaries showing tiny slices of everyday life such as a blacksmith at work or a baby eating breakfast. These films may seem like nothing today, but their first audiences had never seen a photograph move, and the *actualités* were subjects of abject wonder.

Arrival of a Train at La Ciotat, however, produced an unusual reaction. In the film's opening moments, the audience saw a real locomotive heading straight at them. Some audience members jumped back, screamed, or even fled in panic at the prospect of being run over! After all, it wasn't just a drawing or a painting. They could see an *actual train* bearing down on them.

We may chuckle at their innocence. But even today, Walt Disney parks have a ride called Soarin' that immerses you in a filmed image on an extra-wide screen that extends beyond your field of vision, making you feel like you are wrapped in the world of the film. Participants sit in seats that tip as they would if they were banking left and right or diving downward. You may be barely moving, but your inner ear thinks you are actually flying, and your stomach climbs into your throat as you feel like you're rising and falling with the image.

Virtual reality goggles and games have the same effect. If you've ever blundered into furniture or slammed into a wall while playing *Call of Duty: Warzone* or *Beat Saber* in your Oculus Meta Quest, you know that the intellect may not be fooled, but the deep brain can be—just as easily as those audiences at the dawn of moving pictures.

Rhythm Zero

Audiences are so used to certain traditions and behaviors, especially in live theatre, that they are easily flummoxed and made to feel disoriented when these rules are broken. Performance art, as it is called, has provided some of the most noteworthy experiments, many of them the product of the artist's peculiar personal vision.

A classic example was presented in 1974 when Serbian performance artist Maria Abramović performed her *Rhythm Zero* at Studio Morra in Naples, Italy. The piece consisted of Abramović, fully clothed, standing, emotionless, before a long table covered with a white cloth. Arrayed on the cloth were seventy-two items, including flowers, matches, a feather, carpentry nails, a book, an axe, a handkerchief, razor blades, an apple, a whip, a bell, and a gun loaded with a single bullet.

The audience was left in the room with her for a span of six hours, with only the following instructions:

"There are 72 objects on the table that one can use on me as desired.

Performance.

I am the object.

During this period I take full responsibility."

In this experiment/performance, Abramović wanted to see how an utterly untethered an audience would become.

The audience was restrained, sometimes even playful during the first two hours. But then things started to turn ugly. They began to touch her, then to tear her clothes, then to remove her clothes, then to cut her skin and lick her blood. Not everyone participated in the more extreme responses. But that produced a response of its own. Some of the audience followed their instincts to protect Abramović, which made the others more extreme. By the end of the six hours, the audience had formed two gangs or mini armies, displaying both the best and worst of human behavior. It made the audience think of what their responsibilities to others might be. The author/performer described herself as "the object," confronting viewers about how women's bodies are treated. The audience made their own drama.

Abramović later observed, "The experience I drew from this work was that in your own performances you can go very far, but if you leave decisions to the public, you can be killed."

Toxic Comedy

Comedy used to be the most lighthearted of entertainments. As the modern answer to court jesters of old, the comedian was given the freedom to criticize the powerful and to fearlessly point out hypocrisy wherever the comedian found it. Mother-in-law jokes and gags about airline food were their stock in trade—even if they sometimes stepped over the invisible line of taste and propriety.

Over the years since comedy became big business, the tone of comedy has evolved. That invisible line got pushed further and further back, as comedians became more "blue," meaning they dealt more intimately with sexual jokes. There were different standards for different media. Audiences who enjoyed Buddy Hackett's or Don Rickles's naughty interplay with Johnny Carson on *The Tonight Show* were stunned to hear the explosion of profanity they employed in their uncensored Las Vegas shows. *The Smothers Brothers Comedy Hour* introduced mass TV audiences to a stronger mix of political commentary, which increased the "proof" level in the clubs as well.

Late-night talk show monologues became more and more political, until whole shows were devoted to politics—usually with a left-leaning take on the commentary.

Some of this "comedy" still has the ability to shock. When comedienne Kathy Griffin posted a picture of herself in 2017 with a fake severed head of President Donald Trump, it not only derailed her career, it gave permission for right-wing comedians to take their gloves off as well. The violent and antidemocratic "jokes" and stunts got many of them banned from commercial comedy clubs, which just drove them to the internet in communities like onaforums.net, which the *New Republic* described as "a safe space to say what cannot be said offline." The article describes multiple "hate threads" whose titles feature racial and ethnic slurs, as well as an "OFFICIAL Post-Election Voter Fraud THREAD," where one poster called President Joe Biden "a pedophile . . . who's about to die in the oval office." Elsewhere the poster derided the COVID-19 vaccine, casting it as a supposed Asian plot in similarly hateful language.

There is a lot worse to be found down that rabbit hole. But this and other forums have found a willing and appreciative audience. How much of it is merely cheekiness, acting out, and enjoying a moment of transgressive behavior? Versus really feeling that way and stoking oneself to real-world action? Those are some of the main questions facing audiencing in the modern world.

Answers may be found in one major real-world expression of it.

Save America

On January 6, 2021, American democracy nearly came to an end. Ironically, its destruction would have come at the hands of a mob who sincerely believed that they were the ones saving it.

On that date, some two thousand to twenty-five hundred supporters of President Donald Trump converged on the Mall in Washington, DC. They were there because they had been told by Trump and his supporters in the right-wing media that the November 2020 presidential election had been "rigged" by Democratic Party operatives to swing the election to his opponent, Joseph Biden. Though several states had conducted recounts at that point, no evidence of rigging had been found (or has been found since then) that would have swayed the election to Trump. Nevertheless, Trump and his supporters had spent much of the two months after the election putting out the word that the presidency had been "stolen."

In the weeks following the election, the final vote tallies had been certified in state after state. The Electoral College count stood at 306 for Biden, 232 for Trump. Only one procedural step remained: the official Certifying of the Ballots before Congress, a count traditionally certified by the vice president, acting as President of the Senate. This count is usually done pro forma, but Trump saw it as his last chance to overturn the election. In the days before the January 6 certification, Trump had pressured Vice President Mike Pence to reject the counts in states where Trump believed there had been irregularities. Pence argued that he had no power to do that.

So Trump and his supporters in right-wing media outlets called upon his supporters across the nation to converge on Washington, DC, to stage a mass demonstration, called the "Save America" rally, to pressure Pence to reject the tally that had already been certified by all fifty states, or to pressure Congress, meeting in joint session, to reject the tally.

Trump was one of several speakers to address the audience at the Ellipse section of the Mall, just south of the White House. But in the aftermath of the speeches, the crowd marched on the US Capitol where Congress was meeting and engaged in a riot, breaking into the building that had not been attacked in arms since the War of 1812, assaulting police, invading congressional offices, vandalizing and stealing documents and furniture, and threatening to lynch Pence, Democratic leader of the House of Representatives Nancy Pelosi, and other officials.

They failed in their attempted putsch because the nation's elected leaders, including Pence, were hustled into hiding by security services, and the disappointed mob was driven out or dissipated. But several interesting details emerged afterward. Number one, the rioters believed they were the good guys, trying to save American democracy and their favored president from an apparent coup. Number two, interviewed after the fact, participant after participant said they did what they did because President Trump had ordered them to do so in his speech on the Mall. They were only following orders.

Point two presents an interesting case in audience dynamics. Let's take a look at what Trump actually said, and how he said it, versus what the audience heard him say. While at no point did Trump specifically order them to invade the Capitol, smash windows, attack police, take the floor of the Senate, murder Pelosi, and hang Pence—that is what the audience on the Mall heard

Trump say. They were so used to getting coded messages from the president that they assumed—correctly or not—that this was another one of those. They believed they had gotten marching orders from the Commander in Chief, and they marched. With that, the audience was transformed into a mob, and mob rule took over.

Trump spent much of the seventy-one-minute, 11,158-word speech attacking the "fake news" media and "big tech," meaning social media and the electronic voting machines, so they could discount anything they'd heard about recounts finding no evidence of fraud. He also attacked Democrats and "weak" Republicans, especially the Republican governor of Georgia, who had refused to invalidate his state's vote count.

Trump repeatedly called the election "fake," "rigged," and "stolen," and pledged, "We will never give up, we will never concede. It doesn't happen. You don't concede when there's theft involved."

He complimented the audience again and again, calling them "American patriots who are committed to the honesty of our elections and the integrity of our glorious republic." He told them, "Our country has had enough. We will not take it anymore and that's what this is all about. And to use a favorite term that all of you people really came up with: We will stop the steal. . . . We will not let them silence your voices. We're not going to let it happen, I'm not going to let it happen," after which the audience began to chant, "Fight for Trump."

Referring to Vice President Pence and the certification that was scheduled to take place that afternoon, Trump said,

> I hope Mike is going to do the right thing. I hope so. I hope so. Because if Mike Pence does the right thing, we win the election. All he has to do, all this is, this is from the number one, or certainly one of the top, Constitutional lawyers in our country. He has the absolute right to do it. We're supposed to protect our country, support our country, support our Constitution, and protect our Constitution. . . . All Vice President Pence has to do is send it back to the states to recertify and we become president and you are the happiest people.

And I actually, I just spoke to Mike. I said: 'Mike, that doesn't take courage. What takes courage is to do nothing. That takes courage. And then we're stuck with a president who lost the election by a lot and we have to live with that for four more years. We're just not going to let that happen.

Trump then began to ask the crowd to take action.

We're gathered together in the heart of our nation's capital for one very, very basic and simple reason: To save our democracy. . . . We want to go back and we want to get this right because we're going to have somebody in there that should not be in there and our country will be destroyed and we're not going to stand for that. . . . Mike Pence is going to have to come through for us, and if he doesn't, that will be a sad day for our country because you're sworn to uphold our Constitution. Now, it is up to Congress to confront this egregious assault on our democracy. And after this, we're going to walk down, and I'll be there with you, we're going to walk down, we're going to walk down [to the Capitol].

This was Trump's first mention of "walking down" to the Capitol, located more than a mile from where he was giving the speech. To the audience, that "we're going to walk" sounded like Trump would be walking with them to the Capitol.
Trump repeated,

We're going to walk down to the Capitol, and we're going to cheer on our brave senators and congressmen and women, and we're probably not going to be cheering so much for some of them. Because you'll never take back our country with weakness. You have to show strength and you have to be strong. We have come to demand that Congress do the right thing and only count the electors who have been lawfully slated, lawfully slated.

Yes, the audience thought, we will follow him down to the Capitol and be strong and somehow demand it. He will tell us how.

Trump continued, "I know that everyone here will soon be marching over to the Capitol building to peacefully and patriotically make your voices heard."

This was the first mention of a "march," which had a military air to it. Trump clearly and specifically used the words "peacefully and patriotically," but the crowd heard a tinge of sarcasm in his voice. This is what linguists call a dog whistle. Literal dog whistles are whistles pitched so high that human ears can't hear them—but dogs' ears can because they were designed by nature to pick up higher frequency sounds. In political speechifying, a dog whistle is a seemingly innocent phrase that the audience understands as meaning something more sinister or even the reverse, but it is said in a seemingly innocent way to give the speaker plausible deniability.

When the audience heard "peaceful" they understood it to be a false order, a wink, something to cover his ass. He'd done it so many times that they understood "peaceful" to mean "violent" because he had mentioned "fight" elsewhere in his speech, and he would mention it again. So was it to be "peaceful" or a "fight"? They knew Trump never demanded anyone to do anything *literally* peacefully unless it was Black Lives Matter, "Antifa," or other bêtes noires.

Trump continued,

> Today we see a very important event though. Because right over there, right there [the Capitol], we see the event going to take place. And I'm going to be watching. Because history is going to be made. We're going to see whether or not we have great and courageous leaders, or whether or not we have leaders that should be ashamed of themselves throughout history. Throughout eternity they'll be ashamed. And you know what? If they do the wrong thing, we should never, ever forget that they did. Never forget. We should never ever forget.

Shame is a great motivator. The audience knew that the "shame" would be laid at the feet of the "weak" leaders like Pence, but the expression was also a warning for the audience too, about doing what was "right." Many audience members resolved then and there to make sure to be on the "courageous" side and never the side of the "ashamed," no matter what happened.

Also, they heard Trump say that he would be "watching"—not just Pence, but all of them. A minute ago he had said he'd be "marching" alongside them, or something like that, but now he said he'll be "watching." Oh well, it was probably the same thing.

"And Mike Pence," Trump said, returning to his main point.

> I hope you're going to stand up for the good of our Constitution and for the good of our country. And if you're not, I'm going to be very disappointed in you. I will tell you right now. I'm not hearing good stories. . . . The Republicans have to get tougher. You're not going to have a Republican Party if you don't get tougher. They want to play so straight. . . . [They say] the Constitution doesn't allow me to send them back to the States. Well, I say, yes it does, because the Constitution says you have to protect our country and you have to protect our Constitution, and you can't vote on fraud. And fraud breaks up everything, doesn't it? When you catch somebody in a fraud, you're allowed to go by very different rules. So I hope Mike has the courage to do what he has to do. And I hope he doesn't listen to the RINOs [Republicans in Name Only] and the stupid people that he's listening to.

After attacking voter rolls, which he claimed were full of ineligible voters, Trump again called 2020 "the most corrupt election in the history, maybe of the world."

Approaching his conclusion, Trump said,

> Today is not the end, it's just the beginning. . . . Our fight against the big donors, big media, big tech, and others is just getting started. This is the greatest in history. There's never been a movement like that. . . . We must stop the steal and then we must ensure that such outrageous election fraud never happens again, can never be allowed to happen again. And we fight. We fight like hell. And if you don't fight like hell, you're not going to have a country anymore. . . . So we're

going to, we're going to walk down Pennsylvania Avenue. I love Pennsylvania Avenue. And we're going to the Capitol, and we're going to try and give . . . we're going to try and give our Republicans—the weak ones because the strong ones don't need any of our help—We're going to try and give them the kind of pride and boldness that they need to take back our country. So let's walk down Pennsylvania Avenue.

Riled up with talk of "stolen" elections and the imperative need to "fight like hell" for freedom, the audience marched to the Capitol (without Trump, who returned to the White House) and began their "fight"—a rampage that led to the building being damaged and occupied and to police being wounded and killed, while Congress, including Pence, barricaded themselves in safe-rooms. So shocked were the congressional leaders by the attack that once the building was cleared of rioters, Congress came back into session and Pence certified the states' votes that same evening, leading to Trump's (and Pence's) departure from office on January 20, 2021.

Perhaps most interesting of all is how the audience was roused to action by simple old-fashioned oratory. He let them hear what they were dying to hear: a call to arms! Their beloved leader spoke directly to them in person. Not on Twitter or TV—live and in person. And they literally would do anything for him, for their daddy. And he told them to do something. Anything. It would have made nineteenth-century orators proud—but, of course, also horrified and sickened.

A Thousand Points of Darkness

Audiences who confuse comfortable fantasy and complex reality seem to be gaining ground in recent years. This is especially true at the fringes of political discourse. Isolated kooks used to stew in their dark fantasies alone or in small groups. But today, they use the internet to find a thousand points of darkness, to invert President George Bush's phrase, organizing into political groups like QAnon, Proud Boys, neo-Nazis, and ad hoc militias.

Goaded by Russian trolls, they use social media to spread lies and hate, culminating in the January 6, 2021, attempt to overthrow the US government. There are left-leaning groups like this as well, but these rightist groups have come out of hiding and parade their ignorance and hate in a more public way—so far.

RACE, ETHNICITY, AND GENDER

It's impossible to write a history of the audience without grappling with the roles race, ethnicity, and gender have played in its development, and the way it changed over time. Issues that were glossed over or ignored entirely have now moved to the center of discussion, debate, and action throughout Western culture, and throughout the world. It's impossible even to use the expression "Western culture" without touching on these themes, since Western culture is by no means the only culture or the only culture that matters.

Comedians like to believe that humor is universal and transcends culture, but that's wrong. Humor is deeply rooted in culture and often shifts wildly with time and place.

Seeing a comic take a pie in the face may seem like something that would be funny anywhere at any time. But certainly not in the midst of a famine when every crumb of food would be precious. In a less extreme example, comic Sam Kinison's jokes about driving drunk made him seem like a rebel and a bad boy—right up to the day he was killed in a car accident after being struck head-on by a seventeen-year-old driver who was intoxicated.

On a larger scale, stereotyped ethnic humor served as a cornerstone of comedy in late nineteenth-century America. Comedians in minstrel shows and vaudeville used jokes with exaggerated accents or supposed national propensities (Irish were drinkers, Scots were cheap, Italians were emotional, et cetera) to help lubricate the friction between these immigrant groups forced to live cheek by jowl with one another in the burgeoning inner cities of the nation.

In many cases, especially with Black and Asian stereotypes, the fooling took on a grimmer edge, making members of these groups look ridiculous and less than human.

Nevertheless, ethnic humor was broadly popular. Chico Marx adopted an exaggerated Italian persona. Stepin Fetchit (real name Lincoln Theodore Monroe Andrew Perry) was a complex figure whose stage persona presented a Black character who was mentally slow and lazy. Nearly every white actor in the early through the mid-twentieth century, from Al Jolson to Eddie Cantor, performed in blackface at one time or another. *Amos 'n' Andy*, originated by white men Freeman Gosden and Charles Carrell, was such a success on the radio that it became one of the earliest sitcoms on TV.

And blackface wasn't the only racially insensitive programming to reach a mass (i.e., white) audience. Popular film characters Charlie Chan, Fu Manchu, and Ming the Merciless were all played by white actors in yellowface. Latin characters tended to be played by actual Latinx performers, but usually in stereotyped roles.

All these performers were broadly popular—yet, at the same time, would have found themselves blackballed from vaudeville if they had performed "blue" or sexually suggestive material, never mind explicit jokes.

How things have changed. Comedy has turned 180 degrees in the last century. Sexual humor is part and parcel of pop music and family sitcoms on TV, and pornography is freely available on the web. But making an ethnic joke or (long ago) wearing blackface consigns even the biggest stars to career oblivion.

Audiences who once applauded the use of blackface to play the title character in *Othello* or yellowface for opera singers to play Cio-Cio San in *Madame Butterfly*, or Larry Blyden playing Sammy Fong in *Flower Drum Song*, now regard those roles as unplayable by anyone but ethnically appropriate performers. And then there is Mickey Rooney's performance as Mr. Yunioshi in *Breakfast at Tiffany's*, which was seen as offensive even in its own time.

The very first commercially released "talkie" film, *The Jazz Singer*, featured the top star of the age, "America's Foremost Entertainer," Al Jolson, singing "Mammy" in blackface. It changed the entertainment world, but today it is widely regarded as offensive and virtually unscreenable.

Most of the old-time actors and comedians at one time or another performed in blackface, and that includes Bing Crosby, Judy Garland, Frank Sinatra, cartoon characters including Bugs Bunny and Mickey Mouse, even master dancer Fred Astaire.

But, of course, their fans were largely white audiences. They believed they were getting the "Black" experience without having to watch actual Black people. Or perhaps they were oblivious to how offensive these portraits were in the long ago before cultural appropriation was seen for the slap in the (Black) face it is.

Or perhaps they just thought Black performers weren't as good as white performers. Astaire himself put lie to that impression when he called the Nicholas Brothers' (Fayard and Harold Nicholas) performance of "Jumpin' Jive" in the 1943 movie *Stormy Weather* "the greatest dancing he had ever seen on film."

Spike Lee's 2000 film *Bamboozled* parodies all these attitudes, with its story of a fictionalized modern-day televised minstrel show (more on this later in this chapter). Ironically, it was criticized for showing the stereotypes, even though it was made by Black artists to attack those same stereotypes. Mark Twain's *Huckleberry Finn*, the classic novel that excoriates racism and the practice of slavery at a time when slavery was still the law of the land, has been banned in some corners because it shows slavery and includes profoundly offensive terms for Blacks that were a symptom of the very racism the book attacks.

Case in point: *The Mikado*. Once the most popular of the Gilbert and Sullivan operettas, it has become one of the most problematic to perform. Although the story is set in Japan, complete with cartoonish faux-Japanese characters who sport names like

Yum-Yum, Pooh-Bah and Pitti-Sing, the joke isn't on Japan, it's on British society, whose own foibles, hypocrisies, and general ridiculousness are lampooned in the opera—not Japan's. But those "yellow" faces, though. And those names. Yes, the show was traditionally performed in yellowface, with largely Caucasian faces made up to look Asian.

So an opera company that wants to do *The Mikado* today has a few options. Number one: attempt to do a traditional version with white actors playing Japanese characters and run the risk of outraging those who see the play as racist cultural appropriation.

Number two: flip the scenario. The 2013 Mu Performing Arts production in St. Paul, Minnesota, was primarily cast with Asian actors and with the action relocated to England itself. A little bit on the nose, perhaps, but the satire still had a sting.

Number three: some companies have attempted to walk a middle path—keeping the cartoonish Japanese names but doing it in British "drag." For example: the English National Opera's 2013 production moved the action from Japan to a 1920s English seaside resort with a stark black-and-white Edwardian design. Eric Idle of *Monty Python* played Ko-Ko, the Lord High Executioner.

Or, four: cast the cartoonish Japanese roles with ethnically Japanese actors wearing the attire of the city of Titipu.

In any case, the opera has effectively been canceled and companies that want to perform a Gilbert and Sullivan operetta should turn instead to *Iolanthe* or *Patience* or *Pirates of Penzance*. The tainted *Mikado* has largely gone on the shelf, awaiting a more viable satirical approach, or a new era of understanding.

Cultural Appropriation

Most of the world's culture today is the result of hybridization: different cultures coming together through trade, travel, or conquest over the past ten thousand-plus years. But a significant portion of today's culture has come about as the result of cultural appropriation: taking another person's culture without credit or recompense and presenting it as one's own.

That's been going on for a long time "without any complaint." Why is that "suddenly" bad, from the audience's point of view? Because there *have* been complaints, and it *has* been bad, but those responses have been played down or ignored. One part of the audience, the dominant white part, has enjoyed the benefits of Black, Latinx, and Asian culture without paying the price minority groups do.

Those who oppose the teaching of what's known as critical race theory, the racial bias in our legal system and policies leading to the mistreatment of minorities in America, simply ignore the facts of history. For the purposes of this book, we need to look at the co-opting of Black culture, a culture born in Africa, imported to North America along with slavery, and developed as a response to three hundred years of bondage that followed, plus the continued exploitation in the decades that followed the end of slavery after the US Civil War.

Much of what all races enjoy today as American culture is the result of that appropriation, especially in the worlds of music and dance, but extending far beyond those two categories.

Minstrel Shows

By far the most popular indigenous American form of entertainment before the advent of musical theatre and jazz was the minstrel show. Though minstrel shows featured ostensibly Black characters, they were, for most of their existence, created by and for whites. They were designed to suggest types of entertainment that white Southerners witnessed on plantations in the years before slavery was abolished. But while these shows had moments of humor and talent, they represented a grotesquely racist form of cultural appropriation and adulteration.

While it's true that Black slaves invented various ways of easing the agony of enslavement and staying connected with their African roots through music and dancing, they bore little resemblance to the whitewashed version that was presented in minstrel shows. White audiences who had never seen Black people performing their own music, dance, and humor came to believe that what they were seeing was an accurate representation of Black culture, even an "improved" representation, and allowed minstrelsy to form their mental images and assumptions about what Black people were really like.

The minstrel shows all followed variations on the same pattern. They were presented in three sections, but the best-known section is the one where the performers—usually white men in burnt-cork blackface, wearing swallow-tailed coats and striped trousers or other formalwear—would sit in chairs lined up parallel to the audience. In the center sat a man with a top hat, called Mr. Interlocutor or the Leader. At the far left and right were Mr. Tambo who shook a tambourine and Mr. Bones who played a percussion instrument, usually bones or clackers designed to suggest the sound of rattling bones.

Mr. Interlocutor would ask questions that were setups for corny jokes; Mr. Tambo and Mr. Bones would give smart-aleck answers. Sometimes the "end men" asked the questions and Mr. Interlocutor would play straight man. This was the source of such corny old jokes as "Why did the chicken cross the road? To get to the other side!" and "Why do firemen wear red suspenders? To keep their pants up!"

> *Tambo*: Say, Mr. Interlocutor, I saw a baby yesterday only six months old and it weighed two hundred and fifty pounds and furthermore—furthermore—they fed it on elephant's milk.
>
> *Interlocutor*: Why Mr. Tambo you must be crazy. Do you really mean to tell me that you saw a baby only six months old that weighed two hundred and fifty pounds and that they fed the baby on elephant's milk? Whose baby was it?
>
> *Bones*: Why an elephant's baby of course!

These simplistic plays on words can be found threaded throughout American humor, from Abbott and Costello's "Who's on First?" to the often retold "My wife and I have sex almost every night . . . *almost* on Monday, *almost* on Tuesday. . . ."

Minstrel shows also featured musical interludes (banjos were a favorite instrument) that would often end with a circle dance called a cakewalk. The cakewalk was borrowed from a number of sources but was primarily a dance competition for couples. The best couple, as judged by the audience, would win a cake. The most popular dance involved extravagantly dressed contestants strutting and kicking up their feet.

It is very hard to overestimate the popularity of minstrel shows during their golden age from 1850 to 1870, but even long after. At one point there were dozens of minstrel companies touring around the United States and Europe, including all-female minstrels and even all-Black minstrels (who were still expected to "black up" their faces to look like white minstrels).

Audiences, especially rural audiences, laughed heartily at the lame jokes because, there being no mass communication yet, they usually had not heard them before. The overall level of sophistication of the American sense of humor has risen drastically since then, but only because we are presented with so much entertainment and many different kinds of humor through the modern mass media. In the nineteenth century, smaller communities often did not have any other form of live entertainment, and when minstrel shows came to town, their cornball yocks passed for high cleverness and wit. The racist part of minstrel shows comes partly from the fact that this dumbbell sense of humor was attributed to "simple" Black people.

Late in their era of popularity, there were some "all-negro" minstrel shows that tried to do the same that the blackface shows did, but they were criticized, as often happens, for not being "Black enough"—code for not dopey enough. Although records show that many Black people attended minstrel shows as well, the shows came under fire from Black commentators even at the height of their popularity. Civil rights leader Frederick Douglass (1817–1895) described the minstrels as "the filthy scum of white society, who have stolen from us a complexion denied them by nature, in which to make money, and pander to the corrupt taste of their white fellow citizens."

Minstrel shows began to die out in the late nineteenth century because they were too racist even for the people of that time. Some whites were genuinely outraged; many just started to feel uncomfortable with *something* about them. But the memory of minstrelsy remained popular in many corners. As late as 1921, author Harold Rossiter published a book for theatre groups titled *How to Put on a Minstrel Show*. Rossiter called it "the one form of entertainment of which the public never seems to tire."

The 1942 Hollywood film *Holiday Inn*, which featured a musical number for each major holiday around the calendar, "celebrated" Lincoln's birthday with a minstrel show tribute titled "Abraham." In 1948's *Easter Parade*, Judy Garland and Fred Astaire did a minstrel tribute. Both numbers are usually edited out of TV rebroadcasts today.

The 1964 World's Fair in New York featured a minstrel show "spoof" titled "America, Be Seated!" It was withdrawn after two performances owing to the public outcry. In England, "The Black and White Minstrel Show" remained a staple of BBC programming beginning in 1958, and was not taken off the air until 1978.

One of the last gasps was the 2010 Broadway musical *The Scottsboro Boys*, which told the true story of a group of Black men unjustly jailed for years on a false rape charge—even after the "victim" confessed that she had lied. The songwriting team of John Kander and Fred Ebb, who had told the story of the rise of Nazism in Germany through the lens of nightclub performances in the musical *Cabaret*, now told the story of the gross miscarriage· of justice through the lens of a minstrel show. But *The Scottsboro Boys* was quickly shot down by critics and audiences for whom the depiction of a minstrel show was grossly offensive, even though it was being used to attack racism, and even though the show also had its supporters, including the primarily Black cast.

The Music Industry

What the minstrel shows did to Black humor, the music industry did to a great degree to Black music, starting with ragtime, and continuing with tap, rock, rap, and many other African American cultural inventions. Often these songs and dances were presented in watered-down arrangements by performers like Pat Boone and Bill Haley to make them palatable to white audiences. Black performers like Ike Turner, Ray Charles, Ruth Brown, Little Richard, Fats Domino, and other seminal rockers of the 1950s had appreciable careers, but their popularity never matched those of the Beatles, the Rolling Stones, and Elvis Presley, billed as "The King of Rock 'n' Roll," a music form that had been born out of the blues created by African Americans.

Visibility and Invisibility

That's just one of the ways people of color were systematically excluded from mass culture. Despite contributing so mightily to American and world culture, Black people themselves were, with very few exceptions, invisible in mass culture for most of its existence. That invisibility gave white audiences the impression that people of color either did not exist, existed in such small numbers that they were irrelevant, or that their stories were not important enough to be told and could safely be ignored.

This invisibility gave audiences of color the feeling that they were living in a culture to which they did not belong. Many books have already been written on this subject. Author Ralph Ellison addressed this problem in his 1952 novel *Invisible Man*. The book won the US National Book Award for Fiction in 1953, a rare mainstream accolade that, ironically, helped make the issue a little bit less invisible.

Where people of color did pop up, they tended to be stereotypes. But things began to change in the 1960s along with the civil rights movement. Public demonstrations were the backbone of the movement in the United States and other Western countries during the 1960s. These included the March on Washington for Jobs and Freedom, the Birmingham Campaign, and the Selma March in Alabama, as well as many other actions large and small in many communities. The word "demonstration" meant that the actions were designed to "demonstrate" both the number and the determination of the participants. But for whom were they demonstrating? The government and industry "powers" who were creating the conditions they were protesting, but also the general public via the news media. The protesters wanted to educate a mass audience about their concerns, to show the sheer size of their numbers for those who might think they were only a fringe, to build concern among those members of the audience who might be sympathetic, and to make clear to their opponents that they weren't going anywhere.

One of the immediate changes brought about by the civil rights movement was a sudden realization among those controlling the levers of power in mass culture that it was time to begin including different faces and different stories. It was both morally right—and good business.

Where once a Louis Armstrong, a Josephine Baker, a Jack Soo, a Ricky Ricardo, an Ethel Waters, a Nichelle Nichols, a Graham Greene, an Omar Sharif, or a George Takei were few and far between, the doors gradually began to open for a more diverse representation in front of the camera. It took much longer for names like these to start appearing in credits lists of people working behind the scenes, and longer still for those names to start appearing in the production offices where the decisions were made.

Black actors were very successful in using their unions to crowbar agreements to cast more Black actors. This led to "tokenism"—that one Black character who kept popping up in minor or secondary roles. But eventually, there started—and only started—to be more opportunities for bigger roles as well.

Asians began pushing for greater representation too. Baayork Lee, who began her Broadway career as one of the Siamese children in the original Broadway production of *The King and I*, and later originated the role of Connie Wong in *A Chorus Line*, won the Isabelle Stevenson Award from Broadway's Tony Awards in 2017 for her work in founding the National Asian Artists Project with Steven Eng and Nina Zoie Lam. Their unusual (but effective) campaign consisted of mounting productions of traditionally "white" musicals like *Oklahoma!*, *Oliver!*, and *Hello, Dolly!*, and casting them almost entirely with Asian actors, to show that, after the first minute or so, they were no different in the roles than any other actor.

These developments had two profound effects on the audience. For traditionally white audiences, if helped make them aware that the world was a more diverse place than they realized, and that ethnic people were more than a collection of stereotyped quirks. Seeing them in a variety of roles helped dissipate their supposed exoticism. They were people who live ordinary lives like anyone else. And once you accept that someone is a real person—just like you—it makes it harder to mistreat or dismiss them.

For audiences of various ethnicities, the effect was even more profound. People who had never seen any representation of themselves in the mass culture gradually began to realize that their stories were part of the great American story after all.

Once people realized a long-locked door was opening, they began to aspire to pass through it. The list of firsts grows longer each year: the first Black playwright on Broadway, first Black director to win an Oscar, gradually turned into first Black justice on the Supreme Court, first Black president, et cetera.

There will be many firsts yet to come.

Gay Rights

Theatre has always been more welcoming of lesbian, gay, bisexual, transgender, queer or questioning (one's sexual or gender identity), intersex, and asexual/aromantic/agender stories than other media—not just as characters or as subjects of stories, but as a place where these people could tell their own stories.

One of the earliest modern plays that touch on this subject was *A Florida Enchantment* by Fergus Redmond and Archibald Clavering Gunter, based on an 1891 novel of the same title. In the play, a woman buys a strange vial of seeds in a curiosity shop. The vial comes with a note that the seeds have the power to change women into men and vice versa. She and her fiancé test the seeds and find themselves changing into stereotyped gay and lesbian characters who are attracted to each other and to others. The play, which was filmed in 1914, has been interpreted as depicting gay, lesbian, transsexual, and bisexual characters.

A more unambiguous depiction of lesbianism on stage came in 1907 with Sholem Asch's Yiddish-language drama *Got Fun Nekome* (*God of Vengeance*), which was a hit in Berlin and then throughout Europe but ran into censorship when an English-language version was produced in New York in 1923. The producer and cast were arrested and charged with "unlawfully advertising, giving, presenting, and participating in an obscene, indecent, immoral, and impure drama or play." They were eventually exonerated, but the play was doomed in America, and later banned in London. *Indecent*, a play about the controversy, was produced on Broadway in 2017. It was nominated for a Tony Award as Best Play and ran 129 performances.

Over the years, nontraditional sexuality was the subject of an increasing number of plays, notably Lillian Hellman's *The Children's Hour* in 1934, Robert Anderson's *Tea and Sympathy* in 1953, Mart Crowley's *The Boys in the Band* in 1968, and Harvey Fierstein's *Torch Song Trilogy* in 1982, which won the Tony Award as Best Play.

Those were all Broadway productions or major off-Broadway productions. But starting in the 1960s, and especially after the Stonewall riots in 1969, smaller theatres off-Broadway and off-off-Broadway, and some nonmainstream movies began exploring the subject of homosexuality. The 1976 Tony-winning musical *A Chorus Line* depicted several three-dimensional gay characters. They may seem unexceptional today, but they broke a serious taboo at the time.

Fierstein's *Torch Song Trilogy* began as three separate short plays about the character of Arnold Beckoff looking for love in the harsh and dangerous world of secret gay bars of the period. The plays were originally produced separately in tiny experimental spaces far from Times Square in the 1970s, but their mainstream success—running 1,222 performances—opened the door for a more serious treatment of gay life and gay characters on the stage and in all media.

A perfect example of the latter was the chant of those fighting for gay rights: "We're here, we're queer. Get used to it."

Fierstein himself went on to have a groundbreaking career as an actor in shows like *Hairspray*, a playwright (*Casa Valentina*), and a librettist on musicals such as *La Cage aux Folles*, *Newsies*, and *Kinky Boots*. A through line in many of his works and appearances is the notion that gays are like anybody else, looking for love and creating ad hoc families when their biological ones turn their backs.

His work helped change not only how the entertainment industry thought of gay subjects, but how audiences perceived gay characters as human beings, not punching bags. But that change had the perhaps unexpected effect on how his own early work was perceived by those audiences.

In his 2022 autobiography *I Was Better Last Night*, Fierstein writes about how he had a chance to witness the stark change when he attended the 2018 Broadway revival of *Torch Song Trilogy*.

> The house was generally gay with a sprinkling of straight folks. . . . The gays were relaxed, social, and festive. That was quite a difference from the pensive, guilty, insular, and cautious feel of the gays we played to in the 1970s and '80s. This bunch felt as if they were comfortably visiting an old friend. Yes, there was a familiarity, almost an ownership, in their attitude. This was their show, their history, their lives that they had come to see. Even the younger members took their seats with an almost impudent anticipation.

As for the performers, Fierstein finds correlating behavior.

> The actors were speaking their truth, giving it their all, but they were performing from a safe place. No one was going to break down the door and arrest them for crimes against nature. I'm not sure how to describe this without making it sound like they should be hiding out in an attic, but the risk, unconscious as it might be, the in-your-face daring, was absent. No one on that stage was going to lose their career for playing a homosexual. None of them would be accused of hiding their sexuality because they were in a play. I don't know how else to express it but to repeat: the danger was gone. The actors were not spouting heresy in the public square. They were not frightened that police were waiting in the wings to handcuff them. The audience was not ashamed to be seen in this place.

Like many successful revolutionaries, he found that the revolution had, to a certain degree, transformed him from a feared radical to a respected gray eminence.

White Privilege

Straight white audiences used to seeing only themselves in the mass media, have, in recent years, begun to see people of various colors and ethnicities in many shows, commercials, sports teams, et cetera. They see nontraditional casting of traditionally white roles with nonwhite actors. "They're everywhere!," white audiences may say, displaying what had been criticized as white privilege.

Well, now they know what it feels like.

But these changes shouldn't be seen as punishment or racial "revenge." Entertainment is about storytelling. The more different kinds of people there are telling the stories, the more varied the stories can be. For example: Disney cartoons. For generations their animated films were mainly populated with Euro-centric characters and stories. The company's few attempts at broadening its ethnic canvas, including *Song of the South,* and individual characters in *Lady and Tramp* and *Dumbo,* hit a sour note with twenty-first-century audiences because they were drawn on racially insensitive stereotypes. In recent years, however, some of Disney's best films, like *Encanto, Moana, Lilo & Stitch, Mulan,* and *The Princess and the Frog,* have told complex new stories, set in new worlds, with multifaceted new characters.

The changes aren't just politically correct. They offer audiences a richer audiencing experience.

Reading back over this whole section of the book, it seems like it is all directed, once again, at straight white readers. Which just shows how difficult white privilege is for cisgendered white people, including myself, to escape.

The Male Gaze

For most of human history, and in virtually every nation around the world, history was told primarily by men; art was made by men; books and plays were written by men, with few exceptions. It's not that women didn't tell stories. They were often denied education and not taught to read and write, so their stories and poetry were transmitted verbally. But most published work came from pens wielded by men—primarily straight men. As a result, characters and situations were seen almost exclusively through heterosexual male eyes. They reflected hetero male attitudes toward just about everything, including their attitudes toward women.

The term "male gaze" itself was created by filmmaker Laura Mulvey in a 1973 monograph "Visual Pleasure and Narrative Cinema" that got more attention a few years later when it was published in *Screen* magazine. The term has gained wider currency in the twenty-first century as the "patriarchy"—including cultural domination by men—has come under greater scrutiny.

Some male writers, such as playwrights Henrik Ibsen and Tennessee Williams, were able to perceive and record female characters as just as fully human as they did men. But they were rare. Men often created female characters who were either saints or whores, emasculating or outright vicious; or nagging mothers-in-law. But, most of all, women were (and to a great extent still are) presented a sex objects. Moreover, these women are depicted as thoroughly *enjoying* being sex objects, reveling in their sexiness, seeking to enhance their sexiness, and mourning the loss of sexiness that supposedly comes with age. Some women do feel that way, as is their right. But most go about their lives unconcerned about how they will be perceived in a relentlessly sexual light.

Women are often presented in body-hugging clothes or otherwise revealing outfits. Sometimes the camera would pan down a woman's body when she made her entrance on screen, just so the men could get a good look.

Once you are aware of this phenomenon, it's difficult to avoid seeing the male gaze in almost every form of entertainment. Many shows, movies, and songs refer to men as "men" but refer to women as "girls." Perhaps this was an attempt to sound "gentlemanly" to women who were considered extra-sensitive about their ages. But it only managed to sound condescending. Even when speaking properly about "men and women" or "boys and girls," the male somehow usually gets top billing. The generic for humans is usually "man" or "mankind."

Many movies also contain scenes in which a female character is topless or entirely nude. It's always explained as "dramatically necessary," but showing men similarly disrobed is extremely rare. Where male epidermis is revealed at all, other than in gay pornography, it's usually what the *Seinfeld* TV show called "full sidal nudity" or "full backal nudity," meaning the man is shown naked from the side or back, with no genitalia in sight. Though that has been changing in recent years owing to what the *New York Times* called "the HBO effect," permitting full frontal male nudity in some of the streaming service's shows.

Beyond the issue of presenting women as sex objects, they have usually been presented exclusively as appendages or accessories of men. Writer and cartoonist Alison Bechdel won a Pulitzer Prize in 2014 for her illustrated memoir *Fun Home*, about growing up in a family that ran a funeral parlor. Exasperated at the way women were treated in mainstream media, she proposed what has come to be known as the Bechdel–Wallace Test, described as "a way of evaluating whether or not a film or other work of fiction portrays women in a way that is sexist or characterized by gender stereotyping. To pass the Bechdel–Wallace Test a work must feature at least two women, these women must talk to each other, and their conversation must concern something other than a man."

Even today, it's harder to pass this test than you might think.

What effect has all this had on the audience? Women who see themselves presented this way are often disgusted, ashamed, demeaned, and annoyed because it's just not necessary. They feel left out of a dialogue between moviemakers and male audiences on which they can only eavesdrop. Traditionally, the best they have been able to do is just endure it until it blows over.

But in recent years, another option has finally emerged, and the only one that will be really effective: women are getting their hands on the levers of media power—writing, directing, and producing works of their own. They are finally shattering the monopoly of the male gaze.

Changing Times

In the meantime, audiences on their own are waking up to the problem. Things that seemed innocuous, even just a few years ago, don't sound right anymore. Problems you may not have seen before are suddenly shockingly obvious, and not just racial or gender issues.

The Three Stooges delighted adult movie audiences in the 1930s and kid TV audiences in the 1960s. Some parents forbade those kids to watch them because they started to imitate the Stooges' comic violence, complete with poked eyes, twisted noses, mallets to the noggin, and punches to the stomach, all set to wacky sound effects. But while the team still has devoted fans, others see the violence as excessive. In their last films, they just looked like a bunch of sad old men hitting each other.

When the film *Arthur* was made in 1981, Dudley Moore's portrait of a rich alcoholic was lauded as a comedy classic. But even by the time its sequel *Arthur 2: On the Rocks* came out in 1988, the portrait had come to be seen as pathetic and sad. Moore was only the latest in a long line of comedic inebriates, including Dean Martin, Marie Dressler, Red Skelton, W. C. Fields, and many others. There are fewer nowadays, because audiences have come to accept that alcoholism isn't really funny.

Modern politics entered the world of the stage several times in recent years. On November 19, 2016, three weeks after the US general election that made Donald Trump president of the United States, Vice President-elect Mike Pence got an earful from the cast of the Broadway musical *Hamilton*.

The show, which used a multiethnic cast to tell the story of the American founding fathers, was then in the first flush of its phenomenal popularity. Pence was met with both boos and cheers when he entered the Richard Rodgers Theatre with several family members.

Actor Brandon Victor Dixon, who played Vice President Aaron Burr in the production, broke character and the fourth wall during curtain calls to acknowledge Pence's presence—and to lecture him about the character of the incoming administration.

The Laughing Audience, Bill of Sale 1733 *by William Hogarth (1697–1764).* The Laughing Audience *is divided into three sections, depicting three classes of people.* Photo12/Ann Ronan Picture Library / Alamy Stock Photo

"Vice President-elect Pence, I see you walking out, but I hope you hear us, just a few more moments." Audience members booed Pence further, but Dixon interrupted them. "There is nothing to boo here ladies and gentlemen, there is nothing to boo here. We are all here sharing a story of love. We have a message for you, sir, and we hope that you will hear us out," Dixon said. "We, sir, we are the diverse America who are alarmed and anxious that your new administration will not protect us, our planet, our children, our parents, or defend us and uphold our inalienable rights, sir. But we truly hope that this show has inspired you to uphold our American values and to work on behalf of all of us."

Lin-Manuel Miranda, writer and original star of the musical, quickly tweeted, "Proud of @HamiltonMusical. Proud of @ BrandonVDixon, for leading with love. And proud to remind you that ALL are welcome at the theater."

But President-elect Trump was not nearly so sanguine, tweeting, "Our wonderful future V.P. Mike Pence was harassed last night at the theater by the cast of *Hamilton*, cameras blazing. This should not happen!" He later added, "The Theater must always be a safe and special place. The cast of *Hamilton* was very rude last night to a very good man, Mike Pence. Apologize!"

They did not. But Pence, perhaps, remembered Dixon's words. On January 6, 2021, when pro-Trump "protesters" stormed the Capitol trying to force Pence to stop certifying Joe Biden's election win over Trump, as described earlier, something stayed Pence's hand. The Veep must have known he might be writing his own political obituary. But he did his constitutional duty and certified, which took both moral courage and physical courage, considering the intense political pressure exerted by his running mate, and considering the mob chanting just outside the window and down the hall calling for him to be lynched. Pence "upheld American values" in a moment when it would have been much easier to do otherwise.

But, back in 2017, the theatre world wasn't finished with Trump yet. The Public Theater production of Shakespeare's *Julius Caesar* at the Delacorte Theater in Central Park depicted the decadent Roman emperor as a caricature of Trump. Conservative news outlets decried the portrait, some corporate sponsors pulled their support, and the audience itself got into the act, either cheering and laughing at the portrait or, in several cases, storming the stage, one chanting "Stop the normalization of political violence against the right!"

Audiences hadn't seen that kind of reverse fourth-wall-breaking since the 1960s.

10

THE PROFESSIONAL AUDIENCE

We train actors, directors, writers, athletes, songwriters, singers, dancers, and all the other creators of content. Sometimes it can start at an early age, and last for many years. We expect to see professionals entertaining us. But for some reason we don't train the most important of their collaborators—their audience. It's accepted as an article of faith that audience members are expected to be amateurs. There are no professional audiences.

Except there are: critics and other commentators.

General audiences don't have the time or patience to sort through the Himalaya of material that is added to world culture on a daily, hourly, even second-by-second basis. They depend on reviewers to sort through what's available, then bestow five stars on the best of it and throw rotten tomatoes at the rest. Prospective audiences read or watch or listen to these commentators partly to decide what is worth their time to experience personally, and partly to stay aware of what's out there, even if they have no intention of experiencing it at all. People want to stay *au courant* simply to stay in touch with what's happening in the culture around them. They want to know what's good and what's bad.

There is a difference between critics and reviewers: reviewers give thumbs up and thumbs down; critics try to give a greater perspective, and therefore they also function as reporters—not to mention as historians. If audiences can't keep up on every-thing happening now, how could they ever hope to know what has happened in the past? Here is where critics are indispens-able to audiences.

At the same time, people are often very skeptical of critics. They are usually viewed as too tough (if they hate what we like) or too lenient (if they like what we hate). That's because many of them *are* too tough and too lenient! They are people like anyone else, full of prejudices. The best way to read or watch a critic is to get to know their biases and measure them against your own. If you know a particular critic hates a particular actor you like, then that critic is very useful to you. If they pan that actor's per-formance, there's a pretty good chance you will like it.

Mark Shenton, former president of the Critics Circle of Lon-don, says, "One of the functions of a critic is to see the shows so you [the ticket buyer] don't have to, but nowadays I prefer to say that it helps to have others out there to offer guidance that enables audiences to make up their OWN minds about whether to see something or not."

The Birth of Criticism

In chapter 1 of this book, we looked at the earliest organized theatrical festival, the Great Dionysia in Athens, Greece. For better or worse, along with the birth of drama came the birth of drama criticism. Ten judges were elected each year, one each from ten different Greek tribes. After watching all the plays, the judges would give awards. These judges were the first recogniz-able critics of artistic merit. But many of the competing poets and members of the audience wondered what their standards were—what was the basis for their awards?

The philosopher Aristotle (384–322 BC), decided to address this problem in one of his masterpieces, *Poetics*, which set forth standards for all areas of theatre. Only his writings on tragedy have survived; his principles of comedy have been lost but can be inferred from the ways comedies were written in the years after *Poetics* was published. His book explores the foundations of story-making, including plot, character development, and theme. He addressed such nuts-and-bolts issues as the ideal length of plays, the different types of characters, and so on. He argued that all plays should observe "unities" of space (all the action should happen in the same physical place), time (everything should happen in no more than a single twenty-four-hour period), and action (the play should deal with a single subject).

For Aristotle, all plays should include six elements: plot, character, thought, diction, music, and spectacle. He set forth how tragedies should be presented, beginning with the *prologue* (setting up the story), *parados* (entrance of the chorus), *episode* (the first scene with the main characters), *stasimon* (comments from the chorus, divided into *strophe* and *antistrophe*), *exodus* (the chorus concludes and leaves), *hamartia* (the revelation of a tragic flaw in the main character), *hubris* (the main character reveals his excessive pride and belief that he is equal to the gods), *anagnorisis* (his recognition that his course of action is wrong, but he proceeds anyway), *peripeteia* (a dramatic reversal of his fortune), *catastrophe* (the moment when the protagonist is destroyed by his own flaw), and *katharsis* (the previously discussed purifying outpouring of terror and pity in the audience, which has continued to present day as the adjective "cathartic," meaning a satisfying release).

Note that each step involves something happening on the stage. But the last step—the *purpose* for all that has come before—is something that happens in the hearts and minds of the audience as well.

Tragedy, by Aristotle's definition, is not the same as "something sad," as many people use the word today. If someone dies in a car crash, it's terribly sad, but not necessarily a *tragedy*. On the other hand, if a habitual heavy drinker imbibes too much at a party (*hamartia*), and tells everyone he is perfectly fine to drive drunk (*hubris*), and everyone warns him not to drive and he ignores them (*anagnorisis*), and he gets into a car accident (*peripeteia*) that kills his beloved daughter, the star of his life (*catastrophe*), and he sobs with agony as he realizes he alone caused her death (*katharsis*), *that's* tragedy.

Playwrights took these principles to heart, and they formed the basis of drama to the present day, though many writers have bent or broken some of them, especially the Unities. Though various playwrights in the years since the Renaissance have rebelled against some or all of these principles, the principles themselves remain durable and satisfying to audiences, whether or not the audience members have ever heard of Aristotle or his *Poetics*.

In judging plays, critics today follow a simpler set of guidelines, usually attributed to the nineteenth-century German writer Johann Wolfgang von Goethe. In an essay titled "On Criticism," he lays out what have come to be known as the three questions of criticism:

- What is the artist trying to accomplish?
- Does he or she succeed?
- Was it worth doing, by which Goethe is taken to have meant, did the critic like it?

This is not a bad way to think about shows, movies, or anything else you might go to see. When friends ask if we liked a show, we still answer Goethe's questions—whether we've heard of him or not.

Goethe also said this: "A man should hear a little music, read a little poetry, and see a fine picture every day of his life, in order that worldly cares may not obliterate the sense of the beautiful which God has implanted in the human soul."

With the coming of newspapers, magazines, and other mass media, criticism moved from universities and scholarly journals to the mass public. Much time has passed, and the arts have expanded enormously since the times of Aristotle and Goethe. But their principles still resonate.

It may be presumptuous of me, but I'd like to add a few more principles, seeing as how I regard critics as professional audiences. It is the responsibility of critics to be trained in their subject, to know something of the background of the people who created the work and who are performing it, and to familiarize themselves with the subject of what they are seeing. It is their responsibility to understand how plays and movies, and other forms of performance, are written, produced, acted, and directed. It is their responsibility to be knowledgeable about sound and lighting design, music composition, orchestration, and other technical aspects of what they are seeing.

And they should approach what they review with an open mind.

Ideally, amateur audiences—which is to say, basically, everyone else—should have a smattering of knowledge about these things too, to enhance their audiencing experience.

Critics and the Audience

I earlier made a distinction between critics and reviewers. One is more literary, the other more consumer-driven. Critics are seen as writers with a deep knowledge of the genre being criticized. Often, they have degrees in the subject area and offer thoughtful commentary, not just on the performers and the fun level (or lack of it), but where it fits into the larger field, history, and context of the society it addresses. Reviewers are perceived as letting potential ticket buyers know if it's worth their time and money, and whether it will be better for children, romantic couples, adrenaline addicts, et cetera. Audiences may sample a bit of both reviewers and critics, or use one for deciding how to spend a Saturday night, and the other for how to understand the world a little better.

Critics and reviewers are all too aware that they live a sort of parasitical life, depending on others' creative efforts for their sustenance. In the best of cases, brilliantly done criticism can rise to a sort of grandeur and stand equal to, and even occasionally above, the thing being criticized.

Among the best in the English-speaking world over the past three generations were theatre critics Brooks Atkinson and Walter Kerr of the *New York Times*, Peter Marks of the *Washington Post*, Elliot Norton and Kevin Kelly in Boston, and Kenneth Tynan in London; movie critics Pauline Kael, Gene Siskel, and Roger Ebert; sports commentator Grantland Rice; social critic Ta-Nehisi Coates, and others.

Literary and social critic Dorothy Parker (1893–1967) was a must-read during her tenure at the *New Yorker*, known for referring to herself in the third person as "Constant Reader." Slitting the throat of A. A. Milne's twee "The House at Pooh Corner," about the toy bear Winnie the Pooh, Parker took special offense at Pooh's use of the word "tiddely-pom" in a song to make it more "hummy."

"And it is that word 'hummy,' my darlings," Parker wrote, "that marks the first place in 'The House at Pooh Corner' at which Tonstant Weader Fwowed up."

Critics rarely hesitate to write a good, juicy pan. But, on the other hand, they are sometimes afraid to praise things too highly, afraid the recipient of the praise will seem less great over time, making the critic look foolish. It takes great insight to recognize when something is really extraordinary and have the courage to say so. Harold Clurman (1901–1980) of the *New Republic* wrote plenty of dismissive reviews. But when he loved something, he didn't hesitate to throw his arms around it. In his original 1949 review of Arthur Miller's *Death of a Salesman*, long before the validation of the Tony Award and the Pulitzer Prize, he writes,

> The play has tremendous impact because it makes its audience recognize itself. Willy Loman is everybody's father, brother, uncle or friend, his family are our cousins; *Death of a Salesman* is a documented history of our lives. It is not a realistic portrait, it is a demonstration both of the facts and of their import. . . . [V]irtually everyone in *Death of a Salesman* is better than good; and the whole marks a high point of significant expression in the American theater of our time.

Nevertheless, while actors and writers (and producers) like to read rave reviews of their work, it's my sad duty to report that readers like to read bad reviews, the more scathing the better, especially when the reviews are spot-on and have been composed by a master.

H. L. Mencken spent most of his career making hamburger of sacred cows wherever he saw them—ruthlessly, controversially, but always with great intelligence and eloquence. Most of his targets were in politics, religion, and the arts. It was he who coined the timeless takedown of democracy American style: "Democracy is the theory that the common people know what they want—and deserve to get it good and hard." But here he took a moment to poke a finger in the eye of the "Great American Pastime": baseball.

> [It stimulates] a childish and orgiastic local pride, a typical American weakness, and . . . it offers an admirable escape for that bad sportsmanship and savage bloodthirst which appear in all the rest of the American's diversions. An American crowd does not go to a . . . [ball] game to see a fair and honest contest, but to see the visiting club walloped and humiliated. If the home club can't achieve the walloping unaided, the crowd helps—usually by means no worse than mocking and reviling, but sometimes with fists and beer bottles. And if, even then, the home club is drubbed, it becomes the butt itself, and is lambasted even more brutally than the visitors. The thirst of the crowd is for victims, and if it can't get them in one way it will get them in another.

Mencken's partner and coeditor on *The Smart Set* and later *The American Mercury* magazines, theatre critic George Jean Nathan (1882–1958), namesake of the annual George Jean Nathan Awards for theatre criticism, vivisected a young playwright named John Howard Lawson, saying:

> The easiest thing in the world is to attract attention to one's self. All that one has to do to do so, as has often been said, is to walk down Broadway without one's pants on. This is the technique embraced by certain of our young playwrights. . . . The latest young playwright to parade the Rialto in his under drawers . . . is Mr. John Howard Lawson. Mr. Lawson's manner of walking down Broadway minus trousers takes the form of what he calls "a jazz symphony of American life." It is entitled "Processional," and the Theatre Guild is its sponsor. Unlike many of his accomplished elders who have been content to attract attention to themselves merely by excellent work in the more or less time honored and approved dramatic form, Mr. Lawson has [pursued] sensational attention within

different works in what may be called a hoochie-coochie form. This frantic struggle for new forms is the most amusing of twentieth century artistic phenomena. Engaged in for the major part by the young—and often lazy—of the aesthetic species it has resulted in a welter of eye-catching but often intrinsically nonsensical methods in manners of expression which are generally found to contain nothing worth expression.

But Nathan wasn't always dismissive. Here is his paean to charismatic Broadway superstar Al Jolson:

The power of Jolson over an audience I have seldom seen equaled. There are actors who, backed up by great dramatists, can clutch an audience in the hollow of their hands and squeeze out its emotions as they choose. There are singers who, backed up by great composers, can do the same. And there are performers of diverse sorts who, aided by external means of one kind or another, can do the same. But I know of none like this Jolson—or, at best, very few—who, with lines of a pre-war vintage and melodies of the cheapest tin piano variety, can lay hold of an audience the moment he comes on stage and never let go for a second thereafter. Possessed of an immensely electrical personality, a rare sense of comedy, considerable histrionic ability, a most unusual music show versatility in the way of song and dance, and, above all, a gift for delivering lines to the full of their effect, he so far outdistances his rivals that they seem like the wrong ends of so many opera glasses. His present background is called "Big Boy." It is the usual thing of its kind made into a merry theatrical evening by this king among clowns.

Critics like Nathan and the best of his calling have a way of reaching into the morass of a performance or a piece of writing and pulling out a particular moment or piece of business and holding it up to illustrate the greatness or worthlessness of the whole. As the audience is watching the proceedings, they may pause for a "wow" or a "yuck" at a particular effect. The professional audience makes time stop, disassembles the moment, and analyzes precisely what makes it tick—or why it fails to do so.

Hitting Back

Not all targets of bad reviews take the criticism sitting down. But composer Max Reger did so in a memorable way. Critic Rudolf Louis of the *Münchener Neueste Nachrichten* panned Reger's Sinfonietta in A major, op. 90 in 1906. Reger riposted, "I am sitting in the smallest room of my house. I have your review before me. In a moment it will be behind me!"

Former *New York Times* theatre critic Frank Rich later settled into a career as an honored and thoughtful political columnist and essayist. But, during his tenure as the *Times*'s first-string Broadway critic, he earned the sobriquet "The Butcher of Broadway" for his occasional slashing review of a show he didn't like. In 1982, the *Times* offices on West 43rd Street in Manhattan were picketed by the cast of the musical adaptation of *Seven Brides for Seven Brothers* after he described the show as "the fifth musical bomb planted at the Alvin [Theatre] in ten months." The cast took up chants including "Frank Rich is anti-American" and "Get Rich!"

In 1992, the pickets returned, but this time the accents were Polish. Angered by Rich's review of the $5 million musical *Metro*, which had been imported from Poland, the cast demonstrated outside the *Times* building. Rich's review had begun, "What's the Polish word for fiasco?"—and somehow went downhill from there.

P.S.: *Metro* closed after thirteen performances; *Seven Brides* after just one. For his part, Rich was a two-time finalist for the Pulitzer Prize for Criticism.

Longtime *New York* magazine critic John Simon was a brilliant essayist, but he pulled no punches in his weekly critiques. He often targeted actors' physical appearance. In a noteworthy review of the musical *The Act*, he describes star Liza Minnelli thus:

> I always thought Miss Minnelli's face deserving of first place in the beagle category. Less aphoristically speaking, it is a face going off in three directions simultaneously: the nose always *en route* to becoming a trunk, blubber lips unable to resist the

pull of gravity, and a chin trying its damnedest to withdraw into the neck, apparently to avoid responsibility for what goes on above it. It is, like any face, one that could be redeemed by genuine talent, but Miss Minnelli has only brashness, pathos and energy.

Minnelli's fans cluster-bombed the magazine with protest, to which Simon responded, "I go to the theatre to see beauty—in costumes, scenery, walks, faces—unless the situation calls for something else. And if we are allowed to invoke aesthetic criteria where other things presented onstage are concerned, why should faces be taboo?"

At least one target of Simon's venom struck back in a famous episode. Actress Sylvia Miles was described by Simon, in his review of *Nellie Toole and Co.*, as "one of New York's leading party girls and gate-crashers." Spotting him at O'Neal's restaurant in New York, Miles said, "I was sitting and chatting cheerfully, and just as I looked up I saw him standing at the bar. He was facing me and talking to [film director] Bob Altman. So I went to the table and filled up a plate with steak tartare, coleslaw, potato salad, and cold cuts." She approached Simon and dumped the contents on his head, saying, "Now you can call me a plate-crasher, too!"

Simon snarled at Miles, calling her "Baggage!" and warned, "I'll be sending you the bill for this suit!" Miles sniffed, "It'll be the first time it's been cleaned."

Getting back at a critic who has panned you, especially when the pan was especially vicious or a cheap shot, is a common fantasy among actors and other entertainment folk. That fantasy was the basis of the 1973 horror movie *Theatre of Blood*, about a soul-wounded Shakespearean actor (Vincent Price, of course) who gets revenge on the critics who killed his career by murdering them one by one, each in a method taken from a Shakespearean play. The vengeful actor delivers this speech to one of his intended victims: "How many people have you destroyed as you destroyed me? How many talented lives have you ruined with your glib attacks? What do you know of the dedication and hard work of the men and women of the noblest craft on earth? Nothing!"

But even here, the critic takes the last word: "Get it over with then, so I don't have to listen to your insane babbling."

Audiences like to read reviews and sometimes will go to see a show or film about which they know little, just because "it got great reviews." But there are also many instances of shows getting slammed by the critics and succeeding nonetheless. Films as varied as Sylvester Stallone's Rambo movies—especially the second in the series, *Rambo: First Blood* (1982)—and Kevin Hart's *Soul Plane* (2004) were ripped by critics but attracted huge and appreciative audiences who liked the star and the story. *The Rocky Horror Picture Show* flopped with both critics and audiences when first released in 1975. They were mostly just confused by it. But the sci-fi/punk musical gradually gathered a devoted following who would see the film over and over, and bring in new acolytes—fresh blood, you might say. *Rocky Horror* now is considered the definition of a cult film.

Under those circumstances, you may hear people crow disparagingly that the critics were "wrong" about the show. But that's not how opinion works. In the comments section of a critic's review, you will sometimes see the clapback, "Well, that's *your* opinion!" Well, of course it is. Who else's opinion should the critic have? Just because it isn't the same as yours doesn't mean it's not legitimate. Different people have different standards, different tastes, and different levels of expertise, depending on whether they are reviewing a Harold Pinter drama, an MGM musical, or a kung-fu action film.

If you look at a roundup of reviews and see that most of the critics felt one way but a couple of them felt a different way, does that make the minority "wrong"? Democracy does not apply to opinions.

The Democratization of Criticism

Or does it?

By the mid-twentieth century, the explosion of mass media of all kinds created the perfect environment for celebrity critics. When movies, dance companies, art exhibitions, TV shows, and especially Broadway shows had their premieres, potential audiences rushed to pick up the newspapers and magazines (and tune in to their radios and TVs) where the critics' hallowed opinions would be delivered from on high. A bad review from Clive Barnes or Frank Rich had the power to close a show virtually overnight.

All that changed with the advent of the internet. In the last two decades, the internet in general and social media in particular have armed the audience to seize power wholesale from professional critics and commentators, though some continue to exert their influence, especially in the political sphere. But for the arts, anyone with a Twitter or TikTok account, Instagram or Facebook page, podcast, or a blog can now make their opinion known to a wide and growing audience. The power of the *New York Times* and other traditional media to set the terms of debate has given way to Rotten Tomatoes, Yelp, Talkin' Broadway's All That Chat, RateMyProfessor.com, and dozens of public and private "rooms" on social media where shows, books, restaurants, teachers, movies, art, fashion, and anything else you can imagine are discussed and evaluated. Instead of having to search back for the original review of a movie to find out what a particular critic thought of it, audience members now have the ability to read, or even solicit, an opinion from one or ten dozen ordinary ticket buyers who didn't get free tickets and perfect seats but paid their hard-earned money to see it.

Veteran users of these services wind up developing a fairly sophisticated bullshit-ometer. They can tell from the wording if the positive review is from a shill, or if the negative review is from a troll or someone with a particular axe to grind. And once people see the show, eat at the restaurant, or read the book for themselves, they have the ability to add their own newly empowered voices to the global chorus of pro and con. Oh, there are still professional critics around, plenty of them, and many are sharply talented. But few members of the general audience could name one of the *New York Times*'s stable of critics today.

The democratization of criticism can have a dark side. Before the web you had a few escalating options if you didn't like something or someone: you could write a letter to the editor, sign a petition, join a picket line, or march on Washington, with corresponding escalation of putting your personal safety on the line. But now, with the power of the web to aggregate and fan the flames of anger, dissatisfaction has become weaponized. The damage to Supreme Court Justice William O. Douglas's idea of a free and open "marketplace of ideas" has been enormous. For example, if a movie has some element, however small, that some people don't like, or someone involved with it has said something controversial at some point in their careers, upset people "review-bomb" the film, overloading audience-review sites with negative assessments (whether they've seen the movie or not) so the overall star rating of the film nosedives.

Referring to the Will Smith slapping incident at the 2022 Academy Awards, Rui Alves in Medium.com, wrote,

> The world has gone from a place where people used to be able to share their opinions freely, to a place where people are afraid to share their opinions for fear of being labeled as racist or smacked on the face for making a harmless joke. In conclusion, the viral content culture is damaging the mental health of people and we need to take action before it gets too late.

The ability to circumvent critics amounts to a revolution. But some revolutions end in a reign of terror.

11

INVOLVING THE AUDIENCE

Since the invention of the proscenium arch and the development of the fourth wall, many writers and directors have sought to break from their confines and involve the audience in innovative ways. A show business tradition holds that audiences like to see something old done in a new way, or something new done in an old way. That leaves a lot of leeway for experimenters.

The simplest and most familiar technique is for a performer to invite audience members to come onto the stage, often as part of an attempt to show that nothing "tricky" is going on. This takes many forms. Magicians like Penn & Teller make great use of audience members to add wonder and verisimilitude to their illusions. Las Vegas animal trainers Siegfried and Roy brought audience members to the stage to help them with their performances with tigers. The climax of every faith healer's performance is to bring audience members to the stage to drive out demons and "heal" them of whatever ailments they may have.

Eighteenth-century performer Franz Anton Mesmer, who gave us the term "mesmerized," even created the field of hypnotism for entertainment. Hypnotists like Mesmer place audience volunteers in a trance and get them to dance, cluck like chickens, break out in sweats from imagined heat, or anything else the hypnotist wants them to do. A snap of the fingers and the trance is broken, with no memory of what they did when they were "under."

Improv groups like Upright Citizens Brigade or Theatre-Sports would ask the audience for a set of unrelated parameters—such as a place, a job, and an article of clothing—then ad-lib a whole scene built around the audience suggestions. *Whose Line Is It Anyway?* did the same on television; rap artists like Common, Eminem, Proof, and Ol' Dirty Bastard do something similar with freestyle rap battles in which the intense rhythm and rhyme of rap, coupled with its storytelling power, is improvised on the spot through the rapper's innate skill. Logic (real name: Sir Robert Bryson Hall II) has been known to freestyle while solving a Rubik's Cube.

The New Vaudeville act the Flying Karamazov Brothers made a practice of challenging audience members to bring in any three items and the Brothers would juggle them. During one performance observed by the author, the audience brought them an axe, a slice of pizza, and a chicken carcass. The Brothers successfully juggled them, though the slice's cheese and the crust went their separate ways during the procedure.

One of the most remarkable such instances of audience involvement took place at "conceptual magician" Derek Del-Gaudio's 2017 off-Broadway show *In & Of Itself*, a live performance that was filmed and shown on Hulu. More than just a magic show, *I&OI* tried to spur the audience to join DelGaudio in his search for "self" through themed card tricks and other illusions. In his most remarkable illusion, DelGaudio asked the audience—the entire audience—to complete the sentence "I am . . . " and write the answer on cards before the show began. He then collected the unsigned cards. The show ended with Del-Gaudio pulling out the cards, looking out at the audience, and somehow being able to match every card with the correct audience member.

Sometimes audience members don't want to come on stage. They're either shy or afraid they will make fools of themselves—or be made to look foolish. It's not unusual for these neophytes to come on stage and freeze up when they look out at the sea of faces, or simply refuse to play along with the primary performer. To control the outcome of such interactions, magicians and other performers sometimes employ "ringers" or "plants" to pretend they are ordinary members of the audience, but actually they are working in cahoots with the primary performer and know how they are supposed to respond. The technical term for this is "cheating."

Tinkerbell

Sometimes breaking the fourth wall and asking the audience to take part in the play is even simpler. One of the best known and cherished is the moment in *Peter Pan* when the fairy Tinkerbell has consumed a cup of poison prepared by Captain Hook to kill Peter. Frantic that Tink is going to die, Peter shatters the fourth wall and addresses the audience directly, begging them to clap their hands to show they believe in fairies. Only that can save her life! In every production of the play in every country where it has been performed, the audience willingly and enthusiastically claps with all their hearts. And, lo and behold, Tinkerbell recovers! The moment is beautifully captured in the film *E.T.* when the mother (Dee Wallace) is reading the story of Peter to her tiny daughter (Drew Barrymore). As they clap, the stranded alien E.T. watches, clearly moved, through a louvered closet and snuggles up with his human friend, Elliott.

The author of this book operated the follow-spot for a grade school production of the show. With zero budget, all he had was the follow-spot itself, which allowed the size of the light beam to iris wider and narrower and the color of the light to be altered through the use of tinted gels. Tinkerbell was created with a golden gel and a tinkling sound effect on an electric spinet. As she drank the poison, the beam turned green and got smaller and smaller. She was dying! After the magical applause, back went the golden gel, the light irised wider, and the beam went looping around the stage in delight. Simple. Silly. Yet even grown-ups could be seen dabbing their eyes.

Follow the Bouncing Ball

One of the more organized attempts to involve the audience in the performance came in 1924 when Max Fleischer, founder of Fleischer Studios, created a series of cartoons, known as the *Ko-Ko Song Car-Tunes*, in which characters would sing a popular ditty of the day and the audience would be invited to sing along. Lyrics appeared at the bottom of the screen in these films, and a red dot (later replaced by other colors) would bounce from syllable to syllable so the audience would know when to sing them.

The practice became known as "follow the bouncing ball," named for the spoken invitation from the film's narrator or one of the animated characters. Later adapted by Paramount's *Screen Songs* series, the process became so popular that it was also used in live-action film shorts, starring singers like Rudy Valee, Ethel Merman, and the Boswell Sisters, among others.

Bandleader Mitch Miller adopted the practice for his TV variety series *Sing Along with Mitch*. That, plus the television syndication of Fleischer cartoons in the 1960s, brought the bouncing ball tradition to the baby boom generation and beyond.

Voting

Sometimes the audience gets to decide the outcome of a show. In this area, audiences for the live theatre have an advantage over other entertainment forms. Rupert Holmes, familiar to the general public as composer and lyricist for the 1979 pop song "Escape" (better known as "The Piña Colada Song"), used it to solve a major problem with a property he was adapting for the stage. He wanted to make a musical of Charles Dickens's final novel, *The Mystery of Edwin Drood*, a murder mystery set in northern England. The problem was, Dickens died suddenly of a stroke in 1870, leaving the novel only half finished, and with the identity of the murderer unrevealed. Nearly all the characters developed by Dickens had motivation to kill—but which one actually did it? That left a real-life mystery inside the fictional mystery.

Other writers over the years have sought to complete the story, naming one character or another as the killer. But Holmes decided to turn the story's biggest problem into its biggest asset. Holmes sat down and wrote multiple endings revealing each of the likely suspects as the culprit—and then left the audience to vote at each performance to choose who the murderer would be, and therefore which *Edwin Drood* ending would be performed that night. The cast had to rehearse all the different endings, and then be ready to perform any of them at a costume-change's notice.

Holmes lightened the mood of the story by framing it as a British Music Hall-style performance, led by a merry chairman who kept things bouncing along and explaining the show's unusual premise. During intermission, the actors playing the various suspects would mingle, in character, with the audience, actually campaigning to be elected the murderer (so they'd get an extra scene to play). It was fun for the actors, fun for the audience, and when the big vote at that year's Tony Awards was complete, *The Mystery of Edwin Drood* was voted Best Musical of the season.

We Interrupt This Program

In 1975, Broadway saw an interesting, if short-lived, experiment with audience participation that presaged bigger things to come. Norman Krasna's thriller *We Interrupt This Program . . .* , seemed to be a typical drawing-room comedy at the start of the show. Lulled by its laughs, the audience was startled when masked and heavily armed terrorists burst onto the stage and announced that the whole audience was being taken captive.

The hostage situation that ensued would likely cause panic, if not heart attacks, these days when terror and unprovoked mass shootings have become horribly commonplace. At the time, however, apart from airplane hijackings to Cuba, this kind of terrorism was regarded as highly unlikely. Once the audience got over its initial shock and realized the threats were part of the show, they actually began to laugh at the hostage takers. Unable to commit any actual atrocities, the poor actors continued to bluster toothlessly, and people who needed to go to the restrooms were allowed to do so. Which certainly took the edge off any threat the playwright, director, and cast (including Holland Taylor, Brandon Maggart, and Taurean Blacque) had hoped to promote.

The problem is that the audience had little experience with such an extreme violation of the fourth wall and refused to play along. Perhaps it was because they had not been warned and thus had been unpleasantly surprised. *We Interrupt This Program . . .* ran only seven performances but opened the door to similar "real" experiences in the years to come that didn't make the same mistake. That movement came to be called immersive theatre.

Immersive Theatre

The immersive theatre movement grew out of the many theatre experiments of the 1920s through the 1970s. One of the best known of these experiments was *Fefu and Her Friends,* written by Cuban American playwright María Irene Fornés. This 1977 feminist drama, with an all-female cast, covers a busy day from noon to late evening as the title characters rehearse a play at Fefu's country house and gradually air accounts of their struggles within a male-dominated society. What sets the play apart is that it is presented in four segments, each one performed in a different part of the theatre. The audience is required to move from performing space to performing space, seeing the same story performed from different points of view.

British playwright Alan Ayckbourn has experimented repeatedly with alternate use of the stage space. His farce *How the Other Half Loves* (1971) shows different couples in different apartments as they are preparing for a party, but they occupy the same stage space. The audience is required to mentally separate the couples, seeing them talking about one another, but remembering that they cannot see or hear each other. Ayckbourn's 1973 *The Norman Conquests* trilogy takes the audience through the same house party three times but shows what happened in three different parts of the house: *Table Manners* in the dining room, *Living Together* in the living room, and *Round and Round the Garden* outdoors.

Immersive theatre first achieved large-scale commercial success in 1988 with *Tony n' Tina's Wedding*, a production created by the off-off-Broadway Artificial Intelligence comedy troupe. Acknowledging that many people enjoy wedding receptions far more than the wedding ceremonies themselves, the actors set about showing a stereotypical Italian American wedding, complete with actors playing the bride and groom and their respective feuding families at a real church. The whole audience was then moved to a real reception hall for a hearty meal at which they were treated as guests and expected to interact with the increasingly intoxicated family members who ad-libbed their way through the party. The production moved off-Broadway where it ran for twenty-two years, spinning off similar productions such as the gay-themed *Joni and Gina's Wedding*, and the black-comedy *Grandma Sylvia's Funeral*.

Perhaps the most successful twenty-first-century immersive play that moves the audience from place to place is the 2009 megahit *Sleep No More*, created by the British troupe Punchdrunk. As of early 2023, the play was still running after more than a decade in New York and elsewhere. The New York production takes place in the run-down McKittrick Hotel in the Chelsea neighborhood. Audiences are required to wear masks and move from room to room, watching different scenes inspired by Shakespeare's *Macbeth*. These scenes are played in different rooms simultaneously, and the actors, having finished one scene, abruptly depart and resume performing another scene in another room. It is up to the individual audience member to decide whether they want to stay in one place and see who shows up, move to another room and see what's happening there, or run after a particular actor to see where they are going and what they are going to do there. Some audience members have seen the production multiple times and still have not experienced the whole thing since it's happening all at once everywhere on different floors throughout the hotel. Because the audience, not the actors, are wearing masks, groups and even couples sometimes get separated and don't finally reunite until the final scene, played with a forest of Christmas trees on wheels to represent Birnam Wood. Though the audience is asked not to interact with the players while they are performing a scene, these audience members surround the action in their creepy white masks. They become silent ghosts, haunting the tragedy as it enacts its multiple murders leading to its grisly finale.

Immersive theatre blurs and erases the fourth wall, allowing participants to do something they may not have done since they were children—to imagine themselves to be someone else. The immersive movement sought to make things called "plays" into something more like "play."

Shock and Eww

Live performance affords many opportunities to involve audiences in different ways. But attempts to do so in the movies have taxed the innovation of cinema owners and operators.

The Tingler, a 1959 Vincent Price sci-fi/horror film about a parasitic creature that lives off the fear of its hosts, encouraged exhibitors to wire their theatre seats to deliver audience members a vibrating sensation during the scenes where the monster went on the attack. The process was trademarked as Percepto! showings of *The Tingler* in these cinemas and were preceded by a filmed warning from director William Castle saying, in part,

> some people are more sensitive to these mysterious electronic impulses than others. These unfortunate, sensitive people will at times feel a strange, tingling sensation; other people will feel it less strongly. But don't be alarmed—you can protect yourself. At any time you are conscious of a tingling sensation, you may obtain immediate relief by screaming.

When the Percepto! moment arrived, Price would break the fourth wall of the film, exhorting the audience, "Ladies and gentlemen, please do not panic. But scream! Scream for your lives! The Tingler is loose in this theatre!"

During the initial run at some larger theatres, Castle hired ringers to sit quietly in the audience until the big moment, then scream and faint in the aisles. Compliant theatre employees would have gurneys ready to wheel the plants out, to impress on the real audience members how truly sca-a-a-a-ry the film was.

More benevolently but even more obtrusively, innovators over the years tried various ways to entertain the noses, as well as the eyes and ears, of spectators. Managers of legitimate theatres experimented with releasing perfumes into theatres as early as 1868 when London's Alhambra Theatre of Variety piped perfume into the audience space during a performance of *The Fairy Acorn Tree*. Similar experiments took place on a theatre-by-theatre basis, but the process was attempted on a slightly grander scale starting around the same time as *The Tingler*, when competing scent-diffusing systems, AromaRama (using the theatre's air ducts) and Smell-o-Vision (directed from each seat) were tested in cinemas. Though receiving approving notices from some audiences and critics, both systems were found to be noisy and the fragrances were not distributed evenly around the theatre spaces, causing some viewers to be overwhelmed and others to smell little or nothing. Other experiments included Odorama and Aromavision, which employed small cards distributed to spectators, who were asked to scratch and sniff numbered circles on the cards at key moments when the appropriate number was flashed on the screen.

In 2013 a group of Japanese researchers unveiled a "smelling screen" system to release scents from a computer peripheral (fueled by tiny gel packets) to add another sense to the computer game experience. No commercial application has been marketed as of press time for this book.

Disney imagineers have taken this general concept and applied it to the audience's other senses, creating rides at the company's theme parks that simulate flight (Soarin' Around the World, Delta Dreamflight, Flight Around the World), the sea spray of boat trips, et cetera.

Cheerleading

Athletes believe they perform better when they are being cheered by an audience. It is considered an article of faith that males, in particular, strive harder when they know females are watching. And their chants help stoke the fans to cheer louder as well. That's the whole philosophy on which cheerleading was founded. There also is a tradition of home field advantage that says teams perform better when they know their hometown fans are watching and, presumably, cheering for them. They feed off the energy of the crowd.

During the COVID-19 quarantines of 2020–2021, when professional sports teams were permitted to play but with reduced or eliminated live audiences, the teams at many stadiums propped up cardboard photos of fans to make the seats look full, and even used the stadiums' public address systems to broadcast recorded crowd sounds that included taped cheers when points were scored by the home team.

And the cutouts were not just any old people. The New York Mets baseball team called this practice the Fan Cutouts Program. Supportive New York fans were charged (and gladly paid) $86 apiece to have a picture of their actual face appear on the cutouts. (The service was free to season ticket holders.) So, to be clear, audience members enthusiastically paid eighty-six hard-earned dollars *not* to attend the games but to have pictures of themselves rooting for the home team. Because they sincerely believed it would help. The charge at pro football stadiums was $100.

Other Experiments

Over the years, theatre artists have tried many theories and experiments designed to jolt the audience or stir the audience to social action of various kinds—nearly all of them with portentous but ultimately misleading names conferred on them by their inventors or by critics. Epic theatre wasn't epic. The theatre of cruelty wasn't cruel. The theatre of the absurd . . . well, it was indeed sometimes absurd—but often grounded in all-too-vivid reality.

Most of these experiments had a political aim: to "awaken" and motivate audiences, especially working-class audiences or gender-specific audiences. But a few were used to manipulate the audience for a less high-minded goal: to shock it just for fun, like shouting "boo" in a dark room.

We looked at Bertolt Brecht's epic theatre in chapter 2. The proud communist rejected theatre's usual goal to immerse the audience in the "reality" of an obviously artificial scenario. Instead, he embraced theatre's artificiality and used it to wake up audiences to what he believed was the capitalist world's plot to anesthetize audiences with dreams. Brecht wanted to motivate audiences to rebel.

Meanwhile, Antonin Artaud expounded his theory in the seminal works "Manifesto of the Theatre of Cruelty" and *The Theatre and Its Double* in which he demanded "communion between actor and audience in a magic exorcism; gestures, sounds, unusual scenery, and lighting combine to form a language, superior to words, that can be used to subvert thought and logic and to shock or hypnotize the spectator into seeing the baseness of his world." These included scenes of horrific violence, but also startling shrieks of noise, blinding flashes of light, and bursts of raucous music. As it turned out, Artaud applied his theory to just a single production during his lifetime, *Les Cenci* (1935), which flopped in its Paris premiere. But many writers and directors picked up his banner after his death, leading to many of the dark visions we often see in many forms of entertainment.

Playwright Sarah Kane, especially in her work *Blasted*, exposes the audience to rape, other forms of physical and mental abuse, and even murder in as unexpurgated form as possible. Artaud would have approved. Her works strove to dramatize the triggers of post-traumatic stress disorder as a way of inoculating audiences, especially women, against it—or perhaps simply as a cry of her personal agony.

While most of these theories failed to impress a mass audience in their pure and original form, eventually all were absorbed into mainstream theatre as *techniques*. Part of the dramatists' and directors' toolbox, to be used in small doses to make a point in the otherwise dominant realistic theatre. And all these theories, however impractical they may have been, were originally couched as theories of how theatre should be made. But they were really *theories of the audience*. They all asked the same fundamental questions: What is the audience for? Why is it there? What does it get from watching? What *could* it get from watching?

Moving the Audience

There is a long history of both demagogues and garden variety politicians rousing audiences to participate—and by inference to agree—with the points being made by political leaders and would-be leaders when they get up in front of an audience. Whether the chant is "Four more years!," "No justice, no peace!," "Lock her up!," or "Say it loud, I'm Black and proud!" crowds seem to love the call-and-answer style of political rhetoric. A few have changed history.

Campaigning for an unprecedented third term as president in 1940, Democrat Franklin D. Roosevelt gave a speech at Madison Square Garden in New York criticizing three of his Republican political opponents, whom he felt had blocked his efforts to prepare the nation for the threat posed by Nazi Germany and Imperial Japan. The three were Congressmen Joseph Martin, Bruce Barton, and Hamilton Fish III. But rather than naming them separately, he lumped them together into a rhythmic chant, "Martin, Barton and Fish." He made a point of pronouncing the last name with a sneering "Fisssh," making the whole group sound malevolent.

Roosevelt told the crowd, "We tried to pass that one, but unfortunately there was a deep hole dug on the road to progress by Martin, Barton and Fisssh." The partisan crowd loved it. On the second repetition, all he had to say was the first of the three names, and the crowd finished it for him: "Great Britain and a lot of other nations would never have received one ounce of help from us—if the decision had been left to Martin, Barton and Fisssh."

Remembering the speech, playwright Arthur Miller recalled, "He walked out of there and he couldn't lose."

The simple power of the human voice, when motivated by high spiritual purpose, has always given oratory its special power. Winston Churchill's World War II speeches helped his country to keep calm and carry on. William Jennings Bryan may not always have been on the right side of history, but he motivated Americans in rural states to fight for recognition of their interests. Mahatma Gandhi lent a spiritual dimension to India's fight for independence. Patrice Lumumba not only helped lead his home nation of the Congo to independence but gave the nations of Africa a way of looking at themselves as a people who should speak with a united voice. When these orators spoke, they awakened a special sense of purpose in their audiences.

Indeed, some speeches have changed history. They did so because they were said by the right person at the right time in the right place . . . but also because they connected in a unique way with their audience.

Think of Martin Luther King Jr.'s "I Have a Dream" speech, Churchill's "We shall fight them on the beaches," Nelson Mandela's "I am the first accused," Emmeline Pankhurst's "Freedom or Death" speech, or John F. Kennedy's speech at the joint session of Congress on May 25, 1961, when he said, "I believe that this nation should commit itself to achieving the goal, before this decade is out, of landing a man on the Moon and returning him safely to Earth," which motivated his audience in the chamber and across the country to not just mobilize for one of the greatest adventures in human history, but to accept a mighty sense of national purpose.

Of course, not all oratory is great or moving. We've all sat through dull, windy, and self-aggrandizing political speeches. Mencken captured this feeling when remembering President Warren G. Harding's effect upon his listeners:

He writes the worst English that I have ever encountered. It reminds me of a string of wet sponges; it reminds me of tattered washing on the line; it reminds me of stale bean soup, of college yells, of dogs barking idiotically through endless nights. It is so bad that a sort of grandeur creeps into it. It drags itself out of the dark abysm of pish, and crawls insanely up the topmost pinnacle of posh. It is rumble and bumble. It is flap and doodle. It is balder and dash.

CONCLUSION

What's Next?

In the mid-2020s, we stand at the threshold of a new era for audiences. Just as most of the world has now dealt with a pandemic virus, that same world has gone through the experience, made necessary by quarantine, to plunge ever deeper into virtual audiencing.

Virtual reality technology via Meta Quest and a growing number of competing brands currently offers non-immersive, semi-immersive, and fully immersive experiences that are computer-generated and three-dimensional. The gaming world gets credit for advancing graphics to the point where players can feel they are not just watching a three-dimensional world but inhabiting it and manipulating objects within it. Traditional audiences experience stories by observing the behavior of the actors and use empathy to immerse themselves in the characters. The VR experience is still strictly a visual and audio experience, however. Someday soon communications technology may add the other three senses and enable audiences to smell, taste, and feel these experiences as well.

Among other participatory media that connect users with a controlled version of the real world, YouTube, TikTok, Twitter, Facebook, and the like have made us all performers as well as reporters and critics. But Zoom and its analogues have forced us to up our game and made the experience more professional, even as it empowers amateurs. VR now allows us to experience stories from the creators' point of view. The line between performer and audience has rapidly begun to disappear.

That seems primed to continue on an even more profound level. Advances in VR technology will further transform the audiencing experience. Technology may allow audiences to more directly (and perhaps almost literally with the development of "wet-wiring" technologies) broadcast information directly into the brain, to get inside the heads of the performers. At some point, thanks to wet-wiring or other technologies that tap directly into the brain, we may be able to experience actors' sensations, emotions, and thoughts directly.

This is not science fiction anymore. The US Air Force Research Laboratory (AFRL) has been experimenting with neuromodulation, to speed training through direct brain stimulation, known as the Individualized Neural Learning System (iNeuraLS) project. Using the AFRL's 711th Human Performance Wing, it launched an effort to speed up pilot training through brain stimulation.

That's information going straight into the participant's head. But DARPA, the military's research division, has been experimenting with ways to let directives come out as well—to allow humans to interact with physical objects using only their minds. In this case, they are trying to get volunteers to control fighter jets with a brain-computer interface (BCI), which uses electrodes implanted in and on the brain's sensory and motor cortices. Currently only in its experimental stages, the research opens enormous possibilities for the audiences of the future.

Technologies like this would transform the technique of acting, and transform what audiences expect and want from performances. The best actors would be the ones who could suppress their personal side thoughts or merge them completely with the character. Method acting would have a renaissance as the power of the personal memories each actor could command would define their personal acting styles as much as an actor's appearance or voice affect us now. Fans of teary movies would experience the actor's sadness along with their own in response. Sports fans would feel the adrenaline (and injuries) of their favorite players.

Users of pornography (often the pioneers for new technology) would feel every sensation the models felt. Progress in this area is already well under way in the field of what's known as teledildonics. In each case, users of this enhanced virtual reality would be able to switch into the heads of any performer, or even multiple performers simultaneously. This could lead to problems and dangers such as those explored in the 1983 science fiction film *Brainstorm*, which envisioned a world where memories and experiences could be recorded directly from the brain. One user who becomes lost in a recorded sexual experience is driven insane when the scene is played on an endless loop directly into his cortex and he is locked in a permanent state of orgasm until rescued.

Even less lurid recordings could draw an impressionable person into emotional quicksand. Some memories are painful just to think about. Imagine if we had a literal recording of a marriage-ending fight, or the terror of a tornado or earthquake, or the death of a loved one. Referring to *Brainstorm* again, imagine if someone recorded the experience of their death and others played it back for themselves.

Instead of dwelling on such horrors, imagine if we could reexperience the moments when we played with our children when they were young. Not just look at a photo or video, but feel all the sensations as if it were happening again. Or be in the moment of the joy of a wedding day or the thrill of accepting a long-anticipated honor. Instead of just watching a great performance on film or a star athlete winning a championship, we could personally experience what it was like to be the actor giving that performance or the athlete scoring that winning goal. Imagine being inside the head of Serena Williams or Roger Federer when they won a tie break or became a Wimbledon champion. Or Tom Brady realizing that his team was going to win another Super Bowl.

For that matter, imagine being able to sit beside a long-departed parent or child once again, or buy the emotional experience of falling in love, or being able to experience a roller-coaster or a SpaceX craft lifting off for Mars with all the adrenaline and none of the actual physical danger.

The promise of such experiences will no doubt drive new technologies that will turn two-dimensional audiencing into three- and four-dimensional audiencing in the decades to come.

As with social media, and even telephones in their early days, some people will be first-adopters and embrace these new audiencing technologies. But others will find them horrifying or dehumanizing and reject them, especially if they require some sort of implant. Think how intrusive cell phones can be. Imagine if all those annoying calls were coming directly into your mind. As with the phone ringer, most people may opt for the ability to turn them on for work or play, then turn them off to sleep or have a quiet time.

Perhaps some will rebel against these technologies and find new appreciation for *actual*, nonvirtual experiences again. There is ample precedent for this. Look at the sudden retro popularity of acoustic instruments and vinyl records in the face of an overwhelmingly digital musical world. People may come to value in-person "analog" experiences precisely because of the ubiquity of virtual experience. The technology may change, but human nature will always remain the same.

Which brings us to the ultimate audience. For those who believe a God created the world, the question must always be asked—why? Why go through the trouble of creating a universe, and creating something called humankind to run around making so much trouble within it?

Perhaps this God created humankind to entertain Her; to make Her laugh and cry. Shakespeare wrote "All the world's a stage, and all the men and women merely players." The Bard may have been on to something bigger than he realized. Humankind is at its most godlike when it is watching itself, learning about itself, changing its heart and mind as it plays out its own cowardice and courage, its own ignorance and brilliance, and hopefully getting a little smarter, a little nobler, a little more self-aware with everything it sees.

All those intent faces out there in the dark . . . watching.

BIBLIOGRAPHY

Adams, Mike. *Lee de Forest, King of Radio, Television and Film*. New York: Copernicus Books/Springer-Verlag, 2011.

Akehurst, F. R. P., and Judith M. Davis. *A Handbook of the Troubadours*. Berkeley: University of California Press, 1995.

Alchin, L. K. "Elizabethan Theatre Audiences." www.elizabethan-era .org.uk. https://www.elizabethan-era.org.uk/elizabethan-theatre -audiences.htm.

Alford, Henry. *How to Live: A Search for Wisdom from Old People (While They Are Still on This Earth)*. New York: Twelve Books/Hachette Book Group, 2009.

Alves, Rui. "Oscars 2022: Will Smith Slaps Chris Rock, and Cancel Culture Strikes Back." Medium.com, March 28, 2022. https://medium .com/fan-fare/oscars-2022-will-smith-slaps-chris-rock-and-cancel -culture-strikes-back-a3105b9be1bd.

"An Act of Spiritual Communion." My Catholic Life, 2022. https:// mycatholic.life/catholic-prayers/an-act-of-spiritual-communion/.

"Another Early 'Smellie.'" *Variety*, January 6, 1960, 35.

Avila, Pamela. "Patti LuPone Claps Back at Broadway Theatergoer for Not Wearing Mask: 'Who Do You Think You Are?'" *USA Today*, May 12, 2022. https://www.usatoday.com/story/entertainment/ celebrities/2022/05/11/patti-lupone-broadway-theater-mask -policy/9741130002/.

Bader, Robert S. *Four of the Three Musketeers: The Marx Brothers on Stage*. Evanston, IL: Northwestern University Press, 2016.

Barnett, Engrid. "The Tragic True Story of Maria Callas." Grunge .com, May 7, 2021. https://www.grunge.com/404076/the-tragic -true-story-of-maria-callas/?utm_campaign=clip.

Bauch, Marc A. *Gentlemen, Be Seated: The Rise and Fall of the Minstrel Show*. Norderstedt, Germany: Grin Verlag, 2011.

Bendersky, Joseph W. *A Concise History of Nazi Germany: 1919–1945*, pp. 105–6. Lanham, MD: Rowman & Littlefield, 2007.

Bennett, Susan. *Theatre Audiences: A Theory of Production and Reception*, 2nd ed. London: Routledge, 1997.

Bennhold, Katrin. "Of Beards and Bubonic Plague: German Village Prays for a (2nd) Miracle." *New York Times*, April 5, 2020. https://www.nytimes.com/2020/04/05/world/europe/germany -oberammergau-passion-play-coronavirus.html.

Bhasin, Nick. "The Black Artists That Inspired Elvis Presley." SBS.com, May 25, 2018. https://www.sbs.com.au/guide/article/2018/05/25/ black-artists-inspired-elvis-presley.

Bieber, Margarete. *The History of the Greek and Roman Theatre*. Princeton, NJ: Princeton University Press, 1939, 1961.

"Blackface! Minstrel Shows." Black-face.com, undated. https://black -face.com/minstrel-shows.htm.

"Blondel the Minstrel." Lords and Ladies, 2017. https://www.lords andladies.org/blondel-the-minstrel.htm.

Bogar, Thomas A. *American Presidents Attend the Theatre*. Jefferson, NC: MacFarland & Co., 2006.

———. *Backstage at the Lincoln Assassination: The Untold Story of the Actors and Stagehands at Ford's Theatre*. Washington, DC: Regnery History, 2013.

Bosse, Katharina, and Cécile Camart. *New Burlesque*. New York: DAP Books, 2004.

Brecht, Bertolt. *Brecht on Theatre: The Development of An Aesthetic*. Edited and translated by John Willett. New York: Hill and Wang, 1964.

Brenman-Gibson, Margaret. *Clifford Odets: American Playwright: The Years from 1906 to 1940*. New York: Applause Books, 2002.

Bullock, Darryl W. *Florence! Foster!! Jenkins!!!: The Life of the World's Worst Opera Singer*. New York: Overlook Press, 2016.

Burnim, Kalman A. "David Garrick, 1717–1779: A Theatrical Life." Folgerpedia, August 27, 2018. https://folgerpedia.folger.edu/David _Garrick,_1717–1779:_A_Theatrical_Life.

Butsch, Richard. *The Making of American Audiences: From Stage to Television, 1750–1990*. Cambridge: Cambridge University Press, 2000.

Cagney, James. *Cagney by Cagney*. Garden City, NY: Doubleday and Company, 1976.

Carlson, Marvin. *Theories of the Theatre*. Ithaca, NY: Cornell University Press, 1984, 1993.

Case, Sue-Ellen. *Feminism and Theatre*. New York: Methuen Inc., 1988.

Castells, Manuel, with contributions by David Gelernter, Juan Vázquez, Evgeni Morozov, and Mikko Hyppönen. *Change: 19 Key Essays on How the Internet Is Changing Our Lives*. Nashville: Turner Publishing, 2014.

Chan, Sharon Pian. "The Yellowface of 'The Mikado' in Your Face." *Seattle Times*, July 13, 2014. https://www.seattletimes.com/opinion/the-yellowface-of-ldquothe-mikadordquo-in-your-face/.

Choi, Hyangmi, Peter Bull, and Darren Reed. "Audience Responses and the Context of Political Speeches." *Journal of Social and Political Psychology* 4, no. 2 (2016): 601–22. https://doi.org/10.5964/jspp.v4i2.618.

Clurman, Harold. "Attention! Harold Clurman reviews *Death of a Salesman*." *New Republic*, February 28, 1949.

———. *The Collected Works of Harold Clurman*. Edited by Marjorie Loggia. New York: Applause Books, 2000.

Coleridge, Samuel Taylor. *Biographia Literaria*, chapter 11, 1817.

Crabbe, Jerome P. "Theatre of the Absurd." Theatre Database, September 3, 2006.

Craig, Douglas B. *Fireside Politics: Radio and Political Culture in the United States, 1920–1940*. Baltimore: Johns Hopkins University Press, 2000.

Csapo, Eric, and William J. Slater. *The Content of Ancient Drama*. Ann Arbor: University of Michigan Press, 1994.

Davis, Lee. *Scandals and Follies: The Rise and Fall of the Great Broadway Revues*. New York: Limelight Editions, 2000.

Debord, Guy. *Society of the Spectacle*. Detroit: Black & Red Publishers, 1983.

De Leon, Walter. "The 'Wow' Finish." *Saturday Evening Post*, February 14, 1925.

De Vos, Laurens, and Graham Saunders, eds. *Sarah Kane in Context*. Manchester: Manchester University Press, 2010.

Dooley, Ben, and Hisako Ueno. "This Man Married a Fictional Character. He'd Like You to Hear Him Out." *New York Times*, April 24, 2022. https://www.nytimes.com/2022/04/24/business/akihiko-kondo-fictional-character-relationships.html.

Duch, Jakub. "Trauma and Trauma Theory in Sarah Kane's *Blasted*." Seminar paper. Germany: University of Hamburg, 2015.

Easwaran, Eknath. *Passage Meditation: Bringing the Deep Wisdom of the Heart into Daily Life*. Surry Hills, Australia: Read How You Want Publishing, 2010.

"Eighteenth-Century English Theatre: Publication Beyond Print." Thesis project supervised by Ros Ballaster and Abigail Williams (with Cristina Neagu). University of Oxford, undated. https://www.humanities.ox.ac.uk/eighteenth-century-english-theatre-publication-beyond-print.

Elber, Lynn, and David Bauder. "Will Smith's Oscars Slap Felt by Comedians Beyond Chris Rock." Associated Press, March 31, 2022.

Ellison, Harlan. *The Glass Teat*. New York: Ace Books, 1969.

———. *The Other Glass Teat*. New York: Ace Books, 1970.

Encyclopædia Britannica. 11th ed. s.v. "applause." Cambridge: Cambridge University Press, 1911.

Errett, Benjamin. "Scratch That Glitch: The Human Compulsion to Correct Each Other Is Now an Algorithmic Growth Hack." Slate.com. February 3, 2023.

Esslin, Martin. *Theatre of the Absurd*. New York: Doubleday Anchor, 1961.

Farber, Donald C., and Robert Viagas. *The Amazing Story of The Fantasticks*. New York: Citadel Press, 1991.

Farias, Juan Carlos. "The One Who Sings Prays Twice: Planting Seeds among the Oaxacan Youth." *Faith of Grand Rapids*, May 2020. https://grdiocese.org/the-one-who-sings-prays-twice/.

Fierstein, Harvey. *I Was Better Last Night: A Memoir*. New York: Knopf, 2022.

Filewod, Alan. "Agitprop Theatre." *Routledge Encyclopedia of Modernism*, January 10, 2017. https://www.rem.routledge.com/articles/agitprop-theatre.

"The First Black Person Is Seen on an American Television Show." African American Registry, undated. https://aaregistry.org/story/first-black-seen-on-television/.

Fordin, Hugh, *Getting to Know Him: A Biography of Oscar Hammerstein II*. New York: Random House, 1977.

Freedman, Samuel G. "Sunday Religion, Inspired by Saturday Nights." *New York Times*, December 1, 2007, retrieved November 25, 2018. https://www.nytimes.com/2007/12/01/us/01religion.html.

Gan, Vicky. "The Story Behind the Failed Minstrel Show at the 1964 World's Fair." *Smithsonian Magazine*, April 28, 2014. https://www.smithsonianmag.com/history/minstrel-show-1964-worlds-fair-180951239/.

Gaston, Anne-Marie. *Bharata Natyam: From Temple to Theatre.* New Delhi: Manohar Publishers, 1996.

Gavin, James. *Intimate Nights.* New York: Grove Weidenfeld Books, 1991.

Goodwin, Doris Kearns. *No Ordinary Time: Franklin & Eleanor Roosevelt: The Home Front in World War II.* New York: Touchstone Books/Simon & Schuster, 1994.

Graf, Stefanie. "Rhythm 0: A Scandalous Performance by Marina Abramović." The Collector, June 29, 2022. https://www.thecollector .com/rhythm-0-by-marina-abramovic/.

Grout, James. "Venationes." In *Encyclopedia Romana.* University of Chicago, undated. http://penelope.uchicago.edu/~grout/encyclopaedia _romana/gladiators/venationes.html.

Gussow, Mel, and Arthur Miller. *Conversations with Miller.* New York: Applause Books, 2002.

Hall, Stuart. "Encoding and Decoding in the Television Discourse." Paper for the Council of Europe colloquy on "Training and the Critical Reading of Television Language." University of Birmingham, September 1973.

Halnon, Mary. "Some Enchanted Evenings: American Picture Palaces." American Studies at the University of Virginia, January 1998. https://xroads.virginia.edu/~CAP/PALACE/home.html.

Hand, Richard J., and Michael Wilson. *Grand-Guignol, The French Theatre of Horror.* Exeter: University of Exeter Press, 2002.

Hauser, Christine. "Benedict Cumberbatch to Fans: No Cellphones, Please." *New York Times,* August 10, 2015.

Herr, Norman. "Television Statistics." Csun.edu, 2007. http://www .csun.edu/science/health/docs/tv&health.html.

Hirshberg, Peter. "First the Media, Then Us: How the Internet Changed the Fundamental Nature of the Communication and Its Relationship with the Audience." BBVA OpenMind, undated. https://www .bbvaopenmind.com/en/articles/first-the-media-then-us-how-the -internet-changed-the-fundamental-nature-of-the-communication -and-its-relationship-with-the-audience/.

"Historically Banned and Challenged Plays." SchoolTheatre.org, January 24, 2016.https://schooltheatre.org/historically-banned-and -challenged-plays/.

"Hostage Crisis in Moscow Theater." History.com, October 23, 2002. https://www.history.com/this-day-in-history/hostage-crisis-in -moscow-theater.

Howarth, W. D. *Moliere: A Playwright and His Audience*. Cambridge: Cambridge University Press, 1982.

"Internet Pornography by the Numbers." Webroot.com, undated. https://www.webroot.com/us/en/resources/tips-articles/internet -pornography-by-the-numbers.

Jacobson, Kelsey, and Kelsey Blair. "Theatre Audience Etiquette and Norms Have Always Shifted with the Times." TheConversation .com, November 21, 2021. https://theconversation.com/theatre -audience-etiquette-and-norms-have-always-shifted-with-the-times -169834.

Keil, Braden. "After More Than 30 Years at *New York* Mag 'Insatiable' Critic Gael Greene Calls for . . . Check, Please!" *New York Post*, August 16, 2000. https://nypost.com/2000/08/16/after-more-than -30-years-at-new-york-mag-insatiable-critic-gael-greene-calls-for -check-please/.

Kennedy, Mark. "Unauthorized Video of Jesse Williams Onstage Prompts Outrage." Associated Press, May 11, 2022. https://www.msn .com/en-us/news/us/unauthorized-video-of-jesse-williams-on stage-prompts-outrage/ar-AAXa07P.

King, Stephen. *Stephen King's Danse Macabre*. New York: Berkley Books, 1981.

Knox, James Suydam. "Eyewitness to Lincoln's Assassination." Letter to Rev. J. P. Knox. Abraham Lincoln Papers, Manuscript Division, Library of Congress, 1865. https://www.loc.gov/exhibits/civil-war -in-america/ext/cw0197.html.

Kooser, Amanda. "Japanese Scientists Create 'Smell-O-Vision' Screen." CNET, April 2, 2013.

Koster, Jo. "Elizabethan London." Winthrop University, Rock Hill, SC. Undated. http://faculty.winthrop.edu/kosterj/engl203/over views/shakespeareantheatre.asp.

Kozak, Mariusz. "How Music and Chants Bring Protesters Together." *Washington Post*, July 7, 2020.

Kramer, Andrew E., Michael Schwirtz, and Eric Nagourney. "Ukraine President Says Hundreds Still Trapped Under Bombed Theatre in Mariupol." Reuters, March 18, 2022.

Kreps, Daniel. "British Lawmaker to Resign After Being Caught Watching Porn in Parliament." RollingStone.com, April 30, 2022. https://www.rollingstone.com/politics/politics-news/british-lawmaker -resigns-porn-parliament-1345477/.

Lacan, Jacques. "The Subversion of the Subject and the Dialectic of Desire." 1960. http://mission17.org/documents/SubversionOfThe Subject_LACAN.pdf.

Larlham, Peter. "Theatre in Transition: The Cultural Struggle in South Africa." *TDR* vol. 35, no. 1 (Spring 1991): 200–11.

Leonard, Kim. "What Is the Male Gaze? Definition and Examples in Film." StudioBinder, April 25, 2021. https://www.studiobinder .com/blog/what-is-the-male-gaze-definition/.

Leopold, Todd. "Broadway Legend Grabs Phone from Texter, Laments Future." CNN, July 9, 2015. https://www.cnn.com/2015/07/09/ entertainment/feat-patti-lupone-cell-phone/index.html.

Levitin, Daniel, J. *This Is Your Brain on Music: The Science of a Human Obsession.* New York: Dutton/Penguin Group, 2006.

Liu, Siyuan, ed. *Routledge Handbook of Asian Theatre.* London: Routledge Books, Taylor and Francis Group, 2016.

Mackay, Charles. *Extraordinary Delusions and the Madness of Crowds.* London: Richard Bentley, 1841.

Mahar, William J. *Behind the Burnt Cork Mask: Early Blackface Minstrelsy and Antebellum American Popular Culture.* Urbana: University of Illinois Press, 1999.

Mann, Theodore. *Journeys in the Night.* New York: Applause Theatre and Cinema Books, 2007.

Margaritoff, Marco. "Meet Valeria Lukyanova, the 'Human Barbie' Who Claims She's Only Had One Plastic Surgery." ATI, January 2, 2022, updated January 14, 2022. https://allthatsinteresting.com/ human-barbie-valeria-lukyanova.

Mazower, David. "10 Things You Need to Know about *God of Vengeance.*" Digital Yiddish Theatre Project, February 28, 2018. https:// web.uwm.edu/yiddish-stage/10-things-you-need-to-know-about -god-of-vengeance.

McLaughlin, Kelly. "2 Women Were Banned from MLB Games Indefinitely after Flashing an Astros Pitcher on Live TV." *USA Today*, October 28, 2019. https://www.insider.com/women-banned-mlb -baseball-flashing-breasts-2019-10.

McLuhan, Marshall, and Lewis H. Lapham. *Understanding Media: The Extensions of Man.* Boston: MIT Press, 1991. First published in 1964.

"Medieval Drama: Staging Contexts." Folger.edu, undated. https:// folgerpedia.folger.edu/Medieval_Drama:_Staging_Contexts.

Melrose, Kevin. "Movie Legends Revealed: How Did the Internet Change *Snakes on a Plane*?". CBR.com, July 29, 2015. https://www

.cbr.com/movie-legends-revealed-how-did-the-internet-change -snakes-on-a-plane/.

Mencken, H. L. *A Religious Orgy in Tennessee: A Reporter's Account of the Scopes Monkey Trial.* Introduction by Art Winslow. Hoboken: Melville House Publishing, 2006.

Meola, Tony. "Finding Pianissimo," in *The Alchemy of Theatre.* New York: Playbill Books, 2006.

Merritt, Jonathan. "'Glorious Glitter Bomb': Critics Loved *Jesus Christ Superstar,* But Much of Religious America Was Unimpressed." *Washington Post,* April 2, 2018. https://www.washingtonpost.com/ news/acts-of-faith/wp/2018/04/02/glorious-glitter-bomb-critics -loved-jesus-christ-superstar-but-much-of-religious-america-was -unimpressed/.

Milani-Santarpia, Giovanni. "Shows with Wild Beasts at the Colosseum." MariaMilani.com, 2017. https://mariamilani.com/colosseum/ colosseum_wild_beasts_shows.htm.

Miller, Arthur. *Timebends: A Life.* New York: Penguin Books, 1995.

Milling, Jane, and Peter Thomson. *The Cambridge History of British Theatre.* Cambridge: Cambridge University Press, 2004, p. 439.

Morin, Rebecca. "Trump: *Hamilton* Cast Harassed Pence." Vox.com, November 19, 2016.

Mulvey, Laura. "Visual Pleasure and Narrative Cinema." *Screen* 16, no. 3, 1975: 6–18. Anthologized by ColumbiaUniversity.edu. https:// www.asu.edu/courses/fms504/total-readings/mulvey-visual pleasure.pdf. https://doi.org/10.1093/screen/16.3.6.

Nagler, A. M., ed. *A Sourcebook in Theatrical History: Twenty-five Centuries of Stage History in More Than 300 Basic Documents and Other Primary Material.* New York: Dover Publications, 1952.

Nathan, George Jean. "The American: His Morals." *Smart Set,* July 1913, 88.

———. "The Theatre." *The American Mercury* 4, no. 15 (March 1925).

Nicola, James B. *Playing the Audience.* New York: Applause Books, 2002.

Novak, Sara. "Why Do People Throw Tomatoes?" HowStuffWorks .com, February 19, 2021. https://recipes.howstuffworks.com/why -do-people-throw-tomatoes.htm.

"Number of TV Households in America, 1950–1978." American Century, November 15, 2014. https://americancentury.omeka.wlu.edu/ items/show/136.

O'Shea, Janet. *At Home in the World: Bharata Natyam on the Global Stage.* Middletown CT: Wesleyan University Press, 2007.

Parker, Dorothy. "Far from Well." *New Yorker,* October 12, 1928.

Paulson, Michael. "After Nude Jesse Williams Video, Theater Turns Camera on Audience." *New York Times,* May 11, 2022. https://www.nytimes.com/2022/05/11/theater/jesse-williams-leaked-nude-video.html.

Peterson, Chris. "'The Mikado' Performed in Yellowface and Why It's Not Okay." OnstageBlog.com, September 16, 2015. https://www.onstageblog.com/columns/2015/9/16/the-mikado-performed-in-yellowface-and-why-its-not-okay.

Plato. *The Republic.* Translated by Desmond Lee. New York: Penguin Classics, 2007. First published 375 BC.

Plotkin, Fred. "Send Me No Flowers." Operavore/WQXR, March 27, 2013. https://www.wqxr.org/story/278395-send-me-no-flowers/.

Pointer, Ray. *The Art and Inventions of Max Fleischer: American Animation Pioneer.* Jefferson, NC: McFarland & Co., 2016.

Porges, Eric C., and Jean Decety. "Violence as a Source of Pleasure or Displeasure Is Associated with Specific Functional Connectivity with the Nucleus Accumbens." *Frontiers in Human Neuroscience,* August 13, 2013. https://pubmed.ncbi.nlm.nih.gov/23964226/.

"Porn Addiction Stats—Pornography Addiction Statistics, Percentages, Numbers, & Info." Tech Addiction, undated. http://www.techaddiction.ca/pornography-addiction-statistics.html.

"Pornography Statistics." CovenantEyes.com, undated. https://www.covenanteyes.com/pornstats/.

Price, Jason. *Modern Popular Theatre.* New York: Palgrave Macmillan, 2016.

Raiders of the Lost Ark. Directed by Steven Spielberg, screenplay by Lawrence Kasdan, story by George Lucas and Philip Kaufman. Lucasfilm Ltd./Paramount Pictures, 1981. https://www.youtube.com/watch?v=yqQD8sVtfA4.

Reim, Garrett. "US Air Force Aims to Train Pilots Faster Using Brain Electrode." FlightGlobal.com, October 12, 2020. https://www.flightglobal.com/defence/us-air-force-aims-to-train-pilots-faster-using-brain-electrode/140554.article.

Rheingold, Howard. *Virtual Reality.* New York: Summit Books, 1991.

Rigg, Diana. *No Turn Unstoned: The Worst Ever Theatrical Reviews.* London: Elm Tree Books, 1982.

Robitzski, Dan. "Military Pilots Can Control Three Jets at Once Via a Neural Implant." The Byte, September 19, 2018. https://futurism.com/the-byte/jets-pilots-mind-control-darpa.

Rossiter, Harold. *How to Put on a Minstrel Show.* Chicago: Max Stein Publishing House, 1921.

Schonberg, Harold. "Nobody Wants to Play Max Reger." *New York Times*, December 2, 1973. Retrieved October 23, 2019.

Schwertly, Scott. "The History of Booing." Ethos3.com, undated. https://ethos3.com/the-history-of-booing/.

Schwab, Justin Jon. "The Birth of the Mob: Representations of Crowds in Archaic and Classical Greek Literature." PhD diss., University of California, Berkeley, Fall 2011. https://digitalassets.lib.berkeley .edu/etd/ucb/text/Schwab_berkeley_0028E_11974.pdf.

Sedgman, Kirsty. *The Reasonable Audience: The Etiquette, Behavior, Policing and the Live Performance Experience*. Cham, Switzerland: Palgrave Macmillan, 2018.

Senelick, Laurence, ed. *The American Stage: Writing on Theater from Washington Irving to Tony Kushner*. New York: Literary Classics, 2010.

Seymour, Lee. "Coming Soon to Broadway: A New Broadway Theatre." *Forbes*, February 28, 2022. https://www.forbes.com/sites/lee seymour/2022/02/28/coming-soon-to-broadway-a-new-broadway -theatre/?sh=5d314e25f4a7.

Shenton, Mark. "They Shoot Critics, Don't They?" ShentonSTAGE Daily, April 6, 2022. http://shentonstage.com/shenton stage-daily-for-wednesday-april-6/.

Sherman, Howard. "Stop Telling Audiences How to Behave—Let's Encourage People to Enjoy Themselves at the Theatre." The Stage, July 13, 2018. https://www.thestage.co.uk/opinion/howard -sherman-stop-telling-audiences-how-to-behave—lets-encourage -people-to-enjoy-themselves-at-the-theatre.

———. "Vincent Price and Diana Rigg Cut Down Critics in *Theatre of Blood*." Theatermania.com, October 27, 2021. https://www.theater mania.com/new-york-city-theater/news/vincent-price-and-diana -rigg-cut-down-critics_92916.html.

Shteir, Rachel. "Championing Odets, Unfashionable as That Is." *New York Times*, April 27, 1997.

Simon, Ed. "Walking Shadows: Meet the Actors Who First Brought Shakespeare's Characters to Life." *Lapham's Quarterly* (July 12, 2021). https://www.laphamsquarterly.org/roundtable/walking -shadows.

Simon, Jeff. "Simon Took Critical Condition to Extremes." *Buffalo News*, September 25, 2005.

Simon, John. "The Boo Taboo." *New York Magazine*, June 24, 1968.

———. *John Simon on Theater: Criticism 1974–2003*. New York: Applause Books, 2005.

Simon, Neil. *Neil Simon's Memoirs*. New York: Simon & Schuster, 2016.

Simons, Seth. "The Comedy Industry Has a Big Alt-right Prob-lem." *New Republic,* February 9, 2021. https://newrepublic.com/article/161200/alt-right-comedy-gavin-mcinnes-problem.

Soumya. "Wayang Kulit—The Fascinating Art of Indonesian Shadow Puppets." Stories by Soumya, October 17, 2018. https://www.stories bysoumya.com/wayang-kulit-indonesian-shadow-puppets/.

Spencer, Terry. "Florida Man Acquitted in Killing at Movie The-ater Where Popcorn Was Tossed." Associated Press, February 26, 2022. https://www.orlandosentinel.com/news/florida/os-ne -theater-killing-trial-goes-to-jury-in-florida-20220225-ncxo5zam 65hifbfvbemdjdpyme-story.html.

Stafford, Tom. "How Liars Create the Illusion of Truth." BBC, October 20, 2016. https://www.bbc.com/future/article/20161026 -how-liars-create-the-illusion-of-truth.

Stein, Charles W. *American Vaudeville as Seen by Its Contemporaries.* New York: Alfred A Knopf, 1984.

Swaminathan, London. "Origin of Drama in Ancient India and Egypt." Tamil and Vedas. Research article no. 1463, December 6, 2014. https://tamilandvedas.com/2014/12/06/origin-of-drama-in -ancient-india-and-egypt/.

Taffel, Sy, Erika Pearson, Brett Nicholls, Martina Wengenmeir, Khin-Wee Chen, Hazel Phillips, Collette Snowden et al. "Audiences and Audience Research," *Media Studies 101,* undated. BCcampus Open Publishing. https://opentextbc.ca/mediastudies101/chapter/audiences-and-audience-research/.

Terry, Kurt. "Jesse Washington Lynching." Wacohistory.org, undated. https://wacohistory.org/items/show/55.

Tran, Diep. "Building a Better 'Mikado,' Minus the Yellowface." *American Theatre,* April 20, 2016. https://www.americantheatre .org/2016/04/20/building-a-better-mikado-minus-the-yellowface/.

"Transcript of Trump's Speech at Rally Before US Capitol Riot." Associated Press, January 13, 2021. https://apnews.com/article/election-2020-joe-biden-donald-trump-capitol-siege-media-e79eb516 4613d6718e9f4502eb471f27.

"TV Violence and Children." American Academy of Child and Ado-lescent Psychiatry. No. 13, updated December 2017. https://www .aacap.org/AACAP/Families_and_Youth/Facts_for_Families/FFF -Guide/Children-And-TV-Violence-013.aspx.

Tynan, Kenneth. *The Sound of Two Hands Clapping.* New York: Da Capo Press, 1975.

"Unique Stage Structures: Dynamic Stage Sets." KabukiWeb.net, undated. https://www.kabukiweb.net/about/kabuki/unique _stage_structures_dynamic_stage_sets.html.

Varrasi, John. "Global Cooling: The History of Air Conditioning." *American Society of Mechanical Engineers*, June 6, 2011. https://www .asme.org/topics-resources/content/global-cooling-the-history-of -air-conditioning.

Viagas, Robert, ed. *The Alchemy of Theatre*. New York: Playbill Books, 2006.

———. "Meet the Guy Who Tried to Charge His Phone on Stage at *Hand to God*." Playbill.com, July 9, 2015.

Weill, Kelly. "The Mask-Defying Church at Center of Disastrous Maine Wedding Linked to 3 Deaths, 144 Virus Cases." *The Daily Beast*, September 5, 2020. https://www.thedailybeast.com/disastrous -maine-wedding-tied-to-3-deaths-144-coronavirus-cases-and-a-mask -defying-church.

Whitton, Joseph. *The Naked Truth! An Inside History of* The Black Crook. Philadelphia: H. W. Shaw Co., 1897.

"Who Were These people? Audiences in Shakespeare's Day." Seattle-Shakespeare.org, undated. https://www.seattleshakespeare.org/ who-were-these-people/.

Wilkinson, Alissa. "Why Outrage over Shakespeare in the Park's Trump-Like *Julius Caesar* Is So Misplaced." Vox.com, updated June 19, 2017.

Willson, Jacki. *The Happy Stripper: Pleasures and Politics of the New Burlesque*. London and New York: IB Tauris, 2008.

Wong, Lisa, and Robert Viagas. *Scales to Scalpels*. New York: Pegasus Books, 2012.

"WPA Opera Put On as Private Show; *The Cradle Will Rock* Is Given Commercially at the Venice Theatre Here." *New York Times*, June 19, 1937.

Index